SELECTED LETTERS OF
ANDRÉ GIDE
AND DOROTHY BUSSY

SELECTED LETTERS OF
André Gide
and
Dorothy Bussy

EDITED BY

RICHARD TEDESCHI

WITH AN INTRODUCTION BY

JEAN LAMBERT

Oxford New York

OXFORD UNIVERSITY PRESS

1983

Oxford University Press, Walton Street, Oxford OX2 6DP

London Glasgow New York Toronto
Delhi Bombay Calcutta Madras Karachi
Kuala Lumpur Singapore Hong Kong Tokyo
Nairobi Dar es Salaam Cape Town
Melbourne Auckland
and associates in
Beirut Berlin Ibadan Mexico City Nicosia

First published as Correspondance André Gide–Dorothy Bussy
© Editions Gallimard, 1979, 1981, 1982
This selection and English translation © Oxford University Press, 1983

British Library Cataloguing in Publication Data
Gide, André
Selected letters of André Gide and Dorothy Bussy.
1. Gide, André—Correspondence, reminiscences, etc.
2. Bussy, Dorothy—Correspondence, reminiscences, etc.
I. Title   II. Bussy, Dorothy
III. Lambert, Jean   IV. Tedeschi, Richard
846.912   PQ2613.12
ISBN 0-19-212224-X

Library of Congress Cataloging in Publication Data
Gide, André, 1869–1951.
Selected letters of André Gide and Dorothy Bussy.
Translation of selections from: Correspondance André Gide–Dorothy Bussy.
Includes index.
1. Gide, André, 1869–1951—Correspondence.
2. Bussy, Dorothy Strachey—Correspondence.
3. Authors, French—20th century—Correspondence.
4. Authors, English—20th century—Correspondence.
I. Bussy, Dorothy Strachey. Correspondence. English.
Selections. 1983.   II. Lambert, Jean, 1914–   .
III. Tedeschi, Richard.   IV. Title.
PQ2613.I2Z56313   1983   848'.91209 [B]   82-14317
ISBN 0-19-212224-X

Set by Oxprint Ltd, Oxford
Printed in Great Britain by
Butler & Tanner Ltd,
Frome, Somerset

CONTENTS

INTRODUCTION

In July 1918 André Gide arrived in Cambridge in the company of a young friend, Marc Allégret, who was going to spend three months with a tutor in Grantchester. Gide had a letter of introduction to Simon Bussy. Lady Strachey was then in residence in Cambridge, where she had rented a house for the summer, and Gide paid her a visit. Her daughter Dorothy Bussy was staying with her, and since Gide wanted to brush up his English, she offered to give him lessons. In the *Hommage à André Gide* published after his death in 1951, she recalled the circumstances of their meeting and of the following days – little suspecting that this was to be the beginning of a thirty-year attachment: 'He had already read widely in English and liked to learn verses by heart. I asked him to recite the last verses he had learned and he started immediately:

> Was this the face that launched a thousand ships
> And burnt the topless towers of Ilium?

When he had finished reciting those magnificent lines, I understood I was in front of a great mind and a lofty intelligence. But I didn't yet realise that Marlowe's *Faustus* was a sort of allegory and I might say a summary of Gide's entire life: the theatre of the eternal struggle, of the eternal coexistence of Heaven and Hell in man's soul.'

A year later, writing to Gide from Venice, she would conjure up this time – what she called 'the "camaraderie" of the Cambridge days': 'Oh, happy Cambridge days, when I was just your dictionary and your grammar, convenient and helpful. And you had the same kind of friendly feeling for me that one has for a dictionary. I understood *that* perfectly. And you didn't notice – you were too much engrossed by other things – that your dictionary had eyes and a heart, was watching you and wondering at you, was charmed and thrilled and shaken by you.'

The two aspects, intellectual and sentimental, of a relationship lasting up to Gide's death and even beyond are already contained in these sentences.

The readers of Michael Holroyd's remarkable biography of Lytton Strachey have already had some glimpses of the writer's sister

Dorothy, fourteen years older than he, who supervised his development with a motherly tenderness. In a letter to Gide written after
Lytton's death in 1932, she gives way to her deepest feelings: 'I can't
take a step in my mind (not to speak of my affections) without
meeting his figure – and one other's – in all the dearest corners. I shall
never be able to read Shakespeare again or Racine without a pang. I
think of him too as a little boy when I had so much to do with looking
after him, nursed him in his illness, took him to the sea-side, read to
him, told him stories.'

Shakespeare and Racine – no names could better symbolize the
two cultures in which she felt equally at ease, as England and France
were the two countries where she would have chosen to live, had they
not already been hers by birth and marriage. Her mother felt a deep
affection for the headmistress of a girls' school near Fontainebleau;
on one of her pupils this Marie Souvestre seems to have made a
strong enough impression to have inspired the character of
Mademoiselle Julie in *Olivia*, the anonymous story published thirty
years after the meeting with Gide, and whose author we may as well
recognize here as Dorothy Bussy.

The first pages of *Olivia* offer a picture of the London home of the
Stracheys, the parents and the ten children (Dorothy was the third
child, twenty years older than James, the youngest son). Dorothy
could hardly have dreamed of being born in a more perfectly British
family: England, Scotland (on her mother's side) and the passage
through India, where her parents met. The house where she spent the
greater part of her youth still exists, at Lancaster Gate, near Kensing-
ton Gardens. Lytton Strachey has left an amusing description of the
large, uncomfortable house and with almost perverse pleasure enu-
merated the signs of the 'decline and fall' of a once prosperous family.

After having refused several proposals of marriage, Dorothy, at
thirty-seven (she was born on 24 July 1865 and died peacefully on
1 May 1960), became the heroine of a family revolution. She had met
a young French painter, Simon Bussy (1870–1954), who then
worked in London. He was very poor and, though the Stracheys
patronized him, this son of a cobbler seemed anything but a desirable
match for a Strachey girl. However, Dorothy knew better. 'Lancaster
Gate', says her brother Lytton, 'was shaken to its foundations', but
the wedding took place – a discreet wedding, without ceremony, but
with a ball in the huge drawing-room – and the not-so-young couple
settled in a small house in the south of France, near the village of

Roquebrune, facing the bay of Monte Carlo; the splendour of the view made up for the unpretentiousness of the house and the garden (which was greatly improved during the following years). To all appearances they led a very happy life there, especially after a daughter, Janie, was born in 1906. 'La Souco', the name of the place, where Gide often came, plays a prominent part in the letters. It was the scene of many secret joys and sorrows for Dorothy, during the long years when her attachment to Gide became an obsession.

Above the house itself Simon Bussy built a studio where, after 1914, abandoning his enormous canvasses, he concentrated on much smaller ones, delicate compositions of plants and animals, mostly in pastel, made after hours of study in the London Zoo or wherever he could observe nature. Besides the chameleons, the owls, and the parakeets, a few humans also sat for him: his brother-in-law Lytton, his daughter (there are portraits of her at all ages), Gide, Valéry, Roger Martin du Gard . . . Since the death of Duncan Grant who bequeathed it, the Ashmolean Museum in Oxford has owned a portrait of Dorothy as a young woman, where more importance seems to be given to the room than to the model herself; but the black touch of the dress makes a pleasant contrast to the bluey-green of the background. Most of Bussy's paintings, apart from the ones his French friends had bought, must today be in private English collections, and it is greatly to be desired that this modest, secretive, hard-working artist should be recognized as a portraitist and as a remarkable interpreter of animal life.

Besides Roquebrune, the other pole of the Bussys' life was London, and more particularly the house at 51 Gordon Square where, after Lytton's death, they occupied the top two floors, the rest of the building being inhabited by diverse members of the family. Quentin Bell's book on his aunt Virginia Woolf, Michael Holroyd's study of Strachey, Carrington's letters, the memoirs of Leonard Woolf and David Garnett have made Gordon Square into one of the most famous haunts of English literary life. When she was still Miss Stephen, Virginia Woolf lived at number 46 with her two brothers and her sister Vanessa. But it is mostly thanks to Lytton Strachey, whose mother came to live there after Lancaster Gate and Belsize Park in Hampstead, that this square became the intellectual and social centre of Bloomsbury.

An important personage in the Bloomsbury story, even though her role remained purely social, was Lady Ottoline Morrell. Her name, when pronounced by Simon Bussy, took on the accents of a devotion close to veneration. She mentions him in the first volume of her memoirs: 'Simon Bussy, the French painter, a brother-in-law of Lytton Strachey, came to do a pastel sketch of me. Unfortunately, he found it impossible to accomplish and had to give it up. But we both enjoyed the sittings – he is an acute, rather mordant observer of life, with a queer subterranean mocking laugh . . .' The Bussys were often guests at Garsington, the home of the Morrells. Gide was once invited with them, and there is a photograph of him and Simon in the album of their hostess.

The names of a good many of the Bloomsbury circle are to be found in the letters of Dorothy Bussy, especially those of Roger Fry, Lady Ottoline, Duncan Grant (a cousin of Dorothy's), Carrington, Harry Norton, Leonard and Virginia Woolf. But she was not a resident of Bloomsbury's enchanted world as fully as her sister Marjorie or her brothers Oliver, Lytton, and James. It was mostly a question of age: Virginia Woolf was exactly the same age as Marjorie, while Dorothy was sixteen years older – almost another generation. But mainly it was because Dorothy only came back to London during the summer. Through all the years of the letters, one finds (except during the war, when England was out of reach) more or less the same pattern: at the end of May, the migration towards London; at the end of September, the trip back to Roquebrune. Paris was a stopping-off point and, from 1918 onwards, Paris meant Gide's apartment, with the hope, the anguish, the delight, the disappointment and the revolt provoked by these intensely desired, intensely dreaded meetings at either end of the summer. Most of the time, the journey included Simon and Janie, but it sometimes happened that Dorothy travelled alone and stopped alone in Paris.

If the friendship initiated in Cambridge lasted more than three decades, and if it became more and more intimate and affectionate, it is because an equal regard, an equal respect existed between the two protagonists. Disparate as their status might have been at the time of their encounter, and if we disregard for the time being the difference in their feelings, there was no natural discrepancy on the intellectual level. The student who came daily to take his lesson in Cambridge was nearly fifty; his teacher was fifty-two. When one considers the sentimental content of their long-lasting relationship, what is most surprising is the age of both partners.

Gide was then approaching the height of his creative powers. He was writing some of his essential works. The period of doubts and misgivings was over; he was convinced of the rightness of his cause and, overriding the advice of his most trusted friends, he was determined to publish *Corydon* and *If it die*, in which, on a theoretical and a personal level, he was advocating homosexuality. He knew what risks he was taking, notably in his relationship with his wife, who was so shy and so easily hurt; but he was willing to incur them. Even more: he was courting scandal and, towards the end of his life, he was to express some regrets for his impunity, since he would not have been averse to being made a martyr. There can be little doubt that the opportunity to express himself freely with his English teacher added to his confidence. He was not judged by her. She knew the young man he was travelling with, she liked him; her broadness of mind and her personal experience of the same kind of feelings made her an ideal confidante. But she was also an ideal teacher, thanks to her knowledge of the two languages and literatures. Gide knew enough English to have been able to translate Conrad's *Typhoon* and several poems of *Leaves of Grass*; he was engaged in the translation of *Antony and Cleopatra*; but his English was in dire need of brushing up – and what better way to do it than to read Shelley or Browning with someone who had spent her life with them?

An English translation of Gide's *Ill-bound Prometheus*, which did not satisfy him, offered the first occasion to discuss the rendering into English of a series of works which she admired all the more since she knew the author. Strangely enough, Gide's writings at that time had hardly attracted any attention in England, but American publishers were beginning to show interest, and nothing could be more natural than for Dorothy to translate some of the books she already knew so well. Here more than ever, translating became a 'labour of love', allowing the translator to dwell intimately in the author's mind and to give his work a new life in another language. However faithful she would always remain to Gide's thought, it is as if she were given some rights of her own in the expression of that thought. While working on it, she could live with him; and it would take long years before he allowed her a closer communion.

Her first translation was that of *Strait is the Gate*. One of the last to be published was *The Fruits of the Earth*, but she had begun working on it fifteen years earlier, very slowly, step by step, as if she were afraid to exhaust her pleasure too soon. Meanwhile, all the major works of Gide were translated by her, elegantly and faithfully: *The Immoralist, The School for Wives, Two Symphonies, If it Die, Return from the USSR, The Vatican Cellars, The Coiners* (severally called *Lafcadio's Adventures* and *The Counterfeiters* in the United States), the two books of travel in the Congo. *Theseus* was to be the cause of bitter contention between author and translator, because Gide wanted it to be done by a man. She protested against his wanting 'a male voice', but he won: it was finally given to John Russell – with *her* approval.

In all these transactions, especially with American publishers, she had ample opportunity to show her fighting spirit, and Gide learnt to respect her advice. He associated her more and more with his literary ventures, asking her for instance to find in Florio's translation of Montaigne the passages he wanted to quote in his anthology for American readers. But, much more important, when he decided to finish his translation of *Hamlet* (he had gone no further than Act I), he sent her, from Tunis where he had exiled himself during the war, a long series of questions, exposing his hesitations and perplexities; her answers were filled with suggestions and commentaries, showing how completely she felt at ease with the most hidden nuances of a text familiar to her since childhood. She had the joy of participating in the re-creation of one of the works she admired most. This was one of her few triumphant moments, and one senses how much she must have savoured it.

There was to be another, more personal one. In 1933 she told Gide she had written a novel and was impatient to show it to him. He answered that he was 'deadly anxious' to read it; he did read it, and said: 'Three evenings I delved into those pathetic remembrances . . . and constantly, as I read, yours was the voice I heard.' But then his interest rapidly evaporated and fourteen years went by. In 1948 Dorothy told him she had shown a few friends the manuscript of that same novel. Rosamund and John Lehmann, and Leonard Woolf as well, had urged her to publish it: 'So now, dear friend, perhaps you will have the glory of having rejected two best sellers – Proust & yours truly! But you won't write me such a nice letter as you wrote him.' In the event, he did write a letter which was much more than nice, saying: 'Your *Olivia* seems to me an extraordinary tale, as accomplished and perfect as possible . . .', and ending: 'You mustn't hide this little *masterpiece* under a bushel.'

They agreed on many subjects. The author of *School for Wives* could hardly fail to be fascinated by Dorothy's dedication to the rights of women (where she was following in the tracks of her mother and several of her sisters). When, after the Second World War, she was at last able to come back to England, she was filled with admiration for her countrywomen, who outnumbered the men by two million and had learned not to depend on them any more: 'They need no longer think it is a virtue to stifle their own personalities and inclinations. They need no longer assume qualities and charms they can't possess to please their masters. And strange to say and very surprising, they have discovered that very often their masters prefer it too!'

But before admiring this 'new woman', Dorothy had considered with misgivings the 'new man' Gide had been announcing while he was flirting with Communism – that is, before his trip to the USSR opened his eyes and led him to say with ingenuous boldness what he felt about this 'paradise'. Well before him she had seen the consequences of his infatuation and had dreaded them. She had understood what kind of dizziness, generous but frightening, had seized him: the need to annihilate himself in the mass, forgetting that man will always have to seek refuge in creation. But if she understood his temptation, she warned him against it with a vehemence which betrayed her anguish. In his hatred for possessions, his thirst for total renunciation, he would be willing to accomplish the greatest of sacrifices. But, she protests, 'but the spirit! To renounce the life of the spirit – ah, that is a sacrifice indeed, that would be worth while, that would leave you really poor. Take care, my dear, take care. The devil, whom you know so well, is very subtle in his ways of approach . . .' In fact, what she told him here his closest friends had tried to tell him without success – she was not more successful, but in retrospect she must have been proud to have spoken as she did.

If, at that time, she felt it her duty to restrain him, there would come a time when she felt bound to entreat him to be more daring. In 1944, while Gide was still in Algiers, she was in Nice and sent him reports on the Paris press after the liberation. He was being abused by Communist intellectuals – notably Aragon – but disdained to defend himself, claiming that he was not at liberty to speak. She protested: 'Why should you of all people be silent when your words may bring support and encouragement to those who think like you? Don't you know that your disciples are longing to hear your great language, to catch your clear accents again?' This is not the voice of a meek disciple, but of a friend conscious of being on a par with the

man she admires most. Gide's fame had grown since that summer in
Cambridge, mainly thanks to her efforts to make him known in
English-speaking countries, an effort which was to lead to his being
given an honorary degree at Oxford, before the worldwide recognition of the Nobel Prize. But her familiarity with him, her confidence
in herself had grown also. She felt bolder (with *Hamlet* and *Olivia*
behind her), at least on the intellectual level, the only level we have
considered so far. But these satisfactions were a prefiguration of a
more subtle, more precious triumph in the domain of feeling; or
rather, since both aspects of their relationship developed in parallel
fashion, while Gide became more conscious of the spiritual value of
his friend, he also came to realize that he was more attached to her.
We must now consider the most unique feature of their friendship,
which is not the least poignant.

When, as early as October 1918, speaking of her brother Lytton and
of the young woman, Dora Carrington, who devoted her life to him,
Dorothy Bussy wrote: 'So much adoration on one side, so much
affection on the other – and the whole thing hopelessly unsuitable',
she little realized she was describing precisely what her relationship
with Gide would be. Alissa's gesture, in *Strait is the Gate*, of putting her hands on Jérôme's shoulders, a gesture which shows her
affection while maintaining the distance between them, is exactly the
attitude Gide tried to keep towards her. It would be wrong, however,
to see her as a victim. She was the one who loved. In a way, *he* was the
victim, because he felt deeply the torture of being loved without
being able to reciprocate. But let us not go too far either: he knew
how to defend himself.

  For it was indeed a matter of defence. He was confronted with a
strong and lucid personality, who said what she wanted to say, even
at the price of her dignity. She often needed courage. She knew she
might provoke irritation, rejection – worse still, silence, not to say
aversion. The only thing which might tire the reader is the repetitious
alternation between complaints and regrets for having complained.
Some pages, one guesses, were written for herself, as a consolation
for what she believed to be coldness, or indifference, or exasperation
on his part. She wrote them at night; the next day, she was unable to
resist posting them. The day after, she regretted it. One could also
speak of an alternation between pride and modesty; but humility
would be more exact, a humility which calls for consolation, and

does not always get it. Even if she kept telling herself the words of Polonius to Ophelia, 'Lord Hamlet is a prince out of thy star', she felt also that she could stand her own ground; she even goes so far as to write: 'And sometimes, dear, with my simple heart, I feel strangely superior to you.'

She knew her place, but did not see it as subordinate. She judged herself, but also others, sometimes with unshakable severity. She judged him too, and her rigour was not always tempered by her love; quite the contrary, since she was more easily wounded, being more vulnerable; and the sincere protestations of innocence he sent her succeeded only in irritating the sensitive spot a little more. For these protestations were sincere. He might play with her, make fun of her, hoping thus to reduce the conflicts to more reasonable proportions; but more often he provoked these conflicts with a kind of unconsciousness, surprising as such a term may be when speaking of a man whom his enemies considered a monster of guile. If so many of his letters seemed horrible to his friend, it was simply because she did not find in them what she expected.

There were many tempests, even though life around her went on with all the appearance of the most peaceful happiness. Simon painted, Janie read. What did Simon think? What did he know?

He remains one of the most mysterious characters of the story. One thing is certain: he felt for Gide total confidence and admiration. And he did not in the least feel obliged to be jealous. The sphere where his wife and their friend met, the sphere of books and ideas, was not his; intellectual exchanges excited him less than his silent dialogues with the animals at the zoo. He probably never suspected how much passion entered, at least on one side, into this spiritual exchange. He lived quietly, innocently, next to this raging fire. His wife once wrote to Gide, fearing obviously that, out of consideration for Simon, he might prove too cautious in the expression of his tenderness, 'Simon never reads your letters. He understands.'

After all, what could he reproach Gide with? With writing affectionately to his wife? But the letters he had received himself from Gide were hardly less affectionate. Gide was also *his* friend, appreciated his art, encouraged him. Friendship more than real choice determined the small collection of paintings owned by Gide; but it would be wrong to think that he bought so many of Bussy's works out of sheer kindness. He valued this form of art. He agreed fully with Dorothy that Simon's success was too modest on both sides of the Channel. For, if spending her long life near this austere and taciturn person, she allowed another man constantly to invade her thoughts, she remained loyal to her companion. How touching are the lines she wrote in 1947, when she and her husband were more than eighty: 'The last ten years he has spent in perfecting his art, materially and spiritually. It has amused me lately to compare him in my mind to La Fontaine. His contemporaries were on the gigantic scale, but it didn't prevent the beauty, the finish, the elegance, the wit etc. etc. of his tiny pieces from being recognised. About animals too! Birds and flowers and fishes! Absurd no doubt.'

No, not absurd at all. And the next year, despite his bad health, Gide used all his prestige to persuade one of the main Parisian galleries to present a large retrospective exhibition of Simon Bussy's works.

If he felt perfectly at ease with Simon, how could Gide have been so with Dorothy, when he knew that his every word would be weighed, scrutinized, interpreted in one sense or the other, but preferably in the sense which would be more likely to produce bitterness and reproach? Hence his understatements; but sometimes also one wonders if he was not overdoing it. Hence also, for him, the obligation to be more precise than he wanted, that is to say, most of the time, to show himself rather cruel. As, for instance, when he writes: 'I have often thought that, had I not promised myself that I would be perfectly natural with you, it would be easy to sound delightful . . .' How many times she says: 'There was a sentence in your last letter . . . How could you write it?' And he tortured himself in order to remember what he might have said. He felt much safer with the purely business letters he sent her about publishers, which he dictated or typed, keeping a copy.

It took years before she could feel something approaching a sort of serenity in their relationship. It was never to be without periods of doubt, sombre times – what she liked to call 'the Slough of Despond'. But, with age, the crises of jealousy became rare and were entirely the product of her too ardent imagination; it was like a habit she was unable to break, like a proof that her love had abdicated nothing of its strength. But it could also be a kind of game, when the objects of her suspicion were only a young lady writing a thesis on Gide, or his secretary. She knew well enough that she had nothing to fear from such rivals. She had others, more real, much more formidable from her point of view.

Or rather, it was she who saw herself as a rival. There was, first of all, Gide's wife. About her, Dorothy never dared to complain: she recognized Madeleine Gide's rights. She met her once in Paris, and the two ladies seem to have liked each other. Gide's wife certainly never felt anything like resentment about the place Dorothy had taken in her husband's life, and the basket of lemons sent one day from Roquebrune to Cuverville was a token of friendship which does not seem to have had a bitter taste. Dorothy was probably the first among Gide's friends to have known about the tragedy provoked at home by his trip to Cambridge with the boy he loved: his wife burnt all his letters to her. It may seem surprising that, hardly four months after their meeting, Gide should confide in his new acquaintance so completely; but, perhaps it is easier to confide in a new friend, especially one who is already prepared to understand and who knows all the elements of the drama. With Lytton, Dorothy had lived in the same atmosphere, and she adored Lytton. Besides, she very much liked young Marc and always spoke of him with unfaltering sympathy. For that reason Gide had no need to hide his feelings; he found in her an already acquiescent listener. Did he not write in his *Journal*, just a few weeks before going to Cambridge: 'The greatest joy, after loving, is to confess one's love'? With her, he could abandon himself completely to that joy. The only person who had ever caused him to experience jealousy was also the one of whom she was never jealous. It was a territory out of her reach, where she could not feel threatened.

Of course, Gide's homosexuality could also be viewed by her as a sufficient reason for his physical coolness. There, she did not deceive herself – except, maybe, when she did not see it as an obstacle. It is vain to imagine what other circumstances might have produced. Would a Gide more attracted to women have responded more easily? Or would he still have invoked his fidelity to his wife? On a purely physical level, this last consideration never weighed much; but in Dorothy's mind, it certainly was one of the reasons she gave herself for Gide's reticence. She would grasp at any twig to prevent herself from falling into the dreaded 'Slough'.

This does not mean that she was completely satisfied. By making her into a spectator or a confidante, Gide could hardly have offered her a more difficult part to play. She might have rejoiced at first that he invited her to enter so easily into his intimacy. But also, he needed to talk, and found in her somebody to talk to. After having started to show himself under her friendly glance as he really was, he was unable to stop when that glance became amorous. He knew her to be intelligent, her soul to be strong; under the pretext that it would be unworthy of her to do otherwise, he played on this strength and spared her nothing.

It is tempting to speak here of cruelty. I would rather call it, as he did himself: thoughtlessness. There was thoughtlessness in this very conscious artist. Or, if we must speak of cruelty, the cruelty was not in his actions or his words, but in their consequences. As he discovered to what degree his friend could be susceptible, he made an ever greater effort to avoid what might wound her; but often his very silences were interpreted in the most wounding sense. As he was continually on the road, she never stopped wondering with whom. Sometimes he told her; sometimes he anticipated her question and said he was alone – even as late as 1934, when he might have begun to feel he had nothing to explain. But that was precisely what she expected from him. It is difficult to love without giving oneself some rights over the loved one. And when this loved one, through his gift of ubiquity, has the art of escaping you, while you are more or less bound to the same place, the torture can become unbearable. As opposed to the regularity, the monotony, of her journeys between Roquebrune, London, and Roquebrune, the ramblings of Gide were maddening for her – all the more so, since, with each new flight of the 'butterfly' (her name for him), she told herself that he found enough time to go *there*, wherever it might be, but no time to come and visit her.

His work was always the pretext for these constant departures. To go away, he felt, was the only means of escaping the countless daily obligations in Paris, of giving himself the periods of freedom he needed. It was also a way of covering his tracks. Moreover, he was often called here and there, especially to the place she dreaded most – which happened to be not very far from Roquebrune. Then, what bitter complaints! ending with the cry: 'Farewell, you who don't know what it is to be jealous!'

Here we touch upon one of the most sensitive points in this story of two intense but discordant sensibilities.

In 1923, during a meeting at Pontigny, the intellectual centre where English writers were often invited, he told her he was going to be a father. But not by his wife. That was a danger she had not foreseen, and it was certainly, for her, the supreme treason. The very possibility that he could be attracted by another woman was too much for her. Shortly before, she had written: '. . . my conscience is clear and perhaps the Fates will be a little kind. I am not trying to cheat them. Not I. Not I. And they *cannot* cheat me. Never, never again. They have done their worst in that direction – and whatever remains to be suffered, it will not be *disappointment*.' How wrong she was about the Fates!

Time was to soften the asperities and in 1946 Simon Bussy, with Janie and Pippa Strachey, was present at Catherine Gide's wedding. Not Dorothy, for she was in England at the time. The following year, when Gide came to Oxford for the honorary degree obtained through the efforts of Enid Starkie, Dorothy did her best to keep his companions (his daughter and son-in-law) at a safe distance; by the end of her life, she had forgiven Catherine for simply existing.

Dorothy was to survive Gide by eight years. She became extremely thin and fragile in extreme old age. Her daughter, who lived for her more than ever, died accidentally two weeks before her, without Dorothy being even conscious of it. The image of Gide, with many others, had already retreated in the fog of her long memory. But, shortly after his death, when the *Nouvelle Revue Française* published its 'Numéro d'Hommage à André Gide', she contributed a few pages on their first meeting in Cambridge; still in full command of her power of evocation, she gave an almost cool account of the beginning of a relationship which was to become so ardent on her part.

The reader will form his own opinion about Gide's attitude. Mine is that he showed great dignity in a delicate situation. Apart from the fact that he never deceived Dorothy about his feelings, the affection and admiration he had for her largely outweighed his irritation. These reactions, in fact, were inextricably mixed. He was more disturbed than flattered by the passion he had aroused: to be loved constrains. And, strange to say when speaking of a novelist, the word passion is not quite familiar to him.

His love for Marc should have helped him to understand; but there, he was the one who loved, and he had no need to defend himself against the expression of feelings he did not share. Let us add immediately that, in his dealings with Dorothy, he very soon learnt the tactic. It was simple: to talk of something else, for instance translations, publishers, a book he had just read; to postpone until a later opportunity, until their next meeting, what he consented to call 'the essential' – knowing very well that they would say nothing essential to each other. A time came when, after having been the one who told her everything, he refrained from such openness, because he understood that she no longer wanted to hear everything and that the only thing she did want to hear was the one thing he declined to say. And yet . . . Yet, it was she who finally triumphed, she to whom he wrote from Algiers in 1945: 'How I long for you!'; from Egypt, a year later: 'My life is only near you, with you – and all your friendly pessimism doesn't prevent you from knowing it'; and, in 1950: 'If I still wrote letters, it would be to you.' And, at the end of that same year, that is to say a few weeks before his death: 'I need to write to you, without however having anything to say.'

The triumph of time, of patience? The impunity of distance, which allows tender accents and sentimental abandon without fear of the consequences? But why not, as well, and much more, the impulse of an affection happy to respond at last to a purified passion? If we insist on finding pathos, it is to be found, without any pretence, any grandiloquence, in this dialogue: She: 'Dear Gide, don't regret your kindness . . . don't disown it. No one will ever know of it. I will not misunderstand it – and yet, you cannot accuse me of extorting it.' He: 'I think you have not realized, modest as you are and as I like you to be, what you have been for me – always, and more and more . . .'

The publication of these letters poses anew the question of discretion towards private lives. But one at least of these two lives ceased being private a long time ago; and inasmuch as her own existence became entangled with it, Dorothy put herself in a position where she could not escape curiosity. Did she know that Gide kept her letters? Yes. He reassured her on several occasions, telling her they were safely preserved. The fact that many of them are undated would invite us to admire her modesty: she did not anticipate the torture this lack of dates would impose on unhappy editors. And that is what one of these editors thought, until he came upon the following lines: 'When your future biographers grub among your papers, how they will pity you, my poor persecuted Gide, and how disgusting they will think my persistence. (Not that I care one brass button or one twopenny damn for your future biographers. I detest and despise them all. There is not the slightest doubt that they will all be thickheaded, blundering fools. It is a pleasure to think that they will read this and I hope that for a moment their equanimity will be disturbed.) They will at any rate never guess my secret consolations, nor the hieroglyphics from which I derive my sustenance.' The last sentence is rather mysterious; as for the rest, there is no mystery at all. After reading this, an editor should feel free of any scruples. Not in order to avenge himself for having been called a blundering fool (and after all he is not a biographer), but because it appears that, as early as 1922, she had foreseen that indiscreet eyes would see her letters.

Did she imagine also that they might be published? She did nothing, at any rate, to prevent it, since these letters were given back to her after Gide's death and she did not destroy them. What is remarkable is that such an eventuality did not incite her to compose a personage different from what she was: passionate, often unhappy, with a great strength of mind and all the lucidity her heart would allow her to show.

In a way, reading Gide's works in Dorothy Bussy's translations (that is to say most of his works, except for the *Journal*, translated by Justin O'Brien, *Theseus*, due to John Russell, and very few other books) might already be an approach to her style. Not quite, though, because she adhered to his prose with a respect he sometimes regretted. There is a letter where she defends her idea of fidelity to the text, saying she is not going to try to improve upon him – it is *his* voice she wants to convey to English (or American) ears. But that she had her own style and very personal images, readers of *Olivia* do not need to be told, and it will be still more obvious for the readers of the present volume.

As for Gide, there is little doubt that this publication brings new dimensions to the picture we have of him. Not only because we see him, for the first time, confronted with a woman's passion; not only because of the rich fund of documentation on some of his major works and his contacts with English literature; but mainly because of the sound of his voice, which here takes on some of its tenderest accents. May the reader of this selection form a just idea of the richness of the whole exchange, of a private story unfolding through thirty years of history. For the student of Anglo-French literary connections, there could hardly exist a more vivid panorama. And finally the translator will find a welcome encouragement in his task, seeing what an eminent part this thankless but nevertheless very rewarding activity has played in two exceptional lives.

The total correspondence comprises about six hundred letters from

Gide and five hundred from Dorothy Bussy. It is to be supposed that quite a few of her letters are missing; one might expect them to be more numerous than his, since one finds sometimes three of hers for one of his. This means that a certain number of hers were lost by him or were never received, as was the case during a few months in 1942 and 1943, when the previously 'free' part of France was occupied by the Germans and connections were severed with North Africa, where Gide was residing at the time.

Nearly all Gide's letters are written by hand; the few typed ones were mainly business letters, dictated to a secretary or typed by him for the sake of exercise. Two or three were written in English and allow us to judge how well acquainted he was with the language. He used to write and speak English, as well as Italian, with a highly literary vocabulary, which gave his style an amusing affectation. Dorothy once corrected him, after complimenting him on his English: 'Only a slight nuance may be pointed out. Though you would say "Ever yours" to anybody you know fairly well without compromising yourself in the least, "for ever yours" is practically equal to a declaration! I am afraid I can't give you the credit of knowing this. But I – fully aware, call myself: For ever yours.'

This letter is signed D.B., as are many others. Through the years, her signature underwent variations: Dorothy Bussy, Dorothy B., Dorothy, D.B., D. – according to the state of her mind or the state of her heart. Gide signed his full name, except for a few times when he used initials. He usually called her 'chère amie' or 'Bien chère amie', occasionally 'Chère, chère amie' or 'Chère Dorothée'. She called him 'Dear Gide', 'Dearest Gide'. Once or twice she risked a 'Cher André', but did not trust herself to do it again.

All her letters but one are written in English. It was not only in order to pursue her task as a teacher but mostly because, perfect as her French was, she felt more secure in English for all the nuances she wanted to suggest, as between *to like* and *to love*. Very conscious of the depreciation undergone by *to love*, she wrote one day: '*Je vous aime*, it sounds better in French.' There was to be in 1948 an '*I love you*' in English from Gide which, three decades earlier, would have overwhelmed her; and it still does at the age of eighty-three, because she answers: 'I hope all this stuff won't bore and tire you. Dear Gide, at any rate it won't make your heart beat as one sentence in your letter made mine beat this morning. But then I say to myself: "He doesn't know English well enough to quite realize what he is saying!"' Then comes a P.S.: 'One word more – a postscript – the postscript of my life. I do believe those three English words in your letter. I believe, I know, you understand, you mean them.'

Three English words she had been dying to hear and had given up the hope of ever hearing since, probably, as long ago as 1918, from the lips which, according to Wilde, had never told a lie. The old Olivia was still willing, still eager to believe them, remembering that her younger self had written once: 'Love has always been the chief business of my life.'

JEAN LAMBERT

NOTE ON THE TEXT

This selection is based on the virtually complete French edition* of the more than one thousand extant letters exchanged by André Gide and Dorothy Bussy during the thirty-three years of their correspondence. So small an assortment, while necessarily reducing the scope, need not necessarily alter that feature which distinguishes the Gide–Bussy letters from the other Gide correspondences of a more purely literary character. It is the delineation of this unique aspect – the correspondents' friendship, its difficulties and development – that the present volume hopes to have preserved, more or less intact.

Most of the letters given are from the early and the late years, from the period when Dorothy Bussy's passion was young (and burdensome to her correspondent), and from the period beginning with Madeleine Gide's death and the Second World War, when Gide's affection becomes more expansive. Precedence given to the personal aspect – a precedence it already enjoys in the correspondence as a whole – does not mean that the two friends' professional concerns and literary quarrels, or that Gide's political involvements, are absent from the selection.

With one exception, indicated in the text, where excision was made to avoid offence to persons living, the letters are all given whole. Gide's were originally written in French, and have here been translated in a manner intended to have pleased Dorothy Bussy, for care was taken to be faithful even to her friend's inconsistencies, to his occasional ambiguities of phrase, and to those expanding yet inconclusive sentences in which he seems to be treading water, and that are as much the mirror of the position in which he found himself as they are the result of hasty composition.

The burden of notes has been much lightened; only those have been retained that help make the text intelligible. For further information on Gide bibliography and pertinent literary history, specialists are asked to refer to the French edition where, it is hoped, they will find satisfaction for their effort.

R.T.

* *Correspondance André Gide–Dorothy Bussy*, 3 vols., édition établie et présentée par Jean Lambert; notes de Richard Tedeschi (Paris, Gallimard, 1979–82).

1. Dorothy Bussy to André Gide

Paris

9th October 1918

Dear Monsieur Gide,

My brother Lytton wants me to ask you whether you think there would be a French public for his book[1] and if so whether you could give him any advice as to what he ought to do to get it translated and published.

We stayed on in London longer than we intended as Janie[2] got ill again but she is all right now and we are on our way South. Before we left we went to a last delightful supper party in Bloomsbury and saw a great many of your friends. The première danseuse[3] and other members of the Russian ballet were there, but it was Lady Ottoline[4] in her pink trousers who executed a *pas seul* for our entertainment and theirs. Then I enjoyed a pleasant conversation with Roger[5] which consisted for the most part in a kind of antiphonal chant in praise of our beloved Gide – though my responses were chiefly uttered silently and in my heart. Duncan Grant[6] was there too and his latest picture – a surprising and most welcome return to tradition ... I expect it all seems very remote to you now. I hope you have recovered from your fatigues and have settled down again satisfactorily to work. I think of you very often and am looking forward to hearing the sequel of all the stories of which you told me the beginnings.

Simon and Janie send you all sorts of messages.

Your affectionate friend
Dorothy Bussy

[1] *Eminent Victorians*, published in the spring of that year.
[2] The Bussys' daughter was then twelve years old.
[3] Lydia Lopokova, who became the wife of Maynard Keynes in 1925.
[4] Lady Ottoline Morrell (1874–1938) whose home at Garsington in Oxfordshire was a meeting place for artists and intellectuals. See Introduction, pp. ix–x.
[5] Roger Fry (1866–1934) had met Gide in Cambridge in August and discussed with him his translations of Mallarmé's poems (these were not published until after Fry's death). The meeting was extremely cordial, and Fry considered Gide already 'an old friend' (*v. The Letters of Roger Fry*, ed. Denys Sutton, London, Chatto & Windus, 1972, vol II).
[6] The painter Duncan Grant (1885–1978) was D.B.'s cousin.

P.S. In case you are kind enough to answer about Lytton my address until October 25th is

    Aux soins de Madame LeRoy Dapré
      Naudet
        par Vianne
          Lot-et-Garonne

and after that

    La Souco
      Roquebrune-Cap-Martin
        Alpes-Maritimes

As for yours I haven't the faintest notion what it is so I am sending this to the Nouvelle Revue Française[7] & hope you will get it eventually.

There seems to be a chance now that the war will be over before your Marc gets to fighting.[8]

2. André Gide to Dorothy Bussy

Cuverville
par Criquetot L'Esneval
Seine-Inférieure

18 Oct. 18

Dear friend[1]

Had I sooner got your address, you already would have received a lettre from me. I wrote to Lady Strachey, last week, enquiring after it. (Just her kind answer reaches me). Welcome is your letter which restore the clue between us! Your account about that last supper-party in Bloomsbury nettles my heart and my brain; but nothing was more chafing for me than the discovery I made in the pocket of my overcoat, the first day of my return at home, of your brother's letter, that letter you were speaking of and I told you I had not received,

---

[7] The publishing firm of which Gide was a founder. It is generally referrred to by its initials N.R.F., which, when italicized, indicate the review.

[8] Marc Allégret (1900–73), whose three older brothers were in the French army, was then doing military service in England (*v. The Correspondence of André Gide and Edmund Gosse*, ed. Linette F. Brugmans, New York University Press, 1959, pp. 162–4.)

LETTER 2

[1] With the exception of the last paragraph, the entire letter was written by Gide in English. Throughout this volume, words, phrases, sentences, etc., that were in English in Gide's text will be given in italics. Words which he underlined have been, wherever feasible, underlined in the English translation.

*which was waiting in this cover I don't know how long, unopened
. . . a letter inviting Mark and me to meet you and to spend with you
the week-end at Tidmarsh,[2] so kindly urging a letter that I couldn't
but yield to its prompting had I only received it in due time. I
answered it immediately, no more able alas! to accept. I did relate to
Mark the whole story, and we both remain, he, furious, and I,
inconsolable! 'All is as God overrules.'*

Eminent Victorians *lies on our sitting room's table and is constantly* 'en lecture'. *One of my sisters-in-law,[3] who converted some
years ago after having read Newman's writings, is particularly interested, and somewhat ruffled, however agreably. – Yet I'm not sure
this book may find in France many readers. I will consult some
friends, next week in Paris, about the question of a possible translation.[4]*

*I spent a few days in Paris, in the beginning of this month,
dreadfully tired; and couldn't find any friend, all of them being still
in the country, or in the army. Yet I met Lady R.[5] She told me the
Dragonnière was let for months and she didn't intend to steer
southward this winter. Notwithstanding I convinced her to postpone the publication of the* Ill Bound Prometheus *until I should be
able to afford new improvements – and if you allow me to bring with
me the manuscript to Roquebrune and be kind enough to read it
again with me . . . so much the better.*

*Take care, little Janie! Don't catch the grippe. I hope you enjoy a
radiant weather in Lot et Garonne. Here it pours so plenteously I
hope it remains not a single drop for you.*

*I duck and dive into Browning, with the greatest amazement. How
magnificent is such poem as 'Prospice'! How piercing 'Mr. Sludge'!
(you know, of course?) How fascinating . . . I don't remember to
ever have feel so complete and satisfactory a delight in any english
poet – but Shakespeare.*

[2] The weekend of 28–29 September, D.B. went along to Mill House, Tidmarsh,
where Lytton and Dora Carrington had been living for nearly a year.

[3] Mme Marcel Gilbert, née Valentine Rondeau, was the sister of Gide's wife.

[4] *Victoriens éminents* (translation by Jacques Heurgon under the pseudonym of
Jacques Dombale) was not published until a year after Strachey's death (N.R.F.,
1933).

[5] Lady Lillian Rothermere (d. 1937) whose 'literal translation' of the *Prométhée
mal enchaîné* was published in 1919 by Chatto & Windus. A new translation by
George Painter, dedicated 'To Dorothy Bussy, Gide's incomparable translator and
friend and "one of the most remarkable Englishwomen of her generation"', was
published by Secker & Warburg in 1953 in the Standard Edition of Gide's works.

Mille souvenirs à Simon Bussy, je vous prie. Ah! Je pense à vous bien souvent! Votre ami

André Gide

3. Dorothy Bussy to André Gide

La Souco
Roquebrune-Cap-Martin

31st Oct. 1918

My dear Friend,

– Do you know that this beginning to a letter which is such an ordinary one in French is very unusual in English? But it is a nice one all the same and I like it. –

It was a great pleasure getting your letter. I was particularly glad to hear of your 'ducking and diving' into Browning. I don't know whether he is the English poet I like or even admire most but he is without doubt the one I have most frequented – except Shakespeare. What a nuisance it is always being obliged to add 'except Shakespeare' – but one must. 'Mr. Sludge' is indeed amazingly good. I have heard that towards the end of the time at Florence, Elizabeth became perfectly infatuated with spiritualism, which he hated, and indeed that it almost cast a shadow over their last years together. But in spite of that 'Mr. Sludge' is *fair* – everything that can be said for him *is* said not only in justice but in sympathy. Do you know the other great study of dishonesty which one can't help setting as a pendant to Mr. Sludge though it is so different – I mean 'Bishop Blougram?'

I know Lytton was greatly disappointed that you didn't accept his lost invitation. The ruling of God upon that occasion was more than usually provoking. When the instrument of His will is Necessity one submits in silence, but when He uses the most futile of accidents to bring about His purposes – a bitterness is added – and a revolt.

It was a deplorably wet and melancholy Sunday at Tidmarsh. I was there all alone with Lytton and Miss Carrington – a pathetic ménage if ever there was one. So much adoration on one side, so much affection on the other – and the whole thing hopelessly unsuitable.

We are back again at Roquebrune and delighted to be in our own little home again. Simon has begun a picture of two crows from one of his Zoo studies – two grim, ravening crows. He had never read the gruesome old Scottish song *The Twa Corbies* – but even so they must have looked.

Janie is pretty well. Both he and she send you heaps of kind remembrances. As for me I am completely absorbed in putting my house tidy – my chief relaxation being that I am reading my two little girls[1] *Hamlet* and it is astonishing how much there is in it that they can feel.

And you? . . . A question mark that asks such an enormous lot that it knows well enough it will never get answered.

Oh! The *Ill-bound Prometheus*. What a mercy that you have managed to stave off its publication. Of course you must bring it with you when you come and we will have another go at it – only you must bring the original too or it will be no good.

Ever yours – do you know that this ending to a letter which would sound so terrific in French is very common in English and just implies a pleasant friendly intimacy? –

Yours ever
Dorothy Bussy

Is it possible to write a letter to a friend to-day – and that friend a Frenchman – without saying a word of thankfulness for France's deliverance? I say it with all the fervour that is in me. –

4. André Gide to Dorothy Bussy

Sunday 10th [November 1918]

Dear friend (I write that word with all my heart)

Allow me to write in French because I have precise things to tell you and am afraid of not being clear enough.

Lady R. was a bit miffed by a letter she received from Chatto & W[indus]. They, concerned that the translation they are to publish is

[1] Janie and Zoum, the daughter of their neighbour, the Belgian painter Jean Vanden Eeckhoudt. For a nostalgic account of these 'English lessons' and of life at La Souco, see the posthumously published memoirs, *Pour Sylvie*, by Zoum Walter, ed. Jacques Antoine (Bruxelles, 1975).

more 'literal' than . . . good, propose she have it looked at by a professional. Lady R. imagined that I had been influenced by Ch. & W., so I had some difficulty reassuring her. Today she accepts less willingly than she did yesterday my proposal of revision. Besides which, she fears the additional costs which such a delay (the tying up of type) and such changes would incur. And so here I am in a quandary.[1]

I am taking the liberty of sending you the two texts, English and French, and of presuming once again on your friendship by requesting that you reread the work. Two solutions are possible: either to allow the translation to appear as is, and face the criticism, mockery – or silence –. (I am prepared to do that.) Or to correct the most awkward blunders and give the public an approximation which will satisfy no one but which at least will not be too open to attack. It would be necessary in that case that you be kind enough to make, on the proofs, what you judge to be the most indispensable corrections; – it would be better to make these corrections (the readings you would propose) on a separate sheet, with references to the proofs. What a job I am proposing! What pleasure it would have been to do it with you. A third solution would be to induce Lady R. to renounce publication of the work altogether – but that wouldn't be possible.

It is unbearable to have to write you all this – when I have so much to tell you! But I have a horror of 'mixing genres' – and will write you all the rest another time. – I've had to extend my stay in Paris – where I am living with the Allégrets.[2] Marc is kept at Grantchester by a bad case of the grippe. I expect I'll take him south with his brother André during the Christmas holiday. Perhaps we shall be able to pay you a little visit, in anticipation of the longer one I shall make when my two nephews have left. Au revoir. A thousand affectionate remembrances to Simon Bussy; a thousand smiles for Janie.

I am your very grateful and devoted,
André Gide

I expect to be back in Cuverville in 3 days.

---

[1] With the single exception of his *Oscar Wilde* which had been published in 1905 in Oxford (translation by Stuart Mason), none of Gide's works had yet appeared in England. With Lady Rothermere's *Prometheus* he would make his début, a fact which caused him some anxiety.

[2] Gide was a close friend of the family of the Protestant minister Elie Allégret, but there existed no familial ties; his reference to the Allégret boys as 'nephews' is inexact.

5. André Gide to Dorothy Bussy

Cuverville
par Criquetot L'Esneval
S^{ne} Inf^{re}

19 Nov. 18

Dear friend

*Thousand thanks for your kind letter; it pours hope and gladness
in my heart. What you say about the translation is perfectly sound
and I believe with you the best thing to do would be to let drop the
aphorismes and ratiocinations which follow the tale (the most part
of them being quite silly – even in French – and of no interest at all in
English). I hope I shall be able to persuade Lady R. to let them drop.
Therefore don't trouble any more about that. I am sure that the
corrections you afford to the Prometheus are precisely those I wanted
– and I thank you very much.*

It is possible, probable even, that I will be called upon to leave for
the south as early as mid-December – which would allow me to see
you nearly a month earlier than I had thought. *I hope I shall find
Janie strong and healthy* – so sad to learn that she was poorly again. I
have lately been worried about Marc's health – and still am, since I
am left almost entirely without news. Brief little notes for his mother
is all that has been had from him, after 17 days of being bed-ridden.
I'm afraid he will come out of his grippe terribly weakened . . . I wish
I were with him!

I have just returned from Paris where I was able to attend the
Armistice celebrations. It was splendid; we lived three days in a state
of indescribable exhilaration. Victory doesn't yet seem real; I feel
a bit like one who dreams he has won the sweepstake and who
wonders how he will 'place' all that money! – Prodigious event!

For some time I have been doing less English in order to work
more. My *Symphonie Pastorale* (the young blind girl) was finished
yesterday. I think I might give it to the *Revue des Deux Mondes*, if
they want it.

I have found in Mrs. [Edith] Wharton an enthusiastic reader of
your brother's book – but have searched in vain for a translator. On
Mrs. W's advice, my wife and I have been reading aloud Dana's *Two*

Years Before the Mast ... do you know it? – Of rather special interest – but thrilling.

Is Simon Bussy working? Please give him by best wishes. I think of you with all my heart

and am very amicably yours,
André Gide.

6. Dorothy Bussy to André Gide

La Souco

20th Nov. 1918

Dear Friend

I am returning you by this post the *Prométhée*. Lady R's translation and my suggested corrections – in two parcels. I have also added one or two notes which you might show her if you thought fit.

I hope you will go through the corrections carefully yourself. There seem, I am afraid, a good many, but you will see, I think, that they either involve very little alteration of type or when this is not the case, they are important to the sense – except a few cases where I have altered because the English was too ugly.

In my notes I have just 'épluchéd' *one* passage as I thought she might be interested to see the reasons of my suggestions. I have got no dictionary with me – except Roget. My beloved *Oxford* I left in England as it was so heavy to pack – and I regret it bitterly.

Janie is getting on all right – downstairs today for the first time. I hope Marc is well again too.

But we must not 'mix our genres' so I'll say no more except that I am

Affectionately yours
Dorothy Bussy

It was all I could do not to correct the English of the Preface! Enclosed a snippet from the *Times* – rather lovely.

7. André Gide to Dorothy Bussy

Cuverville

23 Nov. 18

Dear friend,

I received at the same time volume, letter, and annotations. I am embarrassed at the trouble you have taken and more grateful than I can say. What an enormous service you have done me! All your comments, all of them, strike me as excellent. In a few days I return to Paris to get Lady R. to swallow the pill without becoming too red in the face – but I don't doubt, I prefer not to doubt, that she will submit graciously. It is to her advantage as well as mine, for the errors you point out seem to me, for the most part, monstrous. Thank you.

How happy I am to know Janie has recovered – and how delighted that I shall see you all soon. Marc has fallen ill again, and more seriously than before. That trip to the south, which was to have been purely for pleasure, will now be indispensable to assure his convalescence. But he is as yet in no condition to undertake it. The weather is bright but terribly cold. I huddle at a corner of the hearth like an old man.

My wife is deep in your brother's book; it would please you to see the great interest she takes in it.

Au revoir. A thousand best wishes to you. I am very amicably

Yours,
André Gide

8. Dorothy Bussy to André Gide

24th Nov. 1918

Dear Gide

Yesterday I opened unsuspectingly an innocent looking letter and it was an announcement that one of my dearest friends – perhaps the dearest left me – had died of the grippe after three days' illness.[1] It was horrid.

And I thought of the people – there aren't many – whose death would give me the same kind of shock. And I thought of you. Yes, you to whom I am only the tiniest bit more than a mere acquaintance, you in whom I have so little confidence that I am afraid of being impertinent and intrusive when I tell you of a private grief. You have become so oddly important to me that I shiver with apprehension at the idea of your being carried off in three days by this horrible illness. And, you know, no kind relation would write and break the news to me. I shouldn't even see it in the *Petit-Niçois*, which is the only French paper I ever read and which is concerned with more important things than the lives of such people as you. I shouldn't, I *hope* I shouldn't get one of those loathsome 'lettres de faire part' – but I should probably come across an allusion to your 'obsèques' in the Echos of the *Mercure*[2] a fortnight after the event – or somebody would casually say at tea-time 'I suppose you've heard that André Gide . . . etc.' And though a few months ago you were nothing but a name to me I think if I were to hear those words now the world would seem a very dark place. And I shiver with apprehension and all that I feel about you and all the thousand things I care about concerning you seem just to be swallowed up in the single desire that you should keep alive. Well! I can only pray that I shall expire of the grippe before you do – which after all is just as likely, if not more so.

Will this seem ridiculous?

Ah! that appelation you have given me, from your heart, you say – after all it can't mean anything if it doesn't mean that you have given me the right sometimes to tell you what I am feeling.

There is nothing more tiresome, is there, than to answer in cold blood a letter that has been written in emotion, but you know that you needn't. Just drop this into that convenient and capacious waste paper basket of oblivion and ignoring that you always keep so handily beside you. And let your next letter be about Lady R.'s translation or what you will – but let it come some day and let it be kind – as usual.

D.B.

[1] Beatrice Chamberlain (1862–1918), the half-sister of Neville, had been D.B.'s friend since adolescence. She seems to have been the inspiration for the character of Laura in *Olivia*.
[2] The fortnightly review, *Mercure de France*.

9. André Gide to Dorothy Bussy

Cuverville

12 December 18

Dear friend,

My reply to your first letter was delayed by the arrival of your second. Let's talk 'business' first: Lady R. with whom I worked two entire afternoons, has accepted (and with gratitude) all your corrections – or nearly all. I was unfortunately able to write in corrections on only about the first half of the book; I had no time for the remainder; but I carefully read over everything with her, and have no doubt that she corrected the end of the volume as scrupulously as I had done the beginning. In any case, I am to receive a fresh set of proofs and will pass the book for press only when I have assured myself that all corrections have been made. Once more, thank you. You will have been my salvation! – As for the *Pensées* and reflections that follow the *Prometheus*, it is agreed to drop them. Ouf!

Yes, I was going to write to assure you of my sympathy in your grief. You hadn't yet told me who it was, so that I assumed I didn't know the friend you had lost. Having been able to appreciate Miss Chamberlain's rare qualities allows me to share all the more in your sadness. How your letter moved me! And what obscure premonition prompted you to write to me at the very moment I was myself going through a period of such despair that the terrible supposition you had made concerning me was nearly realized. Perhaps, if I were there with you, your patient affection would tempt me to talk to you a little about the catastrophe that has just thrown my life into confusion and wiped out every bright prospect.[1] My heart is shattered, my back broken. Were you to see me now, you would no longer recognize your Cambridge companion. And three weeks of it already! And life goes on ... but it seems I do no more than pretend to live ... But please make no mention of this; my distress must be kept secret, and I can give no better mark of my affection than to let you glimpse it this way.

I had to write to my friends in Saint-Clair[2] that it's painful for me

---

[1] Allusion to the conjugal drama of Cuverville. In a gesture of despair provoked by Gide's journey to England with Marc Allégret, Madeleine destroyed all the letters her husband had ever written to her.

[2] The family of the Belgian painter Théo Van Rysselberghe.

to have to forgo seeing you – at least as soon as I had hoped. Toward the end of winter perhaps I shall be able to come . . . ? but I no longer dare promise or hope anything.

Please don't leave me without news of you, and of Simon Bussy and of Janie. And believe in my very faithful affection.

André Gide

Marc is feeling a bit better; we hope to see him back in Paris towards the end of the month.

10. Dorothy Bussy to André Gide

Roquebrune Cap Martin

18th Dec. 1918

Yes, I had a presentiment – first a terror – and then the feeling that has haunted me day and night, for so many days and nights now, that something dreadful was happening to you. And it is so horrible being in the dark that at first your letter was almost a relief to me. But now the relief is over and I'm sitting face to face with the irreparable. You have been hurt – you are in pain. The beautiful spirit I loved has perhaps been spoilt irretrievably. No – no – I'll not believe it. You will recover. You are strong enough. You must.

Oh! dear Prometheus, the spark of fire you bring us down from Heaven, it's you that must pay the cost of it. Your gift to us poor wretched mortals must be paid for with your heart's blood and we can only look on. But you know – none better – what passionate gratitude we feel for those who bring us fire from Heaven and there are some who will feel that for you. Perhaps it does not seem worth while, but it is your fate – your fate to be a fire-bearer and to suffer.

I said I hadn't confidence in you – but now I have – implicit confidence that you understand and accept my affection. My patient affection. Yes patient for as long as you will, but impatient too. Oh! impatient of all that keeps me so far away from you for ever.

Simon is well and working. Janie well again too. Their disappointment at hearing business prevented you from coming was very great. But I was not disappointed. I knew that it was not to be.

Yours
Dorothy Bussy

11. Dorothy Bussy to André Gide

31st Dec. 1918

Tonight the thought of your unhappiness is so cruelly present to me that I can't prevent myself from writing. You said in that last letter of yours that my '*affreuse supposition*' nearly came true. Do you know that was a torturing thing to say to me and ever since I read it my life has been one sickening anxiety. Will you tell me – if you can truly – that there is no longer any need for that fear?

I care so much – so incredibly much. I can easily bear never seeing you again but not that you should suffer as much as that.

Oh! dear friend, forgive me. I don't know what I'm saying or what I mean. I only know I am in pain too – not for myself, don't think it is for myself, only for you.

Yrs.
Dorothy Bussy

12. André Gide to Dorothy Bussy

Cuverville-en-Caux

21 Jan. 19

Dear friend,

Increased activity doesn't leave me the time to write to you as I should like, but I am afraid my silence might worry you – and I also want to tell you how sweet your last letter was to me – and how good for me still, each time I read it. The fortunate *buoyancy* of my nature has rallied; it still astonishes me and I cannot fully understand where I found the courage to go on living . . . or why I am telling you all this, which I hide from everyone else. And perhaps you would have seen nothing of it, if you had been living near me. For me to speak to you this way, you can see that the affection you have shown me with such exquisite discretion must have touched the best part of my heart.

Au revoir – I don't know when. But you will find me to be

very faithfully, your very fond
André Gide.

A thousand good wishes to Simon Bussy and to Janie.

13. Dorothy Bussy to André Gide

La Souco
Roquebrune-Cap Martin

23d Feb. '19.

Dear Gide

It is one month since I heard from you, close upon two since I wrote to you last. Isn't that long enough to prove that I can practise the virtue of abstention? More, would be self mortification and of that I'm incapable.

Oh! I like sometimes to knock at your door and imagine you letting me in and giving me – I dare to hope – a welcome, like those you gave me once or twice before and which I thought the sweetest and most charming I had ever had. And I should sit down and ask you questions, interminably and boldly – that is, in my dream, you know, and it's unlikely you'll ever suffer from it in reality.

For when I say – What is happening to you? How are you? What are you doing? Are you writing? And what? Are you publishing? What happened about Méral[1] and his review? – just as a beginning – you must remember that I don't really care to ask what you don't care to answer and consider that these aren't questions but just, as it were, sighs.

We have been reading some of your books lately. Simon was so carried away by what you say about art in the two lectures printed in *Prétextes* that he was on the verge of writing to tell you what a pleasure it was to find some one who had the same thoughts as he and could express them like you. But you are a provoking person for most of your books seem unprocurable. When I write for them to the booksellers – I have tried at least three – they simply don't answer – as if I were a mere lunatic and had ordered a slice of the moon or a small star. And yet I want my bit of moon desperately. And to think that Lady Rothermere has books of yours which I have never read enrages me.

We have had a visit from Keynes. Do you remember him? He is in Paris, a delegate at the Peace Conference and a great swell. He had a good many interesting things to tell us – besides gossip about our English friends – as for instance that Roger is 'au dernier bien' with

---

[1] Paul Méral (pseudonym of Paul de Guchtenaere) was then the protégé of Lady Rothermere.

'Lalla'[2] and though he denies the soft impeachment is highly pleased that it should be made. Here I am talking nonsense to you as usual. Oh I wish I could see you smile. And in a fortnight's time the Van Rysselberghes are coming to Menton and I suppose I shall see them and have to talk about you which I detest doing (even with your friends who will only say nice things) and which you may be sure I shall do as little as possible. I take particular pains not to hear and so far I never have heard one single thing about you that you haven't told me yourself.

But alas! the visitor I wanted hasn't come, isn't coming, and I don't care about any of the rest.

Simon is well and working away very eagerly, and on the whole happily, at his beasts – strange, apocalyptic creatures they are. Janie too is well – better than usual that is. They send you their affectionate remembrances.

And Marc? I wonder how he is. I hope he is quite strong again by now.

You wrote me a very kind little note. If you hadn't my heart would have broken and you would never have heard any more of me. But this time it's different and if you are too busy to answer me – or too weary, dear Gide, I shan't mind and in another month or two, I shall come back to knock again – patiently and hopefully.

Your devoted friend
Dorothy Bussy

14. André Gide to Dorothy Bussy

9 rue de la Cure
(Avenue Mozart)
Paris XVI

rec'd. 1st March 1919[1]

Dear friend,

I was hoping for, waiting for, your letter. It arrived this morning

[2] Hélène Frédérique Speyer (1870–1964). She had spent the war years in England with her second husband, the Belgian socialist Emile Vandervelde. There she met Roger Fry who painted her portrait. Together they made a brief journey to France (July 1916) during which Fry met Picasso and Matisse.

LETTER 14
[1] In D.B.'s hand.

and I answer it immediately so that you won't make me wait so long for the next. – I am back in Paris; dreadful weather, icy gusts of wind, grippe and pneumonia everywhere. I don't know how I managed to escape until now, but since yesterday I haven't stopped coughing, and had someone telephone Lady Rothermere that I shall not be able to accept her luncheon invitation today with M. Paul Méral. I have seen neither of them in a long time – and have been waiting for the book from Chatto to whom I sent the proofs over a month ago – having carefully verified that all your corrections had been made.

I managed at last to procure a slow-combustion stove; the work-men are in process of installing it at Villa Montmorency[2] where I hope to return in ten days or so – and to have a visit from you on your trip north. Your letter was lovely. I too answer in imagination those questions which in imagination you ask – and probably much better than either of us should be capable of doing in reality. We shall give it a try nevertheless.

I am housed temporarily at the Allégrets, very agreeably since I can follow Marc's progress from day to day, but not in a way that allows me to collect myself for work. Only by confronting a new piece of work will I know whether last autumn's terrible ordeal hasn't been too crushing. I'm eager to begin.

How glad I am to think that Simon B. is working and Janie is well – which doubtless permits you to be well, too. When can one see this series of animals? Oh, if only I could have come to see you in the south!

I certainly hope, at least, that you'll be able to receive the visit of my friends the Van Rys[selberghe]. – Madame Théo is in Brussels, but Elisabeth and Miss Whitehorn,[3] whom I went off to join near Edinburgh, with Marc if you remember, are still in Saint-Clair. I'd like you to meet them.

Delighted to learn that Simon B. appreciates my *Prétextes*. If you are unable to find some book of mine that you would like to read, tell me – and I shall attempt to procure it for you . . . but it is true that certain of them can hardly be found.

I have been making up my mind to take on direction of the *N.R.F.* which will resume publication in May . . . I hope. It would mean a great deal of work and worry . . .

---

[2] The park in Passy where Gide owned a house.

[3] Gide's intimate friend is referred to as 'Madame Théo' or 'la petite dame'. Elisabeth (1890–1980) is her daughter; Ethel Whitehorn, known as 'Whity', is Elisabeth's English friend.

A thousand fond remembrances and smiles round about you.

> Your faithful,
> André Gide

Excuse this very pale ink . . . I wonder whether you can read me.

15. Dorothy Bussy to André Gide

17th March 1919

Roquebrune Cap Martin

Dear Gide

Yesterday we thought and talked of you. Your friends came – M. Van Rysselberghe and Elisabeth and Miss Whitehorn, Mme Schlumberger and Monica.[1] Of all the party, the one to whom I at once and quite unexpectedly took a fancy was Miss Whitehorn. I thought my young compatriot – was there ever anything more English? – wonderfully refreshing. She gave me such a vivid and delightful account of how she saw you off at Charing Cross and I just loved hearing that you got your English books safely packed and bought yourself boots and a necktie at the Army and Navy!

Elisabeth is a different matter. One doesn't get to the bottom of Elisabeth in half an hour at an afternoon party. She seemed a restless, uneasy, rather tragic person. But I liked her too.

She said she was going to see you soon. Lucky Elisabeth!

And after they had gone I was sad. I seemed to feel, even more acutely than usual, what an immense way off you are. All these people – your friends – who know you so well – who have known you so long –

We are beginning to think of our return to England. We shall probably spend a few days in Paris during the first week in May. I want to take Janie to the Comédie Française and her father wants to show her the Louvre. And there will be a few friends to see – and you – oh! perhaps you?

> Yrs sincerely
> Dorothy Bussy

[1] One of the Schlumberger daughters.

16. André Gide to Dorothy Bussy

Dudelange
Grand Duchy of Luxemburg

29 April 19 (beginning
tomorrow, again: Villa
Montmorency, Paris)

Dear friend,

I have been here in the Grand Duchy of Luxemburg for twelve days, at the home of friends[1] who <u>must</u> soon become yours. I return to Paris this very evening – where I hope to see you shortly, although winter's renewed onslaught can hardly be an incentive for quitting the south just now. Madame Van Rysselberghe, Elisabeth, and Miss Whitehorn are here – and speak to me about you. Marc was with us until the day before yesterday. He precedes me by two days to Paris, where today he resumes his studies – and where his father, back from Africa, is soon to arrive.

I have something very specific to say and shall come straight to the point: Madame Mayrisch de Saint Hubert, the excellent friend with whom I took the trip into Asia Minor a few months before the declaration of war – and at whose home we are now gathered – would like her daughter to go to Cambridge next October. It is a wish we all concur in; I myself have strongly encouraged her – and have no better way of showing you what a fine remembrance I have of last summer. Andrée Mayrisch is eighteen years old. She has just spent a year in Geneva, as a 'student', and would like to pursue her studies in England (her English is already fluent) by taking courses principally in political economy and the social sciences. I don't remember ever meeting a more interesting – or more gifted – girl than she, and should very much like her to enter into relations with the people I met through you, primarily Miss Harrison, your sister, Miss Norton, and Dickinson,[2] who will not fail to take as lively an

[1] The Mayrischs. Aline Mayrisch, known as 'Loup', is the intimate friend of Mme Théo.
[2] The classical scholar Jane Ellen Harrison, J.E. 'Betty' Norton (Gibbon's bibliographer and the sister of Harry Norton), and D.B.'s sister Pernel (Joan) Strachey all taught at Newnham. Dickinson is Goldsworthy Lowes Dickinson of King's College, the friend of Roger Fry and others of the Cambridge–Bloomsbury circle.

interest in her as she will take in everything she can learn from them. I was thinking that the best thing would be for her to enrol as a student at Newnham; but before deciding anything, we shall wait for advice which you are doubtless in a position to give us – since we don't know exactly the admission policy of that college. In any case, if it is by examination, I have no doubt that Andrée Mayrisch is capable of passing – and brilliantly.

Whity (Miss Whitehorn) plans to accompany her, without yet knowing exactly how she herself will settle at Cambridge. She would like to take courses . . . which? All this is to be looked into. You will help me, won't you?

How much more I still have to tell you! I left Paris very tired, but the two weeks of rest here have completely set me up again. I think of you often and should like to talk with you more. How readily I pictured you here among us . . . Soon another letter, but perhaps you will be so kind as to write me a few words beforehand concerning the plans I put to you here.

A thousand affectionate remembrances to Simon Bussy; a thousand smiles to Janie – and from Marc as well. Believe me to be

your very faithful friend
André Gide.

17. Dorothy Bussy to André Gide

27 Grange Road
Cambridge

May 14th 1919

What a relief to be able to write to you without pretending – without pretending to pretend.

Travelling towards you with exhausting slowness, being torn and whirled away from you with despairing swiftness – that is what my whole life seems to have turned into. All my light is behind me now. Soon I shall be in the thick of the tunnel again with the horrid fear of dying, stifled before the faintest little glimmer appears at the other end.

But for the present I am still living on my four days.[1] Oh! I saw your face again. And a great many fears and anxieties dropped away from me. It was pale and tired but the spirit is not broken. The flame was there in all its brightness – the intensity, the eagerness. I suppose you don't know how beautiful your face is – a mille times more beautiful than Marc's. Ah! my friend, I am not like you. Never in all my life has my soul been tempted by youth and its bloom. I have never loved a face that had not the visible marks of thought and suffering upon it ... And afterwards I looked at it for my own particular doom. Writing to you in the dark like that had been very difficult. Two of my senseless letters you had left unanswered. For two months I had had nothing from you. I had been afraid it was worse than indifference – perhaps disgust. But now I have seen your face, I don't think I shall fear that again – at any rate not just yet.

You gave me some words which I carry in my heart, which make my heart stand still when I remember how you said them – It wasn't the day when we were sitting in your room, underneath your wife's portrait, when you could find nothing for me but pity and kindness, when you said – 'Voilà ce que je *craignais*.'[2] No, but the day before in the garden. I will repeat them for I don't want you to forget them yet. 'Cette affection,' you said 'que je ne connaissais pas il y a un an, j'en ai besoin à présent; je ne peux plus m'en passer; ne me la retirez pas.'[3] Oh! it's not your kindness I want – I want my pain to give you pleasure. I want you to be a little glad of it. If my unhappy letters succeed in giving you only so poor a thing as a *literary* satisfaction – why! take it! I am content to suffer even for that. I think I'd be willing to suffer for the rest of my life just to believe that I had warmed the tips of your fingers for a few moments.

But I wouldn't have you think that you have spoiled or lessened or changed my other loves. No, they remain still my daily bread, the very stuff my life is made of. But you are my Kingdom of Heaven – something outside me – a vision – a glory – a despair.

Oh, Gide. I will try and write something more sensible soon. And how can you, how can you say they are all well written when they are so frightfully empty of all I try to put in them?

D. B.

---

[1] The Bussys had spent four days in Paris on their way to England.

[2] 'That's what I was afraid of.'

[3] 'This affection that was unknown to me a year ago I now need, can no longer do without. Don't take it from me.'

18. Dorothy Bussy to André Gide

27 Grange Road
Cambridge

27th May [1919]

Dear Gide

It makes me very happy to feel you are really pleased I should have translated the *Porte Etroite*[1] – I was afraid you wouldn't be. I felt I ought to have asked your leave before starting on a journey which was so clearly to be in sacred ground, but I couldn't, because I didn't know till I got to the last page whether I should be able to finish it. – I spent an odd winter with your book. I remember the first time I read it – years ago. I rebelled against it and shrank from it. I wouldn't let it hurt me. It was cowardice. But this time there was no escaping. I leant upon the sharpness of its point – passionately. I drove it home and turned it round in my heart. It has left me, I think, with my own poor little capacity of thinking and suffering and loving enlarged – and oh! I am sure, with an added intensity of wonder and gratitude for the people who can think and suffer and love really.

And it was my companion. Day and night your voice, your sweet, excruciating voice, spoke to me. I ruminated your words, and their music and their meaning, and let them sink into me and become part of me – I hardly wanted more of you during the winter.

But now that is over. I have nothing to do, and I am here – in Cambridge – without you – without a single hope of you. It is extraordinarily beautiful in this lovely spring – and extraordinarily haunted – and sometimes I find it very difficult to bear.

I shall be so immensely interested in your remarks. I hope there will be numbers of them. I so often wanted your help, so often hesitated, so often didn't know what to choose and what to sacrifice. No, I am very far indeed from feeling sure that it is well done. Let me know as soon as you hear about Conrad, because I've already spoken to Lytton about it. He hasn't read the book and said he couldn't promise anything till he had, but he didn't refuse, didn't seem inclined to refuse.

All the set here are very full of their new review *The Athenaeum* –

---

[1] D.B. had not mentioned the translation to Gide until it was finished. It did not find a publisher, however, until 1924.

edited by Middleton Murry. Have you seen it? Lytton writes for it, but only very occasionally, Roger often, my brother James does the dramatic criticism, and there are a good many bright and advanced people who contribute to it. I see your friend Valéry writes a letter from France[2] so I suppose you know all about it.

By all means let Mlle Mayrisch put her name down for Newnham. But I don't think there's much chance for her – and if that is all we have to rely upon for your keeping up a connection with Cambridge, I'm afraid it's a broken reed. Not that it much matters to me. I don't suppose we shall ever live here again.

Oh, Gide – your letter – real words from you to me. So few, so meagre, so rare, so costly. All such joys seem to have to be bought with a double price – to be earned beforehand with what painful toll, to be paid for afterwards with what pangs. And will any pilgrimage and any penance buy me what most I want – the words that shall be about you and not about me? For in all this (though you reproved me when I tried to say so) it is not my own feelings that interest me – them I endure as best I can, but really, really I don't think much of them, nor am I much pre-occupied as to any regard you may have for me. This is too unimportant and too simple a part of you for me to mind about – much. It is you I think of. To know about you – anything about you – your journeys, your books, your friendships, your adventures – ah! your loves – this is what I long for with a kind of desperate curiosity, which may be base – which at any rate, you seem to have forbidden. And I reflect, somewhat bitterly, that when I liked you less, you told me more. It is perhaps one of the consequences of my liking you, of my showing it to you. Well! if so, if I've lost my chance because of that, it can't be helped – there's nothing to wish otherwise

Your friend
Dorothy Bussy

19. André Gide to Dorothy Bussy

Thursday 5 June 1919

Dear friend,

I should like to write you the letter you expect, for I sense how deserving of it your friendship is . . . Oh, do understand at least that

[2] 'La Crise de l'esprit', on the intellectual crisis resulting from the war, appeared in translation in two instalments (11 April, 2 May, 1919).

my silence implies not the slightest <u>lack of trust</u>, but rather an excessive difficulty in talking about myself. I have often lived in a truly triumphal manner, and yet, as you have guessed – my whole life appears to me at times to be a frightful drama, more terrible than any of those one reads about in books. This past autumn I believe I touched the bottom of horror and despair, and for a long time I no longer understood <u>how</u> I would manage to go on living . . . And yet I do live, and feel in my heart, in my whole being, such a demand for joy that I doubt whether the happiest creature could not yet find room to envy me. This is perhaps precisely the kind of happiness given by the demon one sells one's soul to . . . But the terrible thing is that the devil doesn't scare me – that I sometimes pretend to believe in him, but that finally I don't at all believe in him – And what irritates me, on the other hand, is that that is precisely what he wants: that one not believe in <u>him</u>. That's how he takes possession of the soul. Each time I chat with him (it was not very long ago, in any case, that I made his acquaintance)[1] I hear him murmur: How could you be afraid of me? You know very well I don't exist.

Under pretext of talking about myself, you see what I am led to write! . . . The devil makes me think of Lytton. My friend hadn't yet written to Conrad concerning the preface to *La Porte étroite*, and I told him not to pursue it since you have already spoken to your brother and since it doesn't appear he will refuse. On the contrary, it is in the event of a refusal from Lytton that I would turn again to Conrad. But Lytton won't refuse, will he? In any case, tell him how much I would like it, but in such a way, however, as not to force him.

I have to tell you again, dear friend: I marvel at your translation (the word is not too strong) – as do some friends to whom I gave it to read, fearing that perhaps my affection for you might cloud my perception and distort my judgement. And if now I am eagerly hoping for the book's favourable reception by publisher and public, it is also in the hope (which I hardly dare formulate) that you will be tempted to translate another one soon . . . And I hope that in the meantime my *Prometheus Ill Bound* will not irremediably disgust them!

[1] It was Jacques Raverat who 'introduced' Gide to the Devil in September 1914. Until that time, Gide 'did not yet understand that evil is a positive, active, enterprising principle; [he] used to think . . . that evil was simply a lack of good, as darkness is a lack of light'. See Gide's *Journal*, trans. Justin O'Brien, vol. 2, 1914–1927 p. 84, pp. 187–90 (New York, Knopf, 1948), for a discussion presumably provoked by a reading with Raverat of Milton's ode 'On the Morning of Christ's Nativity'.

Saturday

This is a very unsatisfactory letter; I am within an inch of tearing it up . . . but my silence would pain you even more. Nothing I say about myself is sincere; only what I hide is true. But I feel that you guess what I am hiding, and better than if I had expressed it. How can I thank you enough for your letters? . . . A thousand fond remembrances. I am your friend

André Gide.

20. Dorothy Bussy to André Gide

16th June 1919

I wasn't expecting, wasn't even hoping to hear from you – just thinking: 'My poor Gide, what an intolerable, unpardonable letter I wrote him! He will want to be kind but there's nothing to be done with such things but to leave them unanswered.' I felt that all I deserved was the fate of Rosencrantz and Guildenstern – to be left to perish in England coldly and remorselessly. Would *I* seem to know your stops? Would *I* pluck out the heart of your mystery?[1] Never – never. God forbid!

Your mystery! Senseless that I am, I'm not too senseless to understand that you couldn't reveal it to me even it you wanted to. I know that the darkness through which your light shines is you as much as the light. I don't want the darkness gone – only to come near to it – as near as I dare and you will let me. And sometimes I tremble to think how strangely, unexpectedly near I am.

How glad I am you are really pleased with the translation. I wonder whether Mrs. Wharton was one of the friends to whom you showed it? I can't get any definite answer from Lytton till you send me a copy that he can see. This won't make you hurry over your remarks, will it? I want there to be as many as possible.

Last week I had a silly accident which only hurt me a little. Your letter stopped me from wishing it had killed me. After that I was able to enjoy the new Russian Ballet, *La Boutique Fantasque*, a great success for our countryman Derain, among the general public and the élite as well. Supper afterwards at Gordon Square.[2] It is odd

---

[1] See *Hamlet*, III. ii.

[2] This supper, at which forty guests were served by Duncan Grant, Maynard Keynes and two maids, is described by Clive Bell in 'Paris in the twenties' in *Old Friends* (London, Chatto & Windus, 1956).

doing all the same things as last year. We went to lunch at the Raverats, and Simon encouraged him and looked at his pictures, and I looked out of the window and tried to imagine myself as I was a year ago. Poor Raverat seems better and more hopeful about his health.[3]

I have just been reading a book of yours which I had not read before (I had to wait for Raverat to lend it to me) – the five *Traités* bound up with *L'Enfant Prodigue*. I don't think it's admiration that makes me sink in a heap on the ground at your feet. No, it's *not* admiration. It is just the sound of your words which makes my head swim and loosens my sinews and turns my bones to water, so that my limbs won't hold me up any longer. The only other person who has ever given me that feeling of physical dissolution in a kind of agonising sweetness is – but for the world I wouldn't say it to anybody but you – is Keats himself. Afterwards if I want to admire, I have to pick myself up and try and stand on my feet again.

Oh! Gide – How do I dare? How do I dare write to you? Why do you encourage it? You could easily stop me, you know. When you say it's time to go, I don't wait to be told twice, do I? And every single time it's an eternal good-bye that I say to you. The 'défense' may come from you – or more terrifying still – from me – or from an outside fate – but of course come it must.

Good bye – no – no – not yet.

Yours
D.B.

21. Dorothy Bussy to André Gide

22nd June, 1919

My very dear Friend

What was there in your letter to offend me? I saw in it only your wish to content me by answering my foolish prayer to talk to me about yourself. You needn't be frightened. You didn't reveal anything very terrible – or anything at all for that matter, that I could make out.

Never once I believe have I posted a letter to you without thinking that it would put an end to your friendship and that you would never

[3] Gide had known Jacques Raverat since at least March 1914. Raverat, who died in 1925, was married to Gwen Darwin.

write to me again. (And not without cause? for what is it I don't reveal?) Sometimes I have lived dreary weeks with that thought. But oh I have always waited. I have never begged you to tell me it was not so. That you should have done so shows, doesn't it, that you didn't really believe it. But . . .

No, I've thought of a hundred ways of going on and none will do.

My chief pleasure hitherto has been to speak nothing to you but the truth. To-day my instinct is to hide how much – not your letter but the little note that followed it, has moved me.

You will return now, dear divinity, I know, to the coldest and remotest of your heights. It is best you should. For I think it is only so my mortal flesh can endure you without being consumed.

But don't regret, don't regret too much your little flashing visit to my heart.

Yrs. D.B.

Oh! this letter too is going to torture me like the others.

P.S.

André Gide – André Gide –

This morning a sudden wave of comfort and confidence has come over me.

You are my kind, my 'faithful friend,' as you are fond of signing yourself. And this morning I believe it. You like me and want me. We get on together. We understand each other. What is a joy to me is a pleasure too to you. All the rest is nonsense. Did I say it wasn't affection I feel for you? Oh! how untrue. It is affection – too – the simplest; the commonest, the most comfortable. I want you to be happy in all the great things and all the small.

D.B.

22. Dorothy Bussy to André Gide

24th June, 1919

Dear Gide

Do you believe in telepathy? I do. I think nothing else can explain the odd little episode which has just taken place and to which, no doubt, I am attaching far too much importance. Of course it is one of the symptoms of my malady and you will make allowances for me

with your usual generosity. I have been puzzling myself to death
wondering what on earth there was in your letter to make me put an
end to our friendship and not write to you any more and I simply
cannot make it out. The worst of it is as it was something so very
awful you will certainly never tell me and it must be added to the
heap of never to be solved mysteries which surround you. Perhaps
you thought my English propriety would be too shocked at your
talking about the devil? Those remarks I simply took to be your way
of saying that you have always been preoccupied, are constantly and
have been especially recently preoccupied with the conduct of life.
I daresay you thought when you had written them that they were
rather nonsense – I daresay they were. But goodness gracious! you
didn't suppose I was going to uproot my affection for you and inflict
on myself the most horrible of mutilations simply because you wrote
a little nonsense – and of so very mild a type? No I can give you credit
for a good deal more and a good deal worse than that without being
in the least bit disturbed by it. But as a matter of fact at the very time
you were writing that letter but *before* I got it, I was trying to make
up my mind – for the first time really seriously – not to uproot my
affection for you – how could I do that? but to stop my letters which
would mean to stop every contact with you. I had actually written
the letter to tell you so though I hadn't had the courage to send it and
during all that fortnight I was saying Good-bye to you in my heart –
not because *you* talked nonsense but because *I* did. It seemed to me
that you had got from me everything that could be of the faintest use
to you and that all the rest was pure self indulgence on my part. After
I had written you that odious letter asking you to tell me about
yourself I couldn't bear myself. I felt I was degenerating into a beggar
and a coward and the thought of going on like that and soon
becoming a weariness to you filled me with disgust. Then came your
letter – the letter you thought so absurd and regretted posting. To me
it was a respite. I seemed to feel in it that you weren't quite tired of me
yet. All my resolutions melted – perhaps they had never been sincere
– I answered it, but though I had given up all thoughts of breaking
off, I remember the possibility was still haunting me terribly. And on
the same day you wrote the little note which told me that the fear had
been with you too.

   All this long rigmarole to prove a case of telepathy! I suspect you of
being more sorry for that little lapse into humanity than for the letter
that went before. Don't be. I know you are human but I haven't felt

you so since you said good-bye to me last year in London. Since then you have been inhabiting inaccessible regions. Even your kindness and compassion were absent-minded. Ah! how sweet to feel you human. Yet, dear human friend, doubt is so painful a thing in friendship that though yours has been sweet to me, I wouldn't have you doubt again. Believe that as long as you want my love it is yours – But how can I tell whether you want it really – and you so polite? Why, a miracle has happened to prove to me that you do – a little. I won't exaggerate. And now you may go on writing me the dryest emptiest, blankest letters, *nothing* but about Mlle Mayrisch, and I shan't care a pin. The blanker they are the better pleased I shall be. I am safe. I am happy.

Your
D.B.

P.S. In two days I will send you all the details I can about Mlle Mayrisch. Of course I'm delighted to do what I can – very little.

23. Dorothy Bussy to André Gide

Telephone,   96, South Hill Park
Hampstead 7163   Hampstead Heath, N.W.

July 4th 1919

Dear Friend

I dreamt a little while ago – this is no fable, but a literal and accurate account of what made a very vivid impression on me, and I'm telling it to you so that you may see my sleeping self is not very different from my waking – well, I dreamt that I was walking beside you along a country road, an ordinary country road. You couldn't think of anything to say to me, but I was content because I was beside you. Suddenly a ray of sunshine fell on the branches of some trees that were standing by the roadside and lighted them up with what seemed to me a miracle of golden radiance. An irrepressible impulse made me turn to you and cry out 'How beautiful! Isn't it beautiful?' And you answered with a smile and a shake of your head, 'No, chère amie, there is nothing beautiful. It is a very ordinary road.' . . . Then the light went out and I saw with your eyes how very dull and commonplace the road really was.

I have always felt that I had rather have no relation with you at all than one in which I didn't tell you the truth, and though every time I tell it you I feel I am risking everything. I don't really hesitate. This is one of the most painful things I have ever confessed: if the other day I didn't understand you it was because the idea that you cared for my friendship a little more than I had believed possible – though that's not much – made me – well, it made me think of myself more than of you. Not for long.

I never told you that in the book of yours I have been reading lately, '*les cinq traités*', the one I liked best after *l'Enfant Prodigue* was *Philoctète*. It is not so perfect so pure, so *distilled*, but it melted my heart all the same. And I see that my love goes to Philoctetes and yours to Neoptolemus, mine to the prodigal son himself and yours to his younger brother. Do you think this pains me? At any rate it is a pain that is coeval with my knowledge of you – and I haven't shirked it.

To-day is an anniversary. Perhaps you'll think I mean American Independence Day. I don't keep a diary, only a book where I note engagements I'm likely to forget. Under the date July 4th 1918 I see entered 'Gide lunch.' I often think I should like to write my reminiscences of that time! But I shan't. Oh! why I wonder did such an unimagined, unimaginable thing happen to me? Why should it have been just at that moment of your life and mine, when no other would have done? Why couldn't I have had a nice, sensible friendship with you – without all these odious feelings?

Good-bye, my Gide. The image I have made of you is mine and no one can dispute it me.

I shall try and stay now some time without writing to you.

Your grateful friend
D.B.

The grateful heart for all things blesses.
    Not only joy, but grief endears.
I love you for your few caresses.
    I love you for my many tears.
W.S.L.[1]

[1] From 'The Thankful Heart', Walter Savage Landor.

24. André Gide to Dorothy Bussy

c/o M. Mayrisch
Dudelange
G.D. of Lux.

24 August 19

Dear friend,

Your exquisite letter took only four days to reach me. There, you see I am not at the other end of the earth. I was beginning to grow a little sad for not having received any <u>real</u> letter from you for a long time and for having allowed 'business letters' to take rather exclusive precedence. It is good not to mix genres – provided one genre not supplant the other.

I am answering directly, first to reassure you – and then so that receiving this letter in time, you may still give Lady Strachey my respects and affectionate good wishes. Oh, it's when you are in Venice that I shall feel you are far away! However, I don't despair . . .

Time flies; the difficulties with the new book,[1] on certain days, seem to me insurmountable. Patience, infinite patience and perseverance are required. And then I have been working at several things at the same time, with the result that each progresses only very slowly; everything I have done thus far seems to me like children's games, or like preparatory manoeuvres.

Madame Van Rysselberghe and Elisabeth are here, and the day before yesterday Marc and his elder brother[2] came and joined us; their father, who left us yesterday, accompanied them. Andrée Mayrisch has left for a few days camping.

I have just returned the proofs of *La Symphonie pastorale*, which will appear in October–November in the *Nouvelle Revue Française*.

Jacques Copeau[3] wrote to me recently, eager to know whether a lecture tour (by him) in the principal English cities would be welcomed and considered opportune. Before reopening his theatre, radically changed, he would like to be sure of the sympathy, and to kindle the enthusiasm, of those who are likely to take an interest in his enter-

---

[1] This was *Les Faux-monnayeurs* (*The Coiners*), which he had begun early in July of that year.

[2] Jean-Paul.

[3] Director of the Vieux-Colombier theatre. Copeau and his troupe had returned recently from a two-year residence in New York.

prise. Myself, I find his ideas profoundly interesting and capable of renewing not only dramatic art (I mean interpretation), but even dramatic production, which is needed even more.

Au revoir. No, no, I don't forget you! A thousand friendly wishes to you – and remember me cordially to your brother Lytton. Don't leave me too long without news – and believe me

very much your friend
André Gide.

25. Dorothy Bussy to André Gide

18th September 1919

London

Dear Gide

I wrote you a long letter the other day, addressed it and stamped it and then was afraid to put it in the post. I am certainly getting less courageous than I was and I find it more and more difficult to send you what I write. When I first began, the idea that you were unhappy made the impulse to tell you what I felt over-powering. Now, I don't feel you are unhappy any longer (I am thankful for it – that was worse than anything) and all the old reasons against speaking of myself keep putting their heads up again and there is very seldom now anything in me strong enough to overcome them.

Oh, it's so pointless to go on writing. You know it all. What's the use?

And then I'm afraid, afraid of being more stupid than even you can bear. Or do you think perhaps it's '*les progrès irréguliers de l'oubli*'[1] beginning?

And now I have got to tell you that Lytton has been quite horrid about *La Porte étroite*. He says he is too busy to write a preface. Well that's natural enough. But he won't even look through my translation. Having lately read the French he can't bring himself to read it again in English. I had really believed he would be more friendly and I'm hurt as well as disappointed. But Lytton doesn't easily face being bored. Perhaps you may think he *has* looked at it and doesn't like to tell me he thinks it bad. I had *rather* believe it was that but honestly I

[1] 'The erratic progress of forgetfulness.'

don't. I have shown it besides to two people whose judgment I trust and they say it's all right.

What will you do about it now?

We are starting for Venice on the 25th and shall arrive there I suppose about Oct. 1st.

Why do you say you will feel me further off when I am there? I imagine that it is because you hate it so much that you won't be able to send me even a thought when I am staying there. Is that it? It will be no use giving you my address there? Think of me then as still at 6 Belsize Park Gardens and no further off than usual.

I like getting a letter from you very much and your last was kind, but – aposiopesis as the grammarians call it, is best here.

Oh! I hope you will finish your book – with a selfish hope, and that it won't be one of those exasperating ones that nobody is allowed to read. For in your books I can satisfy some of my soul's thirst: in your books I find you, hear you, feel you, *there* I can get near you – and with that I ought to be content, oughtn't I?

I wonder whether you are still staying with Madame Mayrisch and enjoying this lovely autumn with your friends.

Best '*amitiés*' to Mark. We had news of him a little while ago from Pamela Fry.[2]

> Your affectionate friend
> Dorothy Bussy

26. André Gide to Dorothy Bussy

> Cuverville
>
> 25 Sept. 19

Dear friend,

Your letter reached me at Cuverville where I've been since yesterday . . . But why didn't you send me that other letter which this one speaks of? Your reticence grieves me a great deal. What did I do to deserve it? and what kind of protest will it take to convince you once for all that my affection for you is deep and faithful? – If you needed to think I was sad before you would send that letter, you will make me regret being happy! It's absurd.

---

[2] Roger Fry's daughter, born the same year as Marc Allégret (1902).

And now a change of tone to tell you this: an important American publishing company has asked for the translation rights of *La Porte étroite*. [Alfred] Vallette (the director of the Mercure de France, which published the work), on my instructions has responded, putting forward <u>your</u> translation. It remains to be seen whether the American publisher would consent to take it – and whether <u>you</u> would consent to have it published over there. The conditions which the publisher would offer you also remain to be seen. Is there no way, in any case, of publishing it in America and in England at the same time? I shall let you know the American publisher's reply – and you, tell me what you think of the arrangement and give me your new Venetian address. This letter will waste more than a week chasing after you.

Yes, I am somewhat saddened by Lytton's answer, but not very, for I had no high hopes. Should we look for another prefacer? . . . Mrs. Wharton, for America . . . ? What do you think? I think she would readily accept.[1]

Au revoir. Don't judge my affection from the dryness of this letter. <u>I no longer know how to write letters.</u> A thousand smiling remembrances to Simon Bussy and to Janie.

I am very faithfully your friend
André Gide

27. Dorothy Bussy to André Gide

234 S. Gregorio
Venice

7th Oct. 19

Dear Gide

I have just got your letter. It is an excellent thing that a translation of the *Porte étroite* should come out in America. I hope the publisher will agree to take mine as I feel perfectly certain that anybody else's would be even more unsatisfactory. I worked at it a good deal during the summer and improved it. But supposing the publisher were to insist on having his own translator, please don't mind. I have had my pleasure out of it and I don't suppose a little bit more or less unsatisfactoriness will really matter to your book. Nothing could be

[1] When *Strait is the Gate* was finally published (by A. Knopf in 1924) it was unprefaced.

better than a preface from Mrs. Wharton. I do think a preface would be a help to the sale. It seems to me quite important – from a business point of view – that it should come out at the same time in England, and I don't see why Mrs. Wharton's preface shouldn't do quite as well for the English edition too. I had thought of suggesting Pearsall Smith[1] who is rather '*en vue*' just now in England among select circles but I think Mrs. Wharton would very likely be better.

We are in Venice which in spite of painters and Barrès[2] and motor boats is still beautiful. We shall be here till the end of the month and then spend a week with the Berensons in Florence and then home to Roquebrune.

Are you vexed with me, my dear, because of my 'réticences'? What a strange accusation! And now you have said the very thing the dread of which has so often stopped me from writing to you naturally what is in my heart: '*Quelles protestations attendez vous de moi?*' Rather than you should think I expect or hope or *want* anything more from you . . .

No, no, as you say it's all absurd. Whether I write or whether I don't write it's absurd.

But why should you have the monopoly of not being able to write letters?

Dear Gide, to show you that I believe you are my very good friend and want no further protestations, to show you that I trust you, that I'm not cross or hurt or anything but devotedly yours I will write you a letter soon to make up for the one I tore up.

D.B.

[written in the margin:] My pen has gone wrong, but if I were to write this out again – I can't, so forgive the smudges.

28. Dorothy Bussy to André Gide

Venice

8th October [1919]

So, dear friend, you think that you have made me enough '*protestations*' and that I ought to be content now and believe in your

---

[1] The American, Logan Pearsall Smith (1865–1946), whose niece Rachel ('Ray') Costelloe had married D.B.'s brother Oliver Strachey in 1916.
[2] The reactionary and nationalist writer Maurice Barrès (1862–1923) had dealt with Venice in certain of his books, such as *Un Homme libre* and *Amori et Dolori sacrum*.

profound and faithful friendship? Indeed I'm very willing to, only to tell you the truth those words that you use convey nothing to me and I haven't the faintest idea what you mean by them. The only thing I seem to gather dimly and am beginning sometimes to believe is that you do like me to tell you I do. It may be more or less than this, or it may be something quite other, but at any rate I can't imagine it in the least. It is a feeling that doesn't make you want to see me, or want to write to me, or want to know anything about me or want to tell me anything about yourself. I suppose you'll think I'm complaining or wishing you to do all these things, I'm not in the least. It would be very unnatural if you were to and probably highly inconvenient. I am only trying to explain that I understand your feeling for me is the kind that induces one to give alms – or that makes one like the advances of a dog or a cat . . . Well, whatever it is, it's a great deal more than I ever hoped for . . . Am I irritating you, Gide? I know I am. But it's your fault for not allowing me to tear up the tiresome things I write.

As for me, I should hardly dare call the feeling that I have for you profound. How could it be, with no roots in the past and no hopes for the future? And faithful? Oh! that's a word I gave up using long years ago. But it's acute – it's sometimes even agonising. It's a continual longing to see you again. It's a desperate curiosity for everything that concerns you. It's a constant dreaming of your face and voice. It's an aching desire to expend myself somehow or other in some kind of vain and useless sacrifice for you. And it's complicated by the horrid knowledge of how old I am, of how little right I have to have such feelings and how unfit I am in every way to be your friend. No equality, no communion seems henceforth possible. I have no advantages. I am even only half intelligent. And I have probably by all this forever destroyed what was pleasant between us – the 'camaraderie' of the Cambridge days. Oh! happy Cambridge days, when I was just your dictionary and your grammar, convenient and helpful. And you had the same kind of friendly feeling for me that one has for a dictionary. I understood *that* perfectly. And you didn't notice – you were too much engrossed by other things – that your dictionary had eyes and a heart, was watching you and wondering at you, was charmed and thrilled and shaken by you. I couldn't help it. Gide, I couldn't help it really. Aren't you the strangest and the loveliest and the most disturbing thing I have ever come across in my life? Oh! happy days, when I could love you safely and comfortably without your knowing it, without knowing it myself, without being afraid of anything.

And now, have I been obedient? Have I been unreticent enough not to 'chagriner' you? Have I stripped enough before your careless, inattentive eyes? Or do you want more? There is more and worse if you want it. Are you going to say again that I am waiting for your protestations?

I am afraid this is not one of the letters you call 'exquises'. But perhaps you think I want your compliments too.

Oh! I know I'm unfair and odious. You are as nice as it is possible to be. And it's not only that I'm afraid of displeasing you. I'm afraid as well of saying things that will make it too difficult for you to come and see me, too difficult for me to let you come. Oh! what courage I should need. But I would have it, if you would – Will you come, I wonder, before it's all over? Time flies you know. And now a whole year has gone by during which I've seen you only on four consecutive days for an hour or two each day. A particularly lucky year I expect.

Good night.

Sometimes my sacrifice to you is to keep silent. Tonight it has been to speak.

Please don't allude to this when next you write. I should like your next letter to be *purely* business.

Yours,
D.B.

29. Dorothy Bussy to André Gide

Venice

16th Oct. [1919]

Dear Friend

I am thinking today that you are perhaps reading that last foolish letter of mine. But today if I could speak to you what different things I should say. A letter always arrives too late – one can never catch it up – and this too will be wrong by the time it reaches you. But however much I sway to and fro you know that I am really fast anchored to a belief in your friendship and indulgence – even after that last letter I will believe in them still. And you know that if I didn't there would be an end of me – as far as you are concerned. But did I say I didn't want protestations? How could I? I do. Of course I do. I want just as many as you can possible squeeze out. Supposing you were never to call yourself again my faithful friend how frightful it would be! How much I like it when you do.

Yes. You see today my mood is very different. I am not going to torment myself any more. I am not going to worry you. But I will go on liking you. It is sometimes a divine pleasure to like you. And sometimes I will tell you about it, since you give me leave. That ought to be enough for anyone. It shall be enough for me.

I am enjoying Venice very much. It is lovely and amusing and we are about the only tourists in it. I am enjoying Janie's pleasure in it too. As for the Italians – the people one meets in trains, and hotels and shops, they are all as polite and amiable as it is possible to be, and very often really cordial.

On the 25th we go to the Berensons' for a week (I Tatti, Settignano, Florence)[1] and then home to Roquebrune – I shall be glad to get back to my own house.

> Yours,
> Dorothy Bussy

30. Dorothy Bussy to André Gide

> Roquebrune Cap Martin
>
> 10th Nov. 1919.

My dear Friend

We came back from Florence a few days ago where we spent a very agreeable time with the Berensons though the weather was too bad for much sight seeing. I liked – oh! foolish – being again in a room where you had once sat, and imagining, as I looked at some of the pictures in Florence, that just here you too had stood and looked. But I'll admit there were other pleasures.

When we came back to our own tiny, uncomfortable, charming house, for some reason or other I took to my bed where I still am, though better – happy in fact to lie still & be able to do nothing.

I tell myself stories of how you will come and see me this winter. I

[1] Bernard Berenson had lived at I Tatti since 1900, the year of his marriage to the mother of D.B.'s sister-in-law Ray Strachey.

really think you might trust me. I think I might trust myself. All this is so much the mere weaving of my imagination, has so little the texture of any reality in it, that I think it wouldn't be difficult – for a short time at any rate – to imagine that it didn't exist, to take up the threads that were interrupted on the afternoon when you said good-bye to me in London a year ago – the afternoon when you dropped your cigarette end into your tea-cup and thought, and half-regretted, that there was an end of another of life's little episodes; when you said good-bye to me in the hall and *promised to come and see me*; when you stopped in the road and looked back and tried to thank me. Oh! pleasant half-way house between friendship and love, more pleasant than either but more difficult to remain in – backwards or forwards one must go, and in reality we parted then for ever.

I have been reading the last part of the *Symphonie Pastorale*; it moved me very much, moved me to write you – not criticism – I am totally incapable of criticising what you write – but just useless, useless words of gratitude and praise.

All the same when you publish it as a book take pains to get the dates of the diary right. They make nonsense now and it's provoking.[1]

My friend, I'm anxious. Not a word from you since that insensate stuff I wrote you from Venice. Thank God, I've forgotten every word of it, but I'm afraid it was pretty bad. Supposing it had disgusted you irretrievably. How shall I endure it? The other night I dreamt of you and you – no. I'll not believe it.

Yrs.
D.B.

31. Dorothy Bussy to André Gide

La Souco
Roquebrune
Cap Martin A.M.

4th Jan. 20

Dear Friend (dear Phantom would be truer – dear inhabitant of that remote, visionary world I wonder so much about) may I have a

[1] The dates were given in the wrong order in Part Two of the novel, as printed in the November issue of the *N.R.F.*

message from you soon? Though when it drops upon my poor earth your missive will be nothing, I know, but a dull piece of stone, a bit of cold lead as hard as a bullet – and almost as deadly. (Your last very nearly did for me.) Never mind, such fragments are welcome still and precious – signs that the Heavens are not altogether empty.

Are you well? Are you happy? Are you getting on with your work? Are you still at Cuverville? Are you still reading English? These are only five of the thousand questions – ah! more important, which I should like to ask you and never shall. But let me hear something about you – anything.

I vowed to myself I wouldn't bother you again for two months . . . it is eight weeks to-day since I wrote and I can't hold out another minute. I vowed I wouldn't fill more than this little page, wouldn't allow myself more room than just enough to say only that I am yours devotedly

Dorothy Bussy

[written in the margin:] Simon & Janie are well. They remember you very affectionately.

32. André Gide to Dorothy Bussy

[Dudelange, Luxemburg]

10 January 1920

Dear friend,

I'm very worried about you. I have no news of you – and am not sure that you yourself aren't suffering from this silence, but if you start telling yourself you are the only one who suffers from it, and convincing yourself that I'm not even aware of it . . . that will make it intolerable. But first I should like to make certain that no letter awaits me in Paris – which I won't know for another four or five days, since a bad case of the grippe has detained me here at the home of my friends the Mayrischs and since the post is so slow I have given up having mine forwarded – so that I've been without news of the outside world for a dozen days or so. Then again, perhaps a letter of yours, of earlier date, has gone astray; in any case, I never received an answer to the one I wrote (from Cuverville I think) in which I remember telling you that the time would come when I would need to feel that your friendship was loyal. But did you ever get it? Or worse, might some sentence in that letter have displeased you? I should so like to be reassured, to know for certain that there is no sadness, no renunciation, no heap of virtuous passivity or resignation hiding in the shadow of your silence . . . Or perhaps you are merely waiting for me to write again.

Wherever I look, even to the most distant horizon, the sky is dark with clouds. I don't dare speak of making plans. I force myself to walk with head erect, but at each step the ground may give way.

Please write to me, if only a few lines; let's not allow ourselves to be swallowed up by the darkness. A thousand affectionate good wishes to Simon Bussy and to Janie.

Your friend,
André Gide

33. Dorothy Bussy to André Gide

Jan. 12 '20

My dear Gide

Your tragic letter[1] harrows me. What to answer? But you don't want an answer – only a listener. Well! I listen with all my devotion – inexpressibly touched, grateful that you should still trust in my friendship.

Dear Gide – you know I don't believe in God – but I believe in men – oh passionately I believe in men like you & the importance of their spirit. You mustn't break down now – you mustn't – you mustn't. What does it matter whether you are happy or she? Your spirit must survive. Save your mind & your body, Gide. You must. They are too rare, too beautiful too necessary to the world to let them be spoiled by a private grief. There are some flames so bright that one mustn't count the cost of the fuel which goes to keep them burning.

Your last years, your precious numbered years they must be full of your best work no matter what is sacrificed.

---

[1] The letter from Cuverville which Gide mentions in his of 10 Jan. The letter was not found among the Gide–Bussy papers.

You think I don't want to hear that Marc is not unhappy. You think I am not glad that you have your reward there at any rate. Dear Gide think what you will of me – or rather don't think at all.

Yours
Dorothy Bussy

What a dreadfully stupid letter. It has been a great effort to write it.

34. Dorothy Bussy to André Gide

La Souco
Roquebrune Cap Martin

17th Jan. 1920

Dear Gide

You don't seem a phantom to me to-day, thank goodness, not any longer the inhabitant of that remote, visionary planet, but living in the real world with me, my friend, whom I can hurt and please. I was expecting an answer to my little note. I thought I knew so well what it was going to be like that I hardly dared to open it. And behold! it turned out to be an answer to my prayers, long since despaired of as impossible and at last miraculously granted. I had wanted you so much, so much, to write to me once of your own accord – not to have to feel always that your letters were extorted from your kindness or your politeness. Yes, your last letter from Cuverville (I got it all right) made me feel – but perhaps it was my own conscience – that I had been writing too much, too often, with too little restraint. Yes, I thought you didn't notice my silence, or noticing, that you didn't care enough what became of me to make the slightest movement. And yet believing all that I still wrote to you again. Oh! I don't think my virtues are all passive! It seems to me that in my relations with you, ever since the very beginning I have shown a superhuman courage – a courage I didn't imagine I possessed. You must make up your mind to it. To-day I feel, I feel you friendly. But to-morrow, after this moment's respite of peace and confidence the agony will begin again, the agony of feeling, of knowing that you are being swept away from me, that all the forces of life, every one – are sweeping you away from me – every minute – further and further away. Oh! what does it matter? They can't sweep away the fact that to-day I love you – that you let me.

Your two last letters[1] are horribly frightening. What is happening
to you? What is threatening you? What are you doing? It is a perfect
torment to guess and guess and not understand a thing that you say.
How could I not be faithful to you? In what possible circumstances
could my fidelity be important to you? Are you going to commit –
have you committed – some awful crime? I don't care a button, you
know, what you commit – unless it makes you unhappy and then I
should care. Say or write or do whatever you please. I can imagine
you capable of all kinds of evil things – cruelty, selfishness, follies,
weaknesses – sins – anything you like – but I believe – no I don't
believe, I *know* that you have some virtue besides, which transmutes
all that into something divinely beautiful, and beautiful not in spite
of the evil that is there but because of it.

Oh! Gide here I am talking to you again. After those dismal dreary
weeks, how heavenly. And you missed me! But I wish you didn't have
the grippe so often and so badly.

Yours
Dorothy Bussy

35. André Gide to Dorothy Bussy

Friday
30 Jan. 1920

Very dear friend,

No, don't worry; I am not sick, only overworked – worn out by
the disjointed life I lead and putting off from day to day the letter I
want to write you. I am still provisionally camped at Marc's parents',
much disturbed by the household activity and having great difficulty
finding the time and place to collect myself. (To tell the truth, I have
given up trying.)

You cannot imagine the number of projects I have taken on. I go
out in the morning and come back at night, exhausted.

Saturday

Even that scrap of letter I had to interrupt. An urgent phone call
summoned me to the N.R.F. Our publishing house is growing,
beginning to rank among the most important. There are meetings
with businessmen, lawyers; we are opening two shops, one on the
right bank, one on the left, without counting the one . . . but what

---

[1] The lost letter and the letter of 10 January.

good is it talking about that? My translation of *Antony and Cleopatra* is to be performed at the Opéra in June. I have to tend to costumes and sets and then oversee the rehearsals. In April, they're doing my *Philoctète* at the Comédie Française (single performance) and *Le Roi Candaule* in May at the Vieux Colombier. *La Symphonie pastorale* will appear any day now. I am preparing two volumes of 'Selections', one for adolescent readers!! another, for the N.R.F., for readers of all ages – an undertaking I attach great importance to, and which has been giving me considerable trouble (I'll include a good deal of unpublished material in it). The N.R.F. is at this moment bringing out an edition of my *Prométhée mal enchaîné*, illustrated by Bonnard and one of my *Tentative amoureuse*, illustrated by Marie Laurencin. And, much more serious, I am having printed, on my own, <u>clandestinely</u>, two books not for public sale, neither of which would <u>astonish</u> you very much I suppose, but one of which is of a sort to get me thrown in jail.[1] For this I had to make a special trip to Bruges to give the printer last minute instructions – and there caught a chill (I think I wrote to you about it) and returned with a bad cold that kept me housebound twelve days. Consequently a great delay and a terrible accumulation of work to attend to as soon as I was able to go out.

What else? A cousin who is being operated on (very serious operation) and whom I must look after; friends who claim attention, ask advice. Meanwhile I am waiting for a chance to slip away to Cuverville where I left my wife – since for lack of coal we cannot consider moving back into the Villa[2] before Spring. And because of that: disjointed existence, dispersion of my papers, enormous bother, fatigue, etc., etc.

If you are not disgusted with me after that enumeration, what will it take?

Add to that that I am led to devote to Marc the little time remaining – for amusement as well as for work. The boy is more and more interested in painting, his greatest pleasure is going to exhibitions – and to the Louvre, and mine is going with him.

And now that I have said all that, can I <u>begin</u> my letter?

Dear friend, your letters have overwhelmed me. I have felt, I have known, for a long time that you understood me without explanation,

[1] The first volume of the autobiography *Si le Grain ne meurt (If it Die)* and the dialogues on homosexuality, *Corydon*. The latter was a new edition of an earlier text published anonymously as *C.R.D.N.* in 1911. All three were printed in Bruges by the Imprimerie Sainte-Catherine, but without indication of place or publisher.
[2] Villa Montmorency in Passy.

and that I had no need, really, to make confidences. (I shall make them one day however.) I am even eager to – and to let you read the frightful book I spoke of above, but which (need I say?) I beg you to mention to no one. My intention, let me say at once, is not to keep it secret forever – not even for very long. But for reasons that you can guess, it is premature – it would be needlessly imprudent – to release it to the public just now. It is not a question of being cautious for myself. I would like it to hurt as little as possible, by its repercussions, certain persons who are dear to me. I see a dreadful expanse of country ahead that I shall have to enter and which I must pass through.

There is not a sentence in your letter that does not touch my heart. I repeat what I told you: the time will come, and soon – when your friendship can be of great support –; you won't take it from me, will you?

No, it's not at all true to say that the only love that can aid us is the love we bear others and not that which they bear us. And even if it were true? But do you believe that your letters – and I am thinking of the next-to-last one especially – are not <u>already</u> a great comfort to me? –

Don't be misled by the businessman's life I describe. <u>Essentially</u> I am as calm as ever and all this agitation ruffles only the surface.

I must leave you now. [Jacques] Dresa, who is to design the sets and costumes for *Antony*, is expecting me. One last word: no reply from the American publisher, although it was he who took the initiative. But Dent writes to request a book of mine; I have spoken to him of your translation; he wants to see it; I sent it; nearly certain he'll accept it.

Au revoir. Au revoir. When shall I be able to say: soon. Understand that I am your friend

André Gide.

36. Dorothy Bussy to André Gide

February [1920]

Dear Gide

We had a message the other day from Van Rysselberghe[1] to say that you had commissioned him to choose some of Simon's pastel studies for you, like the ones belonging to Mme. Schlumberger.

[1] The painter Théo, husband of the 'petite dame'.

(That message seemed to signify to me personally the extinction of a private hope that was still lingering desperately on. Since then I've been occupied in burying it. *Don't let it ever raise its head again*!)

Well, some day I hope you'll see Simon's real things in Paris. In the meantime it seems a pity you should have things of his in which his essential qualities don't appear – mere notes which show some of his gifts but not his art. And just now he is beginning, he is now really beginning to do the things he wants with confidence and ease and felicity. And I believe firmly – blindly perhaps you'll say – that they're interesting – intense and rare. Don't believe what Van Rysselberghe says about them. Painters of that kind can't understand what he's driving at. But I expect you would. At any rate Simon quite agrees with me that he would rather you had one of his pictures and has given me leave to propose that you should take, instead of the pastel studies, a little oil painting of two squirrels he did this winter. It is quite a small thing and not at all important but he likes it and would like you to have it. Of course if you don't care for it you can change it when you please.

No need to answer this, my busy friend. Van Rys. will tell us what you want.

Yours,
Dorothy Bussy

37. André Gide to Dorothy Bussy

Cuverville
par Criquetot L'Esneval
Seine-Inférieure
1st March 20

Dear friend,

I was going to announce Théo's visit, but word from you, received yesterday, shows me that you are already advised of it. Has what he said caused you to lose all hope of seeing me in Roquebrune? . . . It were better, in any case, not to count on it. All the same, I don't yet fully resign myself to not coming. The truth is, that although I appear to be the freest of creatures, heaps of 'clauses and conditions' (some of them sentimental) restrain or oblige me – and although, for example, I have resolved to join Elisabeth Van R. and Andrée Mayrisch over the Easter holiday in Florence – I am not at all sure I shall be free to choose my return route – since I shall not be travelling alone.

Regarding what you say of Simon Bussy's little studies and his paintings, don't think that Van R.'s opinion has influenced me, or that I have been prejudiced against the effort toward 'stylisation' that Simon B. had already spoken to me about back in Cambridge. I believe on the contrary that we agreed perfectly on those questions, and I have rarely had more pleasure talking art and painting than with him. But I can only speak of what I have seen. Now I'm <u>mad</u> about the little pastel studies I contemplate each time I visit the Schlumbergers. They even excite in me the most frightful feelings of concupiscence and envy. Will I be as fond of the squirrels? Perhaps even more so . . . Possibly, but how do you expect me to know? – In the meantime, don't allow everything I might like to be carried off by other friends and by the Schl. if they return.

I have been in Cuverville for a week; but it will be a long time before I stay for a longer period, alas! I work <u>too</u> well here; by which I mean that after a short time I can no longer sleep, that my nerves break down. The weather is splendid, but I can't bring myself to make up my mind to go out. A stroll without objective or without someone to lead me is beyond my moral strength. Have been reading a good deal of English these past days (rereading with keen pleasure Marvell's poems that we read together in Cambridge, and others whose acquaintance I owe to you, and yet others I should like to read with you.) I have been looking over a translation (not at all bad) of 'Mr. Sludge the Medium' which was submitted to us for the N.R.F.[1]

Have you already heard that we are going to publish the translation of Keynes's book?[2] I'm delighted. Have corresponded with him about it. The work is underway and will be shortly completed if the printers are not on strike. It is now 18 weeks since I passed the *Symphonie pastorale* for press – and I still haven't seen it. I've told you, haven't I, that my translation of *Antony* is to be performed in June. Where will you be then? All the same, I can't believe we shall not have seen each other before.

I am truly your friend – and you know it, don't you?

André Gide

[1] 'Monsieur Sludge, le Medium', the translation by Paul Alfassa and Gilbert de Voisins, appeared in the April 1921 issue of the *N.R.F.*, with a prefatory notice on Browning signed by Gide and the two translators.
[2] *Les Conséquences économiques de la paix*, translated by Paul Franck (N.R.F., 1920).

38. Dorothy Bussy to André Gide

Roquebrune Cap Martin

5th March [1920]

Dear Gide

Your letter which arrived this morning was full of things that interested me very much – as for instance that you are going to publish a translation of Keynes' book. It seems to me very important that it should be published in French. But it's pretty depressing reading isn't it?

And that you are going to Florence. But really there's no need for you to take such trouble to explain to me so gently that your life and heart are full and that I 'mustn't count' on your finding time or room for me. Goodness knows it isn't necessary. I don't count on anything but having to spend the rest of my life wanting things I can't have.

It doesn't matter. What matters is you. That you should be a little happy. That you should do the things you must. That you should sleep at night.

Dear – my friend, since so you call yourself – that shall be enough for me. Yours

Dorothy Bussy

P.S. 6th March

All right about the squirrels. It shall be of course as you wish.

This letter is very untidy. But this morning I am sick of it. No one would think, would they, that last night I spent two mortal hours on it of effort and of . . .

39. André Gide to Dorothy Bussy

18 March 20

Dear friend,

I have happy news for you: Dent accepts your translation.[1] A few conditions remain to be discussed, for I should like the agreement to be as advantageous for you as possible – and correspondence between London and Paris is slow; but I expect it is now a closed affair and that the book can be published this autumn. We can correspond to

[1] The UK edition of *Strait is the Gate* (1924) was, in fact, published by Jarrolds, not Dent.

ascertain where the proofs should be sent to you – I can't tell you how happy I am to owe this great joy to you! And so long awaited. It will console me for the *Prometheus*.

I had lunch yesterday with Keynes and Duncan Grant. Their acquaintance I also owe to you. It gave me the greatest pleasure to see the former again, and to meet, at last, the latter. The *Conséquences économiques de* is in the hands of the printer and we have every hope it will come out at the end of April. I am satisfied, very satisfied, with the translation.

I have just received your note. It is, indeed, with Marc I leave for Florence; and it is not impossible that the two of us will return by way of Ventimiglia, Roquebrune, Saint-Clair . . . but don't count on it. It's so uncertain that I should best not have mentioned it at all. Rehearsals for my *Cleopatra* begin soon and it will perhaps not be possible for me to be late in returning; besides which, there are heaps of considerations that my decision will depend upon –. But if I don't see you in Roquebrune, your note allows me to hope I shall see you in Paris . . . it won't be the same, alas!

Dear friend, I expect the above good news to fill you with courage and hope – for Dent has already given me to understand that he won't stop there; and for my part I have told him my wish to have the same publisher publish the various books of mine that might be of interest to an English public; you will tell me what are, on this subject, your own wishes.

> Your devoted,
> André Gide

40. Dorothy Bussy to André Gide

10th April [1920]

Dear Gide

I have just thrown away the bit of wall flower you picked,[1] no perfume left in it at all, black, withered, frightful –

Dear Gide. Two lines you said to me once at Cambridge run in my head all the time. Perhaps if I write them down I shall get rid of them.

[1] Gide had made a brief visit to La Souco.

Toute douceur d'amour est détrempée
De fiel amer et de mortel venin.[2]

I can't bear that memory of you to be my last for another year perhaps for ever. I can't. I have never left you before without carrying away some comfort, some courage, some hope. You would give them to me again if I could only see you alone, in peace, for just a few minutes, for just once. Please let me when we come to Paris, please, dear Gide, please – Try to arrange it for me. Simon knows, understands perfectly that I like talking to you alone, that I like keeping your letters to myself. It is quite natural. We shall only be two days in Paris, but you will find a little time on one of them for me, won't you?

Yours,
Dorothy Bussy

41. André Gide to Dorothy Bussy

Cuverville-en-Caux

30 April 20

Dear friend,

Yes, certainly I want to see you when you come through Paris; but your letter doesn't say when you plan to leave Roquebrune. I have had to come back to Cuverville – and shall soon leave again, taking my wife back to Villa Montmorency which we shall try to open, if only to show it off to advantage to the Americans to whom I'm trying to rent it – or sell it, since – what with the difficulties of heating, service, etc. – it is becoming too burdensome.

I might have guessed that that imperfect visit to Roquebrune left you with a rather bitter memory. I wish I had been able to stay longer, as I propose to do another time . . . but this time it wasn't possible – maybe one day I shall tell you why.

Will we be able to talk, in Paris? It pains me to be a cause of sadness to you . . . Where will you go afterwards, if not to Cambridge? Is there any chance of meeting you somewhere, this summer? – My life is so profoundly disorganized that I cannot know where I shall be – it depends upon too many things. But I'd like to be able to work. If the

[2] 'Every sweetness of love is sodden/With bitter gall and deadly venom.' Maurice Scève, *Délie*, CCLXXIII.

exchange rate were not ruinous, I would try to settle for a few months in England . . .

Marc conveyed to me a letter in which you inquire after your nephew.[1] He says he replied with a letter so awkward he hesitated to send it to you. He plans to return to England directly after his exam, that is, in July – and his father has been trying to find him a position as . . . a tutor!! We can also talk about this when you pass through. Tell me quickly when you will come. – A thousand fond remembrances to Simon; a thousand smiles to Janie. I am your friend

André Gide.

New proposals, from another publisher, concerning *La Porte étroite*, will probably come off.

42. André Gide to Dorothy Bussy

Llanberis[1]

8 August 20

Dear friend,

I snatch this pretext to write to you: would you be so kind as to drop this letter in the postbox. I prefer, *for reasons you know*, that it not bear the Llanberis postmark.

I read yesterday in Keats's letters a few lines that clarify for me so admirably what I attempted the other day to express to you: '. . . *What shocks the virtuous philosopher delights the chameleon poet. It does no harm from its relish of the dark side of things, anymore than from its taste for the bright one, because they both end in speculation.* (This isn't always exactly so with me.) (But now this is entirely true:) *A poet . . . has no Identity – he is continually in for – and filling some other body . . . It is a wretched thing to confess; but it is a very fact, that no one word I ever utter can be taken for granted as an opinion growing out of my identical Nature – how can it, when I have no Nature? etc.*' 27 Oct. 1818.[2]

[1] Vincent Rendel, the son of D.B.'s sister Elinor.

LETTER 42

[1] A village in North Wales which D.B. had recommended to Gide for a brief vacation with Marc Allégret. Gide's conjugal difficulties (the 'trial' referred to in his letter) were such that he preferred his wife to believe him to be in London.

[2] From a letter to Richard Woodhouse.

The weather is awful, but *it doesn't matter at all*; the countryside is hideous, but *exactly what suit us*; and we are wonderfully housed. *The trial is sometimes so cruciating for me that I believe I can bear it no longer more. Yet it must be so, and I willed it.*

Au revoir. Soon. Believe in my very grateful affection

André Gide.

I do really need to see you . . . You will write to me, won't you? You don't know the pleasure and the benefit a letter from you would give me. – Au revoir. I've been working almost very well, and am deeply your friend

André Gide.

43. André Gide to Simon Bussy

1 1 August 20

Bodafon
Llanberis, North Wales

My dear friend,

This is the first day . . . I hardly dare say it: of good weather – but without rain. I am writing to you seated on a bench, facing the lake. On my right: Snowdon and slate. On my left: slate. Behind me: slate; before me: slate. Enough to cover a continent. It's of an indefinable shade, not at all blue like our slate at home, but rather the colour of rhinoceros (underside of same). Took advantage of the weather by working, while Marc canoed in the downpour. I pass for a 'painter' here, probably because I wear a flowing cloak. We are lodged in truly comfortable fashion. In the evening we light fires of 'slate' and coal . . .

The day after my arrival I received a packet of letters, which I expect have been forwarded by you. Thank you –. Since then, there has been nothing. You do have my address (above) don't you? and will kindly forward to me here anything that I might receive at Gordon Square. I plan to remain in Llanberis until the 26th of this month – then to see you in London on the way through. I should very much like to make a tour of the Nat. Gal. with you if the Zoo doesn't take too much of your time. Have you established relations with the director?

Au revoir. Soon. With affection and gratitude,

André Gide.

44. Dorothy Bussy to André Gide

Wednesday
[11 August 1920]

Dear Gide,

I always feel in such a fearful panic after I have sent you a letter. I want to go and drown myself. Such intolerable stuff I write you. I can't imagine how you can bear it. Shameless it seems to me after it has gone, and worse than shameless – stupid – often not true. Can you tell what is true and what is false? I suppose you can. I suppose that is why you put up with me and why I always find courage to begin again. Because in reality I'm not ashamed of the essential part – the part that is true. No. I'm proud of it.

Well, the Thursday that you left and the Friday after, I was very busy packing and doing all the countless things that had to be done before leaving London for the country. On Saturday we went down to Lady Ottoline's[1] and on Monday I spent the whole day getting to Haslemere.[2] During these days I found time to read *Corydon* and part of *Si le Grain ne Meurt* – but no time to write to you. I must be alone and quiet when I write. But I thought of you – goodness! how I thought of you, how I think of you! And now I'm going to write to you just whenever I please, as many letters and as long and as stupid as I feel inclined – without any scruple or really, any fear.

It was quite pleasant at the Morrells', a beautiful old Elizabethan manor house and garden, and the hostess very gracious and amusing to look at and in a mood that was not in the least extravagant. When we went away she asked for your address and said that she wanted to invite us again for a week-end to meet you and that she would write to you. Let me know what you answer. If you go I should like to go

[1] At Garsington in Oxfordshire.
[2] Fernhurst, the small village near Haslemere in Surrey, had been since the 1900s a summer gathering place for members of the group with Pearsall Smith connections. The Berensons spent part of the summer there.

too, but it would probably be impossible to speak to you alone and I should be dying to. And perhaps you won't be able to spare more days than that and I dream of one more day with you. I should like you to come to our cottage here for a night. Then if the day missed fire as it probably would with so many people about, we could be certain of a talk in the evening. But I should hardly dare ask you, because it is a *real* cottage, with only absolutely the barest necessities of life, and I'm afraid a very uncomfortable bed. Its present inhabitants are Ray (my sister-in-law) Janie, myself and three babies, but there is a spare room, and it would be joy to have you if you could bear it.

Dear friend, there are such heaps and heaps of things I want to talk to you about. But tonight it's late. I shall write again to you tomorrow. Oh! you don't know how exquisitely delicious to me it is to feel at last that I'm [some words crossed out].

Dorothy Bussy.

My dear. Here I am again in my extasies. Yes I think that's the real word. I have just finished – last night – reading *Si le Grain ne Meurt* and it has left me in an indescribable state of excitement. The other book I read from beginning to end without my heart once beating quicker, absolutely nothing stirred but my brain. But this! That feeling of oppression, of suffocation of an extraordinary *quality* of emotion which all your books give me was here, only intensified to the pitch of being almost agony – almost intolerable – the dissolution of my being in fire. Perhaps you will think that it is because I was in a state of excitement when I began to read or that I'm an excitable person – I assure you that I'm not. I don't really think it is that. And I daresay it's a quality you are not aiming at, that you think it un-important. I don't know, but to me it's so overwhelming that it's only ages afterwards, when at last the grip on my heart relaxes, and I can breathe without gasping and a little strength returns to my limbs, that I can *think* about it at all. And now what has always seemed to me so extraordinary a mystery – how with a few simple words, with a bare and apparently trivial récit, with (oh! such rare intervals) a single, crystalline note – how such things could produce such an effect is explained – no not explained, accounted for. The incredible effect you have upon me as a person too is explained – no accounted for – It is that you *communicate* (how?) that sensation of your own which you felt first at Emil's death . . . I too recognize that *schaudern*.[3]

[3] 'Trembling'.

Gide, 'cette étrange aura' accompanies you. The God Dionysos who inhabits you – it is his power I feel in your books, in your presence. Is it good for us to be moved so? It must be. It is – you know it is – the highest good. Then what is all this talk of vice and virtue? Why should you have been afraid of my reading your book? Oh! my chameleon poet, you have no identity to yourself perhaps, perhaps that makes you suffer, but to me, to anyone who can understand anything, it is that very quality of the chameleon, the alternation of dark and bright which makes your identity, your beauty.

Your friend. (Oh! miracle!)
Dorothy Bussy

Aug. 12th 1920

45. Dorothy Bussy to André Gide

Monday
[16 August 1920]

Last night I dreamt that you were not only divinely but humanly happy – that Amor Sacre e Profano met in you and that you enjoyed them both in a moment of perfect felicity. I imagined that this might be true more this week than any other week in your life and when I woke I prayed that it was so.

We have had two days of perfect summer weather. The country here has what Simon calls 'une incomparable suavité'. I am beginning to wonder whether you will come and see me. If you don't feel inclined to I couldn't bear you to make the slightest effort. I shan't be disappointed as I never expect anything, never hope for anything except for you to believe in my . . . I really don't know what to call it.

I am horribly afraid of your telling me again to 'maîtriser' myself. I *can* do it. I can. But not if I write to you. That is why I didn't want to. And if you ask me to write, what kind of things do you want me to say to you? Things that force themselves from me, that are stronger than my control – are the only ones that are worth while. You know that don't you, so I don't understand what you mean. What you mean by asking me to write.

When I am with you it is easy. I don't have the same temptations as when I write. What do you think that proves? Merely that when you are actually there – I live in you and not at all any more in myself.

And to-morrow perhaps I shall have a wholesome cold douche of a letter from you – Dear Gide

au revoir
D.B.

46. André Gide to Dorothy Bussy

Llanberis

17 August 20

Very dear friend,

Your letters send my heart and mind into corkscrew spirals – but delightfully. Oh, most decidedly I should like to see you, and feel we could talk better than we have yet done. But today I have definite things to tell you:

We expect to leave Llanberis on the 26th and return directly to London. A weekend at Lady Ottoline's, gladly, if you are there. Marc, too? I should like that. Then we'd leave Oxford and England on Monday the 29th.[1]

Were you able to obtain any information concerning the American publisher?

Perhaps if you had the patience to underline the passages in the first four acts of my translation of *Antony* which strike you as defective, we could go over them together, as we did, so profitably, the last two.

Soon.
Your friend
André Gide.

I'm delighted by what you say about *Si le grain ne meurt.*

And how can I thank you for all the addresses you so kindly write on the letters you forward!? . . .

[1] Monday was the 30th.

47. Dorothy Bussy to André Gide

Wednesday Aug. 18, 1920

Dear Gide

The expected cold douche has arrived. May God give me patience!

You say you must speak of 'choses précises', but the very precise invitation I gave you, you don't so much as allude to. I daresay you didn't notice it. What seems clear, however, is that you will be alone with Marc in London and that you don't want to leave him.

I have written to Lady Ottoline to suggest that she invite us all down to Garsington for the week-end on the 28th – But it's very short notice and it's rather unlikely that she'll have room for us all. If she does invite Simon and me too I could come up to London on Friday and see you perhaps that evening. But (though I said I would) I don't think I can very well come to London just on purpose to see you. So the chance of meeting again is precarious. I think however we might do the *Anthony and Cleopatra* [*sic*] quite well by correspondence.

The Berensons had not heard of the American publishers[1] and I'm trying to find out something from elsewhere, but after all I don't see why you should hesitate to accept if they made a decent offer.

Dear Gide, for a novelist, you really haven't got much imagination. 'Ce que vous dites de *Si le Grain ne Meurt* me ravit' – is a sentence you needn't have taken the trouble to add as a postscript.

Yours always
Dorothy Bussy

Of course it isn't I who send on your letters, as I'm not in London, but Pippa.[2]

48. Dorothy Bussy to André Gide

17th Sept. [1920]
London

Cher ami

Wasn't it horrid of me? this morning I actually spent 2d½ in trying to give you a disappointment. Instead of redirecting a letter to you like a sensible person I put it in a fresh envelope so that you should

---

[1] This was most likely not the A. Knopf company (founded in 1915) which eventually published *Strait is the Gate* in 1924.

[2] Philippa Strachey, D.B.'s younger sister.

think it was a letter from me and be disappointed to find that it was one from Lady Ottoline. Were you? I do wonder. I wonder whether you had two penny halfpenny worth of disappointment, or whether the whole investment was pure loss . . . one of the things I shall never know.

I suppose that absurdity astonishes you. I can't forget the way you said I caused you '*de l'étonnement.*' Perhaps you'd be astonished too to know what extraordinary pleasure Lady Ottoline's photographs give me.[1] It's they that have made it possible for me to write to you again. I had forgotten your face already. In spite of all my staring – which was so rude. In spite of my desperate efforts to learn you by heart I had clean forgotten you. For all I could see, you might have had those immense moustaches you told me you had when you wrote *La Porte étroite.* Reason told me that you probably had two eyes and a nose, and knowledge of your character that your mouth is as sinuous as a serpent, but the vision was absent. And now there's something that actually recalls you and I can see that your mouth isn't at all the serpent that it ought to be and that your mask at any rate is sweet to look at. Yes, these photographs help me to see you as I have so often seen you, with a kind of visible emanation coming from you of shining grace and brightness. But it isn't those qualities in your face that make me dream and wonder and long, for those are the qualities of youth and in reality the beauty of youth has never tempted me. The things that make a face beautiful to me are the things that are pre-eminent in yours – thought and suffering and experience – knowledge of good and evil. Oh! how I like to look at your forehead and wonder and wonder what is working behind it, and your eyes which are so eager and so rarely tender, and your lips, your lips, sweet, austere, incredibly mysterious. Amour de tête you will say. Perhaps. But so I can't divide myself up like you. The fire that starts in my spirit doesn't stop there, it goes on burning till it reaches all the rest of me and then I can't distinguish whether it's my brain or my heart or my body that loves any more than I can distinguish whether so to love is pain or pleasure. Pain and pleasure when they reach a certain pitch are identical aren't they? The intensest and most ecstatic sensation of physical pleasure I ever had was when Janie was being born – it was pretty hard – and they gave

[1] Lady Ottoline was fond of photographing her guests. Three of the pictures taken the weekend Gide and the Bussys visited Garsington are included in *Lady Ottoline's Album: Snapshots and Portraits* (Knopf, 1976), p. 62.

me whiffs of chloroform. Not enough to make me unconscious, but just enough to send me in a kind of delirium of joy out of Hell into Heaven. Such another moment I had on the hillside when you put your hand on my shoulder and I doubt whether in all your pursuit of pleasure you get many like it. But it lasts too short a time – too horribly short and the beast has its teeth into me again.

My innocent – Gide! Has no woman ever spoken to you like this before? How I wish I was young and beautiful – not that I imagine there'ld have been any chance for me, no doubt I shouldn't have been allowed to approach even so far – but perhaps I should have felt more – perhaps you would have believed in me more – at any rate it would be more amusing for you.

I had been meaning to write such a different letter. It all comes from looking at photographs. But I want more – about a million more. And I don't care now what I write. There'll be time enough in six months for you to forget it all – even time for me to stop feeling it. Hang it all! one must grow old *some* day.

Dear. I hope you are resting. Do you ever rest? I hope you are well and – ah! happy? Think of me sometimes. Don't write to me till I get back to Roquebrune. There's no need. Though if you feel a perfectly uncontrollable impulse! or if you have a business communication 51 Gordon Sq. will reach me.

Yrs. D. B.

P.S. What will interest you more than the whole of this stupid letter is that Simon is reading *Si le Grain ne meurt* – and likes it *really*.

49. André Gide to Dorothy Bussy

[1 October 1920]

Dear friend,

Where will this letter reach you? I'd like it to be Paris. Isn't this the time you were to pass through? I have been here since yesterday, again alone in this huge Villa where I play at being Robinson Crusoe . . . leaving it however in the morning and only returning to sleep, running as many errands as I can all day long, eager to go home to Cuverville and settle once more to work . . . Looking back, I don't understand how I found the courage or the imprudence to speak to you of a 'situation' that was more hopeless than I could describe to you,[1] and that one couldn't humanly understand. It seemed to me that your solicitude warranted that confidence. – If I were with you, I would perhaps tell you the little effort – the enormous effort – which I made, (giving in to my anguish and to your encouragement) – to lift a corner of the heavy curtain of silence and mendacity that hangs between us. A few words only . . . No, I have already told you. It's all too painful and begins bleeding again at a touch. My <u>punishment</u> is that I am no longer permitted to speak to her.

I admire you if through my reticence you can understand any of this . . . But this little bit I tell you is already too much. Still, I wished you were there the other day when this latest blow was inflicted. Yes, with monstrous selfishness, I wished you were there. And then a moment later, I was glad you were not.

> Very deeply your friend,
> André Gide.

Received your double letter at Colpach. With each new letter from you, I open the envelope with a slight palpitation, with an indefinable feeling in which there is even a measure of curiosity – a somewhat oriental curiosity: your heart has resources that amaze me. I read you with a sort of dumb admiration: What! all this is written to <u>me</u>? And I feel some of the landowner's uneasiness I told you I felt at La Roque when I considered that those so beautiful woods belonged to <u>me</u> . . .

I look <u>frightful</u> in that picture Lady Ottoline took! But it's my punishment for not yet having sent you a better one.

A thousand friendly wishes to Simon. A thousand smiling ones to Janie.

50. André Gide to Dorothy Bussy

> Cuverville en Caux
>
> 14 Oct [1920]

Dear friend,

What a long, dreadful silence![1] I am very worried. I'm always afraid I may have written you I don't know what distressing thing

---

[1] i.e., the strained relationship with his wife.

LETTER 50

[1] Rereading this letter some years later, D.B. commented in the margin: 'Fifteen days! It has certainly changed. D. Bussy 1925.'

which you have interpreted as proof of my dreadful character and of my total indifference to your regard! . . . I beg you to reassure me or to justify my anxiety.

Here life goes on with all the semblance of happiness. Lovely weather. I have been reading the *Old Wives' Tale*[2] and feeling my own novel[3] slowly taking shape inside me, but I'm writing nothing of it yet. Having much trouble working; I spend at the piano, practising, about four hours a day – which is much too much for a novelist. I don't know yet where or how I shall settle this winter, or even whether I shall settle at all. But at least my plan to fasten myself for a while in Roquebrune before spring remains unchanged.

I return to Paris in two days. Your letter from La Souco just arrived. You would have been reassured by the way my heart beat. But today I add nothing to my letter. Friendly wishes to Simon and fond remembrances to Janie.

Your friend
André Gide.

51. André Gide to Dorothy Bussy

28 Oct. 20

Dear friend,

Since you remember the Villa so well, you will easily imagine what solitude can be like here. Impossible to find a servant. From six to seven in the evening a char comes to make up my room. I bring home a bit of cold meat which I eat at a corner of some table. The day before yesterday I spent three hours clearing my heating system. Were it not for the time it took from work, it would all amuse me . . . But I have hopes of seeing an Annamite arrive in a few days;[1] a friend

---

[2] Gide wrote a preface for Marcel de Coppet's translation of Bennett's novel, *Conte de bonnes femmes* (N.R.F., 1931).

[3] *Les Faux-monnayeurs*, which was not published until 1926.

LETTER 51

[1] Gide's friend, André Ruÿters, had 'lent' him an Annamite (Vietnamese) soldier to act as part-time domestic at the Villa Montmorency. His Christian name was Paul, but Gide preferred to call him by his 'real' name, Phong.

who procured him for me has it that colonials are very closely observed and that if this one were to murder me he would have little chance of escaping justice.

What's more, Elisabeth V.R. has been sharing my solitude since yesterday. And Madame V.R. will join her here in four days – which means I shan't have to cope for meals. A boon for work.

Oh please dear friend don't tell me another time that you've written me a long letter and then torn it up – I mean, don't again tear up the letters you write to me. It grieves and enrages me. It matters little that afterwards I receive the most exquisite letters from you, I always think that the one you shredded was still better – or more touching, or more I don't know what – but I should like to <u>know</u>.

Marc repeats his baccalauréat exam in three days and the same evening leaves for Strasbourg (Colonial Infantry) where I think I shall go and see him towards the end of November. I am relying on work alone to console me for his leaving.

Pending the photo I had promised you (I told you that the print I had made for you was unsatisfactory) I am sending you this one in which I am barely distinguishable, but which your imagination will fill in. Full of shadows as it is, it seems better to me than Lady Ottoline's.

Pleased with what you say of Rhys[2] – I'm going to see him one of these days. – Oh no, don't be at all afraid you will bore me with talk of those around you. Young V. d. E.'s misadventure is lamentable; it wrung my heart . . .[3] but you tell me nothing of your lodger.

I am reading *Old Wives' Tale* with interest and even a certain admiration. It's certainly the best one can do if one is to dispense with genius.

The weather has been so radiant I have no trouble imagining La Souco. Au revoir. I think of you much more often than you allow yourself to believe.

> Your friend
> André Gide.

[2] Ernest Rhys (1859–1946), who represented in Paris the Everyman Library series published by Dent, was then beginning a translation of *Les Caves du Vatican*. The published version however was D. B.'s (*Lafcadio's Adventures*, 1928).

[3] Two weeks before the wedding, Zoum Vanden Eeckhoudt broke off her engagement to Maurice Van der Borght. D. B. was much concerned by Zoum's disillusion at eighteen.

52. Dorothy Bussy to André Gide

La Souco

8th Dec. 1920

My dear Gide

It certainly is a disappointment that the American publisher has refused the translation of the *Porte Etroite*. Did he give a reason I wonder? Yes, I have begun the *Symphonie Pastorale*, but I am getting on with it very slowly. In fact for the last month I haven't done any at all, having been too much disturbed inwardly to do any work that I wasn't absolutely obliged to. But I will try again now, since you tell me not to be discouraged.

My young people keep me pretty busy. There are five of them to whom I give lessons and read, now that Zoum Vanden Eeckoudt has come back and Julian Morrell[1] arrived. Zoum, Vincent[2] and Janie are the joy of my life. I am relieved about Zoum. I think she has come out of her trial improved and that she has had the strength to save herself from a horrid fate.

I have always thought that one of my occupations in Heaven (if I were allowed to go there) would be arranging a library in company with a friend. I like books more than flowers – I mean their outsides of course. I like dusting them, sorting them, handling them, dipping into them. And so I envy Madame van Rysselberghe and you. And you, I expect, are sick and tired of your task and would rather be doing other things.

When will you invite me to stay in your house? Shall not I some day dispose of my family and pay you a visit? Am I not quite as respectable as Madame van R? Or perhaps respectability is not the passport? What then?

I have been hearing all about the beautiful estate that Elizabeth is to have the management of.[3] Her father wrote a glowing account of it to our friend Jean Vanden Eeckhoudt. I admire her courage and her enterprise.

Did you see in the *Times Literary Sup.*[a review of your *Antoine*

---

[1] The daughter of Lady Ottoline. The Bussys often took in 'paying guests' or young ladies to whom D.B. gave lessons.

[2] Vincent Rendel, D.B.'s nephew.

[3] 'La Bastide-Franco', near Brignoles, which had recently been acquired by the Mayrischs.

and Cléopâtre?[4] It was stupid – trying to be polite and disagreeable at once, it was simply confused. It chose for disapprobation a passage which is in fact a mistranslation – overlooked by me and for which I feel guilty.

Act V. Sc. II. *Cleopatra.* Dost thou not see my baby at my breast,
That sucks the nurse asleep?

Means: that sucks the nurse till she (the nurse) falls asleep. i.e. the sucking makes the *nurse* fall asleep not the baby.

It is pleasant to hear that you are setting to work on a new book but I am sorry there is going to be no more *Si le Grain ne meurt*, I should like several more volumes of it.

Simon is very well and happy I think, working away with his usual ardour.

You didn't answer any of my questions about Mark. Did you think I didn't mean what I said? I am really not as horrid as all that. I have a very human interest in him quite apart from you. I hope with all my heart he doesn't hate it too much. I should very much like to hear how he is getting on and whether you have been or are going to see him soon. Oh! if you didn't tell me things like that I should indeed be irremediably hurt.

Now I must stop a letter which I send in the hopes – for once – that it won't displease you.

Good-bye.

Your friend
Dorothy Bussy

53. André Gide to Dorothy Bussy

15 Dec. [1920]

Dear friend,

I've been through a terrible time – and am not sure of being past it yet. A mire of discouragement, sadness, stupidity. And no exterior

[4] On 25 November 1920, p. 774. A closing sentence in which Gide's translation is recommended to the reader because it points up certain aspects of the original does little to mitigate the sharp criticism of the review as a whole. Gide is taken to task for constantly 'rectifying' the original, for translating Shakespeare's verse into his own 'accurate prose' which gives the 'sense' but not the 'sting'. The reviewer cites the mistranslation of the lines given here by D.B. as an example of the danger of Gide's method of 'correcting' Shakespeare, which can result in failure to distinguish the literal from the metaphoric.

cause – unless perhaps a conversation with Paul Valéry. That excellent friend is possessed of an aesthetic that is the death of me. Beside him I feel moronic.

You can't know how comforting your letters have been. From them I was again able to draw that confidence in myself which has nothing to do with pride, but without which I do no more than pretend to be alive.

I should like to write to you at length, but have saddled myself with a lecture on Verhaeren,[1] to be done in four days (for next Friday) and under the burden of which I've been agonizing.

One sentence in your letter, among all the others, encourages and uplifts me . . . What! You agree to stay at the Villa when passing through Paris! . . . It would quite simply be marvellous.

But before then I shall have seen you at Roquebrune. Au revoir. Soon.

It was naturally when I was at my lowest that I received a shower of vicious attacks – including the one in *The Times*[2] – which did not serve to lift my spirits.

Your
André Gide.

54. André Gide to Dorothy Bussy

Thursday 17th [February 1921]

Dear friend,

I leave tomorrow evening. It's probably too late to write to me at Toulon Poste Restante – for I shall only stop there a day or two. But I should be very disappointed if I found no word from you

c/o Van Rysselberghe
Saint-Clair
Le Lavandou

telling me when I can make my way to Roquebrune. Need I repeat that I am making La Souco the delightful object of my journey. You will undoubtedly find, not far from you, an inn where I might lodge. As for meals, we can discuss it and find a possible arrangement. If I felt, however little, that I was a bother, you would feel me to be ill at

---

[1] The text of this lecture is included in volume ten of Gide's *Oeuvres complètes* (N.R.F.)

[2] See note 4, Letter 52.

ease . . . I hope to be able to stay nearly until the Easter holiday. I say 'nearly' because I have promised a visit to the Raverats.[1] I am to spend the Easter holiday at Elisabeth V.R.'s, near Brignoles, in the Var, where I shall await a letter from Copeau calling me to Paris. He begins work on *Saül* soon.[2] What joy to be drawing near, and to be able to say: soon. Best regards to Simon. My most affectionate smiles to Janie.

Your,
André Gide

55. Dorothy Bussy to André Gide

Sat. Feb. 18th
1921

Dear Gide

A week ago when I thought of your coming I was full of apprehensions and terrors but now that I know it is really true, that you are on your way, nothing is left but joy – a gentle delicious stream of joy. Je m'y laisse aller.[1]

I am writing you a more sensible letter to Saint Clair.

Yrs.
Dorothy Bussy

56. Dorothy Bussy to André Gide

Sat. Feb. 18th 1921

La Souco
Roquebrune Cap Martin

Dear Gide

How heavenly! Please come the very soonest minute that you can. You couldn't have chosen as far as circumstances go a more con-

---

[1] The Raverats were living in Vence, not far from Roquebrune.
[2] Gide's play opened at the Vieux-Colombier theatre on 16 June 1922, with the director Jacques Copeau in the title-role.

LETTER 55
[1] 'I'm indulging in it.'

venient moment for us. You shall lodge where you please and you mustn't think that I am making designs upon your liberty when I say that it will be more sensible if you come to us at any rate for one night and choose your abode yourself. How can I tell whether you would prefer to be near and comfortable and expensive or a long way off and cheap and picturesque and nasty? I really can't take the responsibility.

You will find nobody in the house here but the little English pensionnaire. Simon and Janie send their loves. They are both extremely rejoiced at the thought of seeing you.

Yours always
Dorothy Bussy

P.S. There is no *need* to let us know the day you mean to arrive but a telegram would be nice the day before.

57. Dorothy Bussy to André Gide

31st March 1921

La Souco

Dear Gide

I am busy clearing up your remains – piano, washerwomen, landlady etc. and soon I will send you your linen & your bill.

I am busy too counting my treasure and I feel as if life wouldn't be long enough.

But don't think I have begun to miss you yet.[1] You are as near me as if you were here – Nearer perhaps.

Yours
Dorothy Bussy

We read the Raverats' p.c! Did you sleep à la belle étoile at Vence? Amitiés to Elisabeth.

D.B.

[1] Gide had spent a week at Roquebrune.

58. André Gide to Dorothy Bussy

Paris

26 April [1921]

Dear friend,

I have just finished reading (in the *Revue de Genève*) a third article by Freud on 'L'Origine et le développement de la psychanalyse' – (I was unable to procure the first two) – and I dash to the desk to write to you. It's decidedly very serious business. To tell the truth, he tells me nothing (Freud) that I haven't already thought, but he clarifies a series of thoughts that remained for me in an undefined state – larval, shall we say. The conclusion of all the reflections which the reading engendered is this: it is imperative that I get in touch with Freud. Your brother knows him, doesn't he, and won't refuse to put me in contact with him?[1] It isn't pressing, however, we'll have time to speak further at our next meeting. I'm already dreaming of a preface by him for the German translation of *Corydon*, which might well perhaps precede publication in France. It's worth investigating. After all, I might perhaps put forth my book as having been 'translated from the German'. It's an idea that has just occurred to me and that I haven't yet examined. A preface by Freud could point up the book's usefulness and timeliness.[2]

What shall I tell you of myself? The day of my arrival (last Saturday) I once again plunged into the life of Paris, going that same evening to the last performance of Schlumberger's play.[3] The following day I had lunch with Tagore.[4] (He is EXQUISITE). And I'm having trouble staving off solicitations and provocations from the outside, but I hold fast and try to devote the better part of my time to work, reading, and even to the piano. When will the Vanden Eeckhoudts be in Brussels? They invited me with such friendly insistence that I shall doubtless accept their hospitality, but should like to know when my

---

[1] James Strachey had gone to Vienna in 1920 to study with Freud. He and his wife Alix Sargant-Florence were to translate *The Complete Psychological Works of Sigmund Freud*, 24 vols (Hogarth Press, 1946–66).

[2] Gide's wish to have *Corydon* prefaced by Freud was never realized.

[3] *La Mort de Sparte*.

[4] In 1914 Gide had translated Tagore's *Post Office* as *Amal ou la lettre du roi*. Although Gide's French version was published in 1922 (Lucien Vogel, Paris), it was not performed until May 1928.

presence there would not be too inconvenient. I need to go to Belgium to tend to the printing (in Bruges) of the second half of *Si le grain ne meurt*[5] – and should like them to say when they will be disposed to receive me. Would you be so kind as to ask them and to advise?

I haven't yet seen Marc who is in Warsaw, but whose return is expected any day.[6]

Been very excited for three days, having suddenly glimpsed the shape of the opening chapters of my novel.[7] I am full of admiration for my discovery, which will doubtless give an impetus to the whole book. Thrilling!

Out of pity for both of us, Oh don't give up writing to me . . . and don't give up writing the account you have begun either.[8] If you agree to believe me, I will agree to tell you that I think of you very often. Your friend,

André Gide.

A thousand remembrances to Simon; a thousand smiles to Janie. Would you believe, my char is going mad, and I'm afraid I shall have to have her confined! . . .

59. Dorothy Bussy to André Gide

3rd May 1921

Dear Gide

I wrote you all these plans too soon.[1] Today I've had a telegram from home asking us to come a few days sooner than we meant to. We shall therefore leave here on May 12th. Simon and I would like to

[5] See note 1 to Letter 35.

[6] While in the military and assigned to the 'courrier extérieur', Marc Allégret was often abroad. In 1922 he became a secretary to the Chef de Cabinet of the War Ministry and had charge of the translation of English newspapers.

[7] *Les Faux-monnayeurs (The Coiners).*

[8] D.B. had begun to keep a journal account of her relationship with Gide, especially of their meetings. They both referred to these pages as her 'black notebook'.

LETTER 59

[1] In two preceding letters D.B. had informed Gide of plans to arrive in Paris on 17 May. Simon and Janie, who were never fond of Paris, were to continue on to London on the 19th, and D.B. was to remain behind for a week at the home of the Hanotaux who were old friends and neighbours in Roquebrune. Gabriel Hanotaux (1853–1944) was a former Minister of Foreign Affairs.

see you very much, if you are free on Saturday afternoon May 14th and perhaps go to some pictures. Simon and Janie will go on to London the next day but I shall stay on with the Hanotaux (if the change of date still suits them) till Thursday the 19th.

The *N.R.F.* arrived with admirable punctuality this month. Just and generous praise. And I was amused by your allusion to Mme. B.[2]

Matisse came to see us on Sunday and talked for four solid hours — one uninterrupted monologue about himself. I'm not a judge of painting, but as a man, how extraordinarily superficial his sensibility.

To think that I wasted my time imagining you at Hyères talking to Mme Wharton and B.B.[3] (Charlie DuBos information) and after all you never went. But by what accident did I learn that?

I remember a dreadful habit you once had of writing me a very dull letter and then winding up by saying 'I have a great many most interesting and important things to tell you but we mustn't mix our genres'! How mad it made me!

I'll not mix tonight

Yours
Dorothy Bussy

60. Dorothy Bussy to André Gide

Sunday [22 May 1921]

(No address on purpose)

When you have nothing to say to me — 'nothing at all' — what *can* I say to you. My resentment? — for I do feel resentment at the hard things you put on me — exacted from me. But I have no *right* to feel resentment and besides my resentment dissolves into pity. My pity? It irritates you to be pitied — and yet perhaps that's the sincerest & most passionate feeling I have for you — My love? Zut! Assez! — My affection? — I don't feel it to-day. My disgust for myself — A disgusting subject — What then? Nothing — nothing.

But it was kind of you to speak to me on the telephone that morning. Do you remember that you did? It was a help. You said

---

[2] In the May issue of the *N.R.F.* appeared Gide's 'Billet à Angèle' in which he relates an anecdote told him by 'Mme B.' who, at twelve years old, was delighted to wear glasses because at last she could see the cobbles of the courtyard.

[3] Bernard Berenson.

'Farewell' in the voice that I like. It was a sigh – so gentle so tender, so musical that the sweetness of it was an agony.

> 'Farewell! thou art too dear for my possessing
> And like enough thou know'st thy estimate.'[1]

I had a very good journey from Paris to Dover and slept and cried alternately the whole way. And from Dover to London I had to 'me priver de mes larmes'[2] so as not to arrive with red eyes – so I read Proust. I found Simon & Janie well and I am very glad to be with them again. But you needn't think I cry often. I hardly ever do. Hardly ever want to. And if I did that day it was just because I was tired.

It wasn't hard meeting your wife. I thought it was going to be, but it wasn't. She looked at me with such beautiful eyes and such a beautiful expression that things seemed easy. And how happy she seemed. It is difficult to believe that she isn't really happy – not like you dear friend – your happiness is not of the same kind.

But you – you are different. You mustn't be happy, whatever you say and sometimes pretend – your virtue lies in *not* being happy..

I hope you have got Marc back again safe & sound. I hope, above all things, that the doctor relieved you.[3] If it weren't that I long to hear this I would ask you – for a change – not to write to me – not just yet. I can't bear any more just yet.

Yours
D.B.

61. Dorothy Bussy to André Gide

July 5th [1921]

We have just come back from Lady Ottoline's. She had on the most wonderful bright yellow dress with voluminous billowy skirts. She sat on the sofa in her little room with orange & tomato coloured cushions behind her and I was alone with her. She began to talk about you in her drawling aristocratic voice. She often tries to pump me but doesn't extract much. This time however, she suddenly said, 'How passionately he loves that boy!' So I answered 'Yes.' . . . And was silent.

---

[1] Shakespeare, Sonnet LXXXVII.
[2] 'Deprive myself of tears'.
[3] From rheumatism.

62. Dorothy Bussy to André Gide

July 1921[1]

The only way I can think of to thank you for sending me the Preface to *Armance* is by giving you some of my own personal experiences. Please, as you read, believe that I am talking only of the past. To-day, at my age, it would be ridiculous to pretend that my feelings can have any bearing on the case of Armance. (It is of *her* of course that I am thinking). But I can remember when I was young.

For seven or eight years at the time when a woman is supposed to be most ardent – from about 27 to 35 – I lived in intimate daily intercourse with a man whom I passionately loved.[2] Circumstances (curious enough) gave us every opportunity, every facility for the completest freedom, but we both resolved not to use it – that is *he* resolved and I consented. Of course he could have taken me easily but from high-mindedness, I thought, he wouldn't do it. Was it high-mindedness entirely? There was probably also a certain want, I suppose, of temperament – (Though he wasn't babylan.)[3] But in spite of that he was a perfect, an exquisite lover. I can't imagine that any woman can ever have been loved more tenderly, more ardently, more *wholly*. And he made me happy – more than happy – *contented*. I never had one single feeling of bitterness against him for I never doubted his love for a single second. Of course I had regrets many and deep when I thought that a woman's natural life was not to be mine. But I gave up the hope of that cheerfully. I never for a moment put it in the balance with the passion of my heart. And since a complete union was or seemed to us impossible I was *grateful* to him for believing that that happiness of unsatisfied love was better for me than marriage with any other man. He knew that the only real bitterness is not to believe that one is loved. The moments of frustrated physical desire – especially for a girl who doesn't know (oh! perhaps still more for a woman who does & has no curiosity) can be borne with comparative ease; they pass; their agony is nothing to the agony of feeling one isn't loved. I have felt them both and I know.

[1] Written after reading Gide's 'Préface à *Armance*' but only sent (as the postscript indicates) on 14 October.

[2] This was probably D.B.'s married cousin, Sydney Foster. See *Two Victorian Families* by Betty Askwith (London, Chatto & Windus, 1971), p. 61.

[3] Or 'babilan' as Stendhal spells it, borrowing it from an archaic Italian word meaning 'impotent'. 'Le babilanisme' and its relation to passion is the subject of *Armance*.

But – and now I know I am going to shock you so that perhaps you'll never like me again – Stendhal knew women I think better than you. Octave would have done right to '*tricher*' (Who are you, dear friend, to scorn 'le tricheur'?)[4] Yes, I have read that cynical letter of his to Mérimée and I understand what I am talking about. Setting aside the grotesque idea of the substitute and a still worse grossness, and drawing the line where each of us draws it, short of depravity (but I'm well aware that that is a varying place according to each one's nature) Octave could have made Armance happy with caresses and kept her for more than three years (Stendhal's limit) – for as long as he loved her. For I believe – and this is another heresy though I was pleased the other day to discover that Rousseau shares it – I believe that total deprivation is more exasperating to the senses than partial indulgence. Yes, it's a curious thing that I have often & often thought of the case of Armance & Octave (more especially I remember thinking of it at the time of Romain Rolland's divorce) and I never could understand how a woman in love could feel such a disability as anything but secondary, when it was caused by a physical defect or by, as in Stendhal's case, the excess of passion. I used to think too like you that passion might be enhanced by it and last longer & more happily in such marriages than in others.

But there's another case which you mention which doesn't seem to me at all the same from the woman's point of view – (it's not honest to pretend that it is the same) the case in which desire is not impotent but merely dissociated from love. I think if Tom Jones had continued all his life preferring to lie with other women and to adore Sophia mystically she would have had a poor time of it. I think it would have been very difficult for her to believe he really loved her, very difficult for her not to suffer from insatisfaction, from jealousy, from fear that after all, since there was nothing essential in that dissociation (essential only for her) some other creature might succeed in dispelling it. But I can imagine even here – and I think it is you who have taught me to imagine – though for my part not to attain to it – a love on both sides so very great that it would rise above all doubt and jealousy and selfishness and turn into a supreme confidence. But oh! let the man remember that if she is denied his physical '*épanchement*' she is in all the more desperate need of every other kind.

There are only six words in all your preface which I thought you might have written thinking of me – '*et qui pis est le lui*

4 'The cheater'.

représentant.'⁵ Insincère! I think perhaps you half thought of me when you wrote the last paragraph. But I am not to be consoled so. I will not be so cowardly as to say because the grapes are out of my reach that they are sour. I still believe I have missed the completest of human experiences. And what's more I don't believe that the ardour of the senses is necessarily followed by repulsion & hatred. When Shakespeare wrote about 'that hell' he meant the gratification of lust without love. Didn't he? You have proved by experience that love can outlive the satisfaction of desire between man & man – why should it not between man & woman? Of course it can. And Alfred de Musset & George Sand prove nothing except that quarrels make more noise than peace. But all of that is nothing to the point. The grapes are out of reach. What is the use of thinking whether they would be sweet or sour?

·················· [D.B.'s line of dots] ···················

I would like to tell you how the passion of my youth ended – not my love for I loved him always. After about 8 years, as I told you, he fell very ill of a violent peculiar illness which affected his brain. In my inexperience I didn't guess what it was. Well, it just was alcoholic poisoning. And in my inexperience I thought that very dreadful. For months more or less I nursed him and prevented other people from guessing what it was and I had the most horrible nightmarish struggle to prevent him from relapsing. He got better but he was never the same again. His brain, his temper, his character were all absolutely different and my feeling for him necessarily changed too. But I believe I should have remained faithful to him if I could have gone on helping him. But I couldn't. His wife (just come out of a lunatic asylum) took him away to Italy and they settled there permanently – out of my reach. He was too changed to be able to resist and nothing was of any good. But when I wrote & told him I was going to marry Simon – ah! the power to help then was living & urgent – I felt as if I was committing murder. I suppose I was. 'For each man kills the thing he loves.'⁶

Janie was born about three years after our marriage. As soon as I was strong enough to write, when she was about a week old, the first letter I wrote was to him. I wanted him so dreadfully to forgive me. I had finished it when Simon came in and told me he was dead. He

⁵ 'And what is worse, showing it to her.'
⁶ Oscar Wilde, 'The Ballad of Reading Gaol', vii.

had died a day or two before my confinement and they had kept it from me. So he never got that letter and Janie's cradle was watered by a good many tears. But afterwards I was happier because he was dead. Is that horrible? And the happiest years of all my life were the first five years when Janie was a baby and I thought I was done with passion & was at peace. But that was false, for my passion then was for Janie, and even that which they say is the *purest* of loves . . . well it was very like all the others. I have never said what I have written here to any human being and I don't know why I want to say it to you. For oh my dear, my dear, though I believe you have some queer sort of kindness for me, I don't believe that you have any *real interest* in me. Why – or how – in Heaven's name should you?

Not a saint – not a boy – just your hopeless and yet not altogether unhappy

Lover
D.B.

P.S. October 14th

But in truth your illustrations from Tom Jones and Marius & Cosette & you might have added a million others are not very convincing – All love – all *amour-passion begins* like that – with no thought of – with terror of physical contact.[7] But, but, ever since I have known you I have been wondering how it is possible for passionate love to grow & live without the desire for physical contact. And I still, alas, cannot answer the question.

63. Dorothy Bussy to André Gide

La Souco

Oct. 3d 1921

Dear Gide

We got home on the 1st and yesterday morning our long delayed post reached us, including, at last, two letters from you.

You *are* horrid to me, aren't you? Horrid – horrid! I wonder why?

---

[7] In his preface Gide cites the refusal of Tom Jones (in Fielding's novel) and Marius (in Victor Hugo's *Les Misérables*) to dishonour, even by lustful thoughts, the women they love.

I wonder, I wonder how you can bear to be. I suppose it must be that you can't really believe in me. Very likely you are right. I daresay I don't deserve to be believed in – yet. But what you don't consider is, that when I do deserve it, it will be too late.

It doesn't matter. Some progress I have made. I am not envious of anybody any more. I wouldn't change places with one of the people you like better than me – not with one of the people you like seeing better than you do me (including Roger Fry!) Our friend the devil couldn't tempt me now by offering me youth & beauty & to be your bien-aimé. I feel as if I had got something better than that. I don't know exactly what it is but something like 'le droit de cité,' only in English they call it the '*freedom* of the city,' which is better. The freedom of your heart! I feel you let me into places where no one else may go. I may wander where I please with impunity. The keys are in my hands. I may sun myself in the open places. I may explore the dark corners. I may listen at secret doors. There is nothing to prevent me from going into the Holy of Holies – except my own awe. Is there a Bluebeard's chamber where I shall be caught & executed at last? Oh! what dreadful nonsense I write. But that's part of the fun. There's nothing I mayn't write – nothing I don't write. Nobody dares write to you what I do. And here's the proof. Last July I wrote you something about Armance – but you hurt my feelings so dreadfully by – I'm sure I don't know what – that I couldn't send it to you. Then I took it to the Tyrol, meaning to give it to you – if you were nice. And now, though you aren't nice, though you are horrid, shall I send it to you? It is rather awful – a kind of confession – but nothing to do with the present – and if it makes you blush it won't be because it has any reference to you. Still I will allow you a few days so that you can 'décommander' it if you want to. I shan't be offended. (I remember that you make the Immoraliste[1] say that the confidences which are volunteered don't interest him – only the ones he surprises.) But if you don't 'décommander' it I will send it you in a registered letter so that you may know what it is and that there's no need to read it in a hurry or to acknowledge it or ever to make an allusion to it. I shall find out quite soon enough if it disgusts you for ever and if it does – oh! I can never do anything, or pretend anything or hide anything in order to make you like me. I have always said to myself 'If he dislikes me for what I *am*, tant pis, there's nothing to be done.' But try and read it when you are in a good mood and then destroy it, <u>please</u> . . .

---

[1] Michel, the protagonist of Gide's novel.

Dear Gide, I very much liked what you wrote to me about Arco, and yet it was sad. I feel you discouraged, anxious. You mustn't regret the time when you wrote an act of *Saül* in one day. You have gained, you know, infinitely more than you have lost – *gained* because you have chosen to live before writing about life. But now, now you have gathered your experience, you are right, you mustn't lose any more time before distilling it. Now, you ought to be as courageous in resisting the call of the outer world as you were before in listening to it. Oh! if your 'defection' had been for *that* I could have borne it better (don't think I say that out of jealousy). I would give up my share of you for *that* without a murmur, though still with an aching – or as you like to call it – *bruised* heart. For *I* haven't enough vitality ever to forget for a single minute how short, how precarious a time is left for love & as you seem able to forget how short & precarious time is left for work.

We have come back here to summer, almost tropical heat. You would be sorry to see our poor countryside. It hasn't rained since April and then very little – and you know how dry it was when you were here. We are all, trees & humans, gasping in the drought and our garden is a desert.

Simon worked a great deal at Toblach – 'collecting documents' he called it. I think he is pleased with what he has brought home – strange landscapes in which to place his strange beasts. It won't be difficult for you to have one when you want one.

How odious to think of you having rheumatism in your hand & writing with difficulty. You needn't write to me you know – *except to notify a change of address.*

Yours
Dorothy Bussy

P.S. That last sentence is discreet & I had vowed I never would be again. Please write to me as often & as much as you possibly can.

P.P.S. I suppose you know the only sentence in your letter that had a drop of comfort in it – the one that you hardly dared write lest it should appear monstrous to me.

I see you racking your brains to try & remember it – rather anxiously too. No, no, you needn't fear – it wasn't really in the least compromising. Oh. Gide. I'm as thirsty as the garden. Goodnight. D.B.

64. André Gide to Dorothy Bussy

Cuverville

12 Oct. 21

Dear friend,

I would have written to you sooner – in immediate reply to your last, long, terrible letter – but I have just <u>agonized</u> five full days on an article promised to the *N.R.F.* (which you will read in the November issue) and from which I didn't dare distract myself.

I know this letter also will disappoint you, but what can I do? Everything I have written you in my imagination since returning to Cuverville, I can't bring myself to send . . . At times I sink into such an abyss of distress that happiness, work, life even, seem impossible, and I only manage to get hold of myself by turning away from the situation.[1] No, I can't, I mustn't speak of this to anyone. Let it suffice you to know that it is to you I would speak most easily of it – and don't torment me too much with reproaches and accusations that affect me much more than you think.

I'm trying to take refuge in work, but have been splashing about in my novel as in a mudhole, a *bog*, a *quagmire* from which I despair of ever getting free. I read and reread the passage in your letter where you say: 'you ought to be as courageous in resisting the call of the outer world as you were before in listening to it.' That's what I say to myself, but I like hearing it said to me. Said by you, I hear it better. Be persuaded that your advice can become a true support for me, that it is already . . .

I recently finished *The Rescue*,[2] without managing to find my way all the time through the plot's ramifications; but as encumbered as the book is, I hold it to be among the most remarkable, and at moments, it touches the most sensitive parts of my heart.

And now I am labouring over Donne's poems.

> *Divorce mee, untie, or breake that knot againe,*
> *Take me to you, imprison mee, for I*
> *Except you enthrall mee, never shall be free. . .*[3]

– apparently influenced by Claudel! . . .

[1] The conjugal tensions at Cuverville.
[2] Conrad's novel, *The Rescue, A Romance of the Shallows* had been published the previous year.
[3] From *Holy Sonnets*, XIV.

And I await, in trepidation, that awful letter you warn me to expect. Address it to the

> Nouvelle Revue Française
> 3, rue de Grenelle – Paris

where I'll pick it up in a few days.

Happy with what you say of Simon's work. Delighted to see soon the studies brought back from the Tyrol – and you.

> Soon, probably. Your friend
> André Gide.

65. André Gide to Dorothy Bussy

> Sunday
> 22 Oct, 21

Dear friend,

I have received the fearful letter . . .[1] Shall I tell you I am deeply grateful to you for writing that way? No, it would annoy you. – Just this brief consideration, instead: to dare resort to 'tricheries', it takes either enormous love or near indifference. But you may be sure that what you say on the subject does not startle me. On this matter there would, to be sure, be a good deal to add to my preface.

And I was, as a matter of fact, thinking especially of you when I wrote the five words you quote . . .

Marc – (what you said of him in another letter is what has surprised, stupefied, me most – since Cambridge)[2] – has 45 days!! of leave time. I'm considering taking him to Rome – unless he goes by himself, in which case I shall return directly to Cuverville. He has just undergone a minor operation (don't ask me for details) which is

---

[1] Letter 62, written in July, but posted only in the middle of October.

[2] Gide is probably alluding to a letter which D. B. had sent him a month earlier (21 September) in which she confessed that she would rather 'a thousand times' that *she* die than Marc Allégret, for whom she felt no particular affection and whose absence would be no loss to her.

keeping him bedridden for a week – which time he is spending here with me, at the Villa – secretly. *I like immensely to nurse him.*

If I do go to Italy, it will be . . . soon – and I'll begin the trip with a two-day visit to La Souco. You may expect me to appear before another week has passed . . . Or, on second thoughts, don't. Don't expect me. Let's say that I shall return to Cuverville. I'll remain undecided until the day I leave here. Your

André Gide

(OVER)

You make no further mention of plans for getting [the translation of] *La Porte étroite* published. And yet, in *The Times*, one reads: '*He* (Robert Curtius) *begins with A.G. of whom – in contrast to the comparative shyness with which English readers have approached this essentially French and difficult critic and artist – the Germans have produced no fewer than eight translated works . . . etc.*'[3] '*Shyness*' is wonderful.

In another connection, I am asked to consider serious proposals made by a London publisher. But *first thing*, I need to know where you are in the steps you said you were taking. You can tell me all this soon, if I come. No, it would be best if you answered me on this matter by return of post, as I might be able to clinch something at once, before leaving Paris.

A.G.

66. André Gide to Dorothy Bussy

Chiusi, Tuesday

[November 1921]

Dear friend,

I wished to write sooner, but the waggons were too [illegible word] *and churning my brains. I hardly could read. Yet I believe I never was more deeply interested than reading this black secret book*

[3] From a review of Ernst Robert Curtius's *Die Literarischen Wegbereiter des Neuen Frankreich* (1919), printed in the *TLS*, 25 August 1921, p. 543a.

of yours.[1] *How strange, how queer, how instructing it is, for one to look at one's own past reflected in an other soul! T'is a pity I couldn't speak immediately with you about that. There were a great deal of commentaries to do. But I think, and I feel, the whole profoundly true. _ I devoured it; but now, I'll read it again; more quietly. What you do say about my politeness made me laugh; I think you cannot understand very well how disconcerting for me were your . . . I don't know how to say . . . sollicitude, attention . . . You couldn't suppose, but I can say (now) that it was the first time a woman paid some attention to me . . . and I felt the need to enwrap myself in this exceeding and formal politeness. I believe it was the unconscious* 'instinct de protection'.

Perhaps what pleased me most was hearing you judge me to be perfectly <u>natural</u> – that's why what pleased me least was the sentence where you say I take pleasure in <u>appearing</u> mysterious. No, what makes me open and close doors so gently, walk noiselessly and so on, is a constant concern not to disturb others – and which I always feel . . . at Cuverville as well as Roquebrune, in Cambridge as well as travelling in Italy with Marc.

Well we spent the night at Ventimiglia, then on to Pisa where a tremendous storm broke as we were approaching the hotel. We spent the following night in Siena, and I'm writing to you from Chiusi where we arrived yesterday evening. The place is admirable but this hotel is freezing and much too uncomfortable for me to consider remaining. And it's raining! I let Marc go alone to see the Etruscan tombs which are quite far off, scattered over the countryside. Directly after lunch we leave for Orvieto. My conspirator's cloak and mysterious air are the cause of my just having been arrested and carried off to the Police Station. I had considerable trouble convincing those worthy carabinieri that I had come to Chiusi 'for pleasure'. They asked me a good ten times: 'What are you doing here?' Also in residence at our inn is a troupe of actors who last night gave a unique and startling performance in the little local theatre. Deadly; but the theatre and the audience were charming.

I think of you much more than you allow yourself to believe . . . Let me say again that I found Vincent exquisite: what distinction, what <u>profound</u> elegance of tone and manners! How much I like his face, still so young, already so serious! – As for Marc, exhausted by

---

[1] See note 8 to Letter 58.

those three days at La Bastide and by his tetanus shot . . . no, don't judge him on the basis of that meeting.

Best wishes to you all, with much more friendship than politeness – your friend

André Gide.

On your advice, I am reading Goldoni. Surprised to understand it so well (*La Locandiera*) and delighted.

67. Dorothy Bussy to André Gide

La Souco

28th Nov. 21

Dear Gide

Your change of address was only half a surprise to me and your letter sounded comforted. How nice! Though you never will believe that I *can* be, that I *am* glad when you are happy.

In the meantime I have done your errands to Lytton. He has already had an application for the German translation of *Queen Victoria* but if on enquiry the applicant turns out to be unsuitable he will be very glad to know of Mme Annette Kolb.[1] I also asked his ideas about the article on English literature in the *N.R.F.* I copy you what he says. 'T. S. Eliot would be very good I think.[2] He is most intelligent and I am sure would be very glad to increase his small income in that way. The only thing is that at the present moment he can do no work as he has had a breakdown and has been ordered a complete rest. However, he'll no doubt emerge fairly soon. He is now abroad. London address: 9 Clarence Gate Gardens, N.W.1. Other- wise there is Murry who is supremely competent in every way – but perhaps he would be too busy . . . But I hope they will have Eliot. That wretch Percy Lubbock! I'm glad he has been removed. The incarnation of priggism.'

I have been reading a book lately which has given me real pleasure – unexpected too. It's a kind of novel that came out last summer by

[1] The Bavarian writer was a friend of Mme Mayrisch. The German translation of *Queen Victoria* however was done by Hans Reisiger (Berlin, S. Fischer, 1925).

[2] Eliot did contribute two 'Lettres d'Angleterre' to the *N.R.F.* the following year, in May (pp. 617–24) and December (pp. 751–6).

Walter de la Mare called the *Memoirs of a Midget*. It is full of very beautiful and interesting things – witty too and uncommon. Much more stuff in it, more emotion, more experience than I had thought him capable of from reading his poetry. It was of course totally misunderstood by all the critics, who took it for a trifling and delicate fantasy, whereas it is really a deeply serious and philosophical account of life told with tragic bitterness. There! emballée as I am very rarely now-a-days. But I don't know whether you would like it. It is too long – like all English books – and difficult to read. But in spite of that, *composed* – an artist's work.

I, who have so much to blush for and who so seldom blush, actually *did* when I thought of a certain passage in my black book about *Le Voyage d'Urien* which you once failed to give me. The gift would have given me immense pleasure at that time – but now, my dear, it's too late. I don't in the least want you to give me your books now – except the ones I can't get otherwise – *those* oh! yes – But please don't bother about the others. The thought that it was that passage of mine which reminded you to send me your *Oeuvres choisies* will make me detest either the white cover or the blue cover[3] – neither of which however has turned up! So perhaps after all my blushes are wasted.

Poor Gide! So hard a job it is for you to please me!

Yrs.
Dorothy Bussy

68. Dorothy Bussy to André Gide

Dec. 8th 1921

Dear Gide

Your delightfully fat little volume in a *blue* cover has arrived. Notwithstanding blushes I am very glad indeed and *proud* to have it – not-withstanding disclaimers it *has* pleased me very much that you should send it.

There are some things I might say about it – but not to-day. This isn't a letter but just an acknowledgment.

I dreamt of you the other night but nothing more interesting than

[3] The limited printing of Gide's books had the blue cover; the white was for the edition popularly sold.

that you were holding and rubbing your wrist – Tut! tut! As if one hadn't got aches and pains enough of one's own!

Yours always
Dorothy Bussy

69. André Gide to Dorothy Bussy

Cuverville

12 Dec. 21

Dear friend,

On your brother's advice, passed along by you, I notified Jacques Rivière[1] directly, and myself wrote to Eliot whose *Sacred Wood* I had in fact just read. If you write to Lytton please thank him as I now thank you, in other words: warmly.

I worked very well the first days of my stay here, but now it's all beginning to break down. I think that what I suffer from, especially in this place – like Oswald in Ibsen's *Ghosts* – is an absence of joy, or rather (since there is joy and suffering wherever there is life) from the absence of that joy's expansion. After a short period, I ache with repressed sensuality, with 'frustrations' à la Freud.

It's a good thing my little blue book had gone off before I received your letter! I wouldn't have dared send it to you. Happy that it pleased you 'all the same'.

I return to Paris in two days (address: Nouvelle Revue Française, 3 rue de Grenelle) to finish preparing a lecture on Dostoevsky[2] which Copeau requested and which I couldn't refuse.

I curb and repress and stifle as best I can memories of Roquebrune – in other words, the growing desire to join you there in early spring . . .

The Vanden E.s are probably with you. Tell them a thousand chosen things for me. Best to you all.

Your
André Gide

I am deep in *The Ring and the Book* – without coming to the end of my admiration.

[1] Gide's intimate friend was then editor of the *N.R.F.*
[2] There were to be six lectures in all, published in 1923 as *Dostoïevski (Articles et Causeries)*. The book was translated by D.B. and published in 1925 by J. M. Dent.

70. André Gide to Dorothy Bussy

7 April 22

Dear friend,

Dreadful weather, but I have felt better for the past few days, despite persistent vertigo. What I missed this winter was a little (or long) visit to La Souco! You cannot imagine how imbued with nostalgia that name is for me . . . But I am over my head in work. I must completely redictate my Dostoevsky lectures, and besides that, a few articles – among which one, very important, on the intellectual plight of Europe, requested by the *Revue de Genève*. All this delays my novel which I am impatient to re-immerse myself in. *Saül* will not open before the end of May. But I 'caress the dream' of having you a few days at the Villa. It all depends on what domestic arrangement my wife can find, since she will be your hostess. Without domestic help – impossible, but she writes that she has hopes of finding something suitable. She plans to spend May here, and perhaps the beginning of June. But my brother-in-law's family[1] will be staying at Cuverville for the Easter holiday, and despite the great pleasure it will give her to receive them, I'm afraid it will cause my wife, considering the absence of servants, considerable fatigue . . . Vedremo.

But what I am definitely counting on is your presence at Pontigny[2] this summer – from the 17th to the 26th of August. Desjardins tells me he has also invited your sister from Newnham[3] and indirectly sounded Lytton . . . I look forward to that *meeting*.

Do you know what Marc is doing at present? . . . Become secretary to the chief adjunct of the Cabinet; for the War Ministry he translates English and American newspaper articles dealing with French politics! Needless to add, he is intensely interested by his new duties.

Saw Roger Fry and Pamela (charming) – and the terrible Lady Colefax, who is certainly the most tiresome person the good lord ever conceived of. I *shun* social intercourse as much as I can and

[1] The Marcel Drouins; Jeanne Rondeau Drouin was Madeleine Gide's sister.
[2] Each year in the restored abbey at Pontigny, Paul Desjardins organized ten-day sessions (called *décades*) at which French and other intellectuals joined to discuss aesthetic and political questions.
[3] Pernel Strachey.

closet myself with a new secretary, a living elegy, engaged for two months.

Tell me quick you will come to Pontigny so I can rejoice!

Your
André Gide

Pitoëff[4] asks me for a translation of *Hamlet* – and in spite of Schwob's, I accept, for the pleasure of going over it with you.

I am also working (for the *N.R.F.*, June issue)[5] on a translation of *The Marriage of Heaven and Hell* by the admirable Blake (abundantly quoted in my lectures).

How the devil would you translate:

'*The selfish smiling fool, and the sullen frowning fool, shall be both thought wise, that they may be a rod*' . . . Don't understand *the secret meaning* . . .

71. Dorothy Bussy to André Gide

51 Gordon Square

5th June, 1922

Dear Gide

Thank you for your note which made me feel remorseful that I should add to your fatigue by giving extra burdens of reading and writing.

I am sorry I sent you the translation.[1] It isn't worth while your reading it. It is the slightest of things; only I was carried away by the argument of masks. Since you are converted – that is all that I want – not in the least that you should notice one of my thousand 'baguettes' . . . More than a thousand by now!

Your letter made me laugh too. Was there ever a more ludicrous correspondence than ours?

[4] Georges Pitoëff (1884–1939), the Russian-born actor-director, had lived in Paris since 1919.

[5] Gide's Blake translation appeared in the August issue of the *N.R.F.*

LETTER 71

[1] *Les Baguettes*, a translation D.B. had made, presumably from English, of a Noh play. The text has been lost.

When your future biographers grub among your papers, how they will pity you, my poor persecuted Gide, and how disgusting they will think my persistence. (Not that I care one brass button or one twopenny damn for your future biographers. I detest and despise them all. There is not the slightest doubt that they will all be thick headed, blundering fools. It is a pleasure to think that they will read this and I hope that for a moment their equanimity will be disturbed.) They will at any rate never guess my secret consolations, nor the hieroglyphics from which I derive my sustinence [*sic*].

I hope you are going at once to set about getting visas for

Austria

Switzerland

Italy

in case, *in case* you feel inclined to join us in the Tyrol. I feel sure that Cook would undertake the whole business for you. All you have to do is to give them your passport or tell Marc to take it to them.

I have settled to go to Pontigny. As it will not be to see you, as it is an understood thing that you will not speak to me, my conscience is clear and perhaps the Fates will be a little kind. I am not trying to cheat them. Not I. Not I. And they *cannot* cheat me. Never, never again. They have done their worst in that direction – and whatever remains to be suffered it will not be *disappointment*.

We have come to the conclusion that it will be better not to take Janie with me. I shall be able to make some other arrangement for her.

Ought I to do anything official about accepting for myself?

I am so glad the Vandens are going to be at the first night of *Saül*. I shall have a faithful account of it from Zoum. I think she will be coming to stay with us in London a few days later.

It is nice to think that the Vanden's friendship – Zoum's in particular – is a pleasure to you. I admire you, dear Gide, for so generously finding and accepting pleasures.

There-there – I had best stop now or you will be laughing at me as usual.

Yours,

D.B.

I am trying to take steps about the *Porte Etroite* & so far have been recommended to do nothing as yet with the American publishers as it is better to make the arrangement simultaneously with the English.

72. André Gide to Dorothy Bussy

Bastide Franco
Brignoles Var

23-7-22

Dear friend,

I am a monster for remaining so long without writing; cannot go on another day . . . It's 5:30 in the morning. In ½ an hour we[1] leave by car for Sainte Baume – and tonight when I return, I shall probably be too tired. It will only be a word, but at least it will reassure you. Since my last letter . . . first there was a brief stay at Cuverville, then a flight to the south, to Porquerolles first (the island facing Hyères) where I met the Martin du Gards[2] – and where I took lots of sea and sun baths and slipped into a total oblivion of time (as you noticed) – then to Hyères Plage, where I had already been last summer. More oblivion. Oblivion of time at La Bastide where I have been for the past week.

I felt so tired before leaving Paris that I longed for complete inaction. But no sooner at Porquerolles than I threw myself madly into the translation of *Hamlet* which Pitoëff has asked of me. I laboured terribly through the entire first act, now complete, but can go no further.[3] We shall speak again of *Hamlet* at Pontigny . . . Translating those redundancies, those absurd images, those limping metaphors, those useless repetitions, that hedging, that quibbling – is an acrobatic feat in which I find no recompense but the pride of having got through it. I reread directly afterwards an act of *Lear* in order to convince myself that this style is peculiar to *Hamlet*. And I told you, I think in Paris, in what a trance of admiration I read *Othello*. – Schwob's translation is perfectly ridiculous. I can't believe that was the text Sarah Bernhardt performed.[4] – His sentences, because he doesn't allow them to stray from the English, are perfect monsters of syntax, as cacophonic and awkward on the tongue as you could wish. Ouf!

[1] Gide, Mme Théo, and Elisabeth.

[2] The French novelist and 1937 Nobel laureate Roger Martin du Gard and his wife Hélène who lived at Hyères Plage.

[3] At the request of Jean-Louis Barrault, Gide did complete his translation of *Hamlet* in 1942. See Letter 187 ff.

[4] It *was*, however, Schwob's text which Bernhardt performed, though modified through collaboration with Eugene Morand.

Dismayed by your desertion from the Tyrol.[5] My travelling papers were in order . . . At least don't drop Pontigny. I am counting on you absolutely, and only the hope of seeing you soon somewhat excused – in my own eyes – my long silence.

What else is there to tell you? The car is waiting –

Soon. My best wishes and respectful and affectionate remembrances to Lady Strachey. Thousands of everything to Simon and Janie.

Your friend
A.G.

73. André Gide to Dorothy Bussy

28 July [1922]

Dear friend

I never wrote a letter which left me more unsatisfied than the last one I sent to you. I am afraid it will have brought you more deception than pleasure and I only sent it lest you would be still more grieved by my silence. I never felt my pen so distant from my thougts [sic], *and my brain so empty. As for the sentiments, what does it matter if I am totally unable to utter them?*

Perhaps in english it comes out better. The working goes as badly as the letters; what I have done since I abandoned the translation of Hamlet *is equal to 0. But I read very much these last times, and principally english matters. We read aloud* The Devils disciple *which is the finest play I have read from Shaw; it delighted us immensely. We tried to read* A Laodicean *(do you know this flat and tasteless novel?) but the book dropped from our hands before we got through the first third of it. And then some sketches from Thackeray,[1] but I couldn't bear this kind of witt* [sic].

And (how could I forget!) a canto from The Ring and the Book *(Pompilia) I already knew.*

[5] The Bussys had planned to spend the summer touring Austria, Switzerland, and Italy. D.B. had invited Gide to join them in the Tyrol, but later announced that the family would spend the summer in England instead.

LETTER 73
[1] The *Character Sketches.*

Privately I dip into wine of W. Pater's Essays,[2] and into King Lear, which is as easy and magnificent as Hamlet was treacherous, swampy and full of snares.

I read again, with you, the beautiful hymn to Bacchus, from Endymion, and a great deal of poetry.

I can not yet realize the idea of not going with you in the Tyrol; it was a great deception to learn that; but I forbear to express it lest you wouldn't trust me.

I don't know at all what I shall be doing, and where I shall be going after leaving (in a few days) la Bastide – before Pontigny; probably some sea bathes more, in the neighborhood of Marseille . . .

And in a fortnight I shall see you again – how it rejoices me, you don't allow me to tell . . .

truly yours
André Gide

Excuse this awkward letter . . . all my sentences begin by 'I' . . shame! –

74. André Gide to Dorothy Bussy

Colpach
Gd Duchy of Luxemburg

29 Aug. [1922]

Dear friend,

I had to cling very hard (to I don't know what) to leave you that way the last evening.[1] I think that, at bottom, only the fear of spoiling our good-bye held me back – as it did the next morning, from accompanying you to the station. What more could we have said . . . ? But your pencilled letter,[2] which I find at my arrival here, is extraordinarily affecting. I need very much to hear you say you don't keep too cruel a memory of that last meeting; . . . what I told you at

[2] Probably in *Greek Studies*, which Gide mentions in his *Journal* on 4 August.

LETTER 74

[1] On the last night of the *décade* at Pontigny, Gide told D.B. that Elisabeth Van Rysselberghe was pregnant with his child.

[2] The letter was subsequently lost.

Pontigny, I could only tell you quickly – and I couldn't keep it from you.

Au revoir. I am your friend

André Gide.

Taking some papers from my valise, I find the letter[3] I thought I had given you. Here it is.

75. Dorothy Bussy to André Gide

[1–3] Sept. 1922

I am glad I was able to find the words you wanted in that pencil letter I wrote in the hotel on my last night in Paris. The radiance of your presence was still lighting me. Since then I have had horrid moments of terror that when that light has quite faded I shall find myself more alone & more in the dark than ever – that, after all, what you have done is to show me that every single way of approach to you is barred not by the obstacles put there by fate, but by that more terribly insurmountable one of your will – your *défense* . . . that you are sitting behind your barriers safe and in reality exulting in your safety. These are the bitterest thoughts I have of you and even in these I am not bitter. Keep up your barriers. I shall not try – you know I never try to get round them or through them. I cannot, I cannot want what you do not want. I take your part against myself. I always want *you* to have the victory. And I know very well what *I* 'cramponner' myself to. If I resist – as I do resist – taking some moments of sweetness that might be mine, it is not like you, through pride, 'sachant une chose si forte de me sentir plus fort encore et de la vaincre.'[1] No, no, it is because I love you best so, best when I am resisting for *your* sake.

Dear, I am thankful that I didn't hate *you* for a single second. I was afraid that I might. But I didn't. I don't. I think I am safe now. I don't

---

[3] From an American publisher.

LETTER 75
[1] 'Knowing a thing to be strong by feeling myself to be stronger still, and by conquering it.'

understand. But that is different. Why should I understand you? What preposterous presumption it would be to think that I can understand you! Vous *comprendre*! *Vous* pouvez me comprendre mais moi – vous.[2] Never. What a reversal of axioms it would be. It is because you are incomprehensible that I love you.

But though I can't understand I can *see* beauty. I have confidence in the judgment of my soul. My soul is not so blind but that it can recognize beauty. It isn't faith I have in your essential beauty. It is certainty. It is knowledge.

Do I hate *her*? Not really. I hope. I think not really. But it made me physically sick to look at her. And in order to be near you I had to force myself to look at her – to think – to think of her body, and what she is carrying.

Dear Gide. What is this horrible instinct of jealousy. You haven't got it. Do you think it is altogether unnatural, false? I mean not genuine, just inculcated by habit and literature?

I have never *really* felt it before.

You must help.

And now you will see, I think you will see, that I have confidence in your feeling for me. I never had it before. I couldn't have it. You used to be astonished. 'That you shouldn't believe in my affection,' you said to me once, 'after I have talked to you like that – (You had been talking of course about your wife) cela me dépasse!' But it was a pleasure to you to talk to me; a relief – and you knew that everything you said could only enhance the image I had of you in my heart – could only make me feel greater love and greater pity.

This time your confidences were different. You suffered more when you told me than I as I listened. It was horrible for you to have to hurt me so. It was horrible for you to risk losing me. But you did it because you cared for me really. You need not have told me. If you hadn't cared really you wouldn't have told me. I know that. I know. I know now that you care.

But oh what awful prices one has to pay for one's joys. Our last day together in Paris was a success, wasn't it? Our day of friendship. I am proud of it. You didn't believe I could do it. But I did. You thought I should spoil it. But I didn't. I was able to be happy, to make you feel that I was happy.

What fun it was. You can't imagine how I like the *little* things. When you pay for my dinner. When you give me books and cigarettes.

[2] '*Understand* you! *You* can understand *me*, but I – you, never.'

When you carry my coat. And remember when I am likely to be cold. And tell me that you like my dress – or my voice – and I smile to myself & remember one of your heroes who describes how he can't abide 'les petits soins'! But with you I feel these things are not little. You never gave them to me when they would have been little. And now – now – they are much. But you needn't be afraid that I shall ever expect them. Each one of them comes each time as a new and particular and overwhelming astonishment.

I was glad though you didn't stay to dinner or come next morning to the station. It was better so.

And you will find that what I say is true. *When once I believe*, I am not susceptible.

Incredible thing that it is *this* should make me believe!

Your amanuensis is glad that it was not she who mislaid the letter of the American publishers. The answer to it has been posted.

I am alone in the house with my mother for a few days after having spent a week in the country with Simon & Janie. I found them both well & happy and we were very glad to see each other again.

I send you all these incoherent contradictory scribblings – a bundle of contradictions which, taken together, make a very simple whole.

Yrs.
D.

76. Dorothy Bussy to André Gide

La Souco

Saturday Oct 21st [1922]

Dear Gide

We arrived here yesterday.[1] It was Friday, the day you settled to go and fetch your spectacles. Did you go? I said to myself, 'To-day he will have been obliged to think of me once. He couldn't go to that spectacle shop without remembering me and the afternoon we went there together.' . . . And yet I don't know. I give you credit for an infinite capacity of forgetting.

Dear Gide, an extraordinary thing has happened to me. I am happy. Perhaps it is wicked to be so happy. No – but dangerous. Millionaires are always detestable people and besides they go in

---

[1] From London, via Paris.

constant fear of being ruined – whereas, when one hasn't a penny-piece it doesn't matter what one does.

To walk up & down the Luxembourg, to listen to your voice repeating the Nightingale,[2] to feel your hand on my arm, to feel you near, to feel you kind – oh! wonderful life, that there should still be such moments as that in it!

And yet it was that same afternoon, just after I had been feeling nearer to you than almost ever before that I talked nonsense to you – nonsense you called it. Yes it was – nonsense, ungrateful & untrue.

Oh! how hard it is to speak the truth! But there is one thing I want to say which I think is true. I think I was really *glad* to hear you speak more tenderly of Beth than I had ever heard you. It would be too dreadful if you didn't feel tenderly for her. No, no, you needn't hide that feeling from me. You must have it. I wouldn't have you not have it.

Why should I be jealous? I am too bound to you. 'Ne vous en allez pas de moi,' you said, '*vous n'en avez plus le droit.*'[3] And my heart leapt with joy. Bound to you, beloved friend, by duty as well as by love. How is it possible not to be happy?

Ah! but the test will come with your next letter. Never mind! Courage! I shall survive even that.

I would never have given you letters to post but that I wanted you to look at the address on one. Did you? Just yes or no, please.

Your dutiful
Dorothy B.

77. Dorothy Bussy to André Gide

La Souco

Nov. 22d 1922

Dear Gide

I am very glad you have forwarded me the objections of the American publisher. (Not that it is of much good, but one likes to know where one is.) I am afraid though that what he really objects to is not *my* translation but *your* book. It is quite certain that if he or you want me to improve upon the *Porte Etroite* or to alter it, I resign

[2] Keats's ode.
[3] 'Don't go away from me. *You no longer have the right to.*'

at once. I am not only incapable of doing it – I don't want to do it. Of course I am not so stupid as not to know that fidelity to the letter may betray the spirit. But I know too that the spirit is very often inherent in the letter. I tried to be faithful to both. I tried to give the book's intensity, its acuity, its aridity and I knew these things depended also on the severity, the nudity, the purity of the language. It pleased me to accentuate rather in that direction than to allow myself any softenings and relaxations. Even your curious method of leaving out the conjunctions that other people put in – it *amused* me to keep – no, I was *right* to keep in English. It is odd in French. Why shouldn't it be odd in English?

But the result of it all is that it isn't a *pleasant* book to read in English any more than in French. It is, I hope, almost as agonising to read in English as in French. It has also I hope kept the impression of *beauty* in the style. Perhaps you'll think it ridiculous to say so – but I believe that – at any rate in parts – it has.

Dear me! I am having the most awful argument on the same subject with the translator of *Queen Victoria*.[1] He has the most beautiful French style – worthy of a distinguished place in the *Revue des Deux Mondes* – (a budding Julius de Baraglioul)[2] and when he insists on translating into its smooth and elegant periods *both* Lytton's irreverences and the grotesque naïvetés of Queen Victoria's journals, he pleads the right of the translator to be unfaithful. 'Je ne veux pas déparer *mon* (!) texte'[3] says he, and simply omits when he thinks the author flippant and undignified, and attenuates when he thinks his humour coarse or his feelings exaggerated, and colours when really he seems not quite sentimental enough. (& makes H.M. correct & sensible!) (Is that the kind of translator you & the American publisher want?) No, dear Gide, when *you* translate Conrad or Shakespeare, or Fitzgerald, Omar Khayyam, you may allow yourselves liberties – that is another affair – (though I don't know why you should expect Heaven to send *you* such an interpreter.) But when M. Cornaz & I set out to translate Lytton & you, our chief merits must be First *Comprehension* – and then *respect*, *fidelity*, & *abnegation*. (It really sounds like advice to the newly married instead of to translators!) Now, for *Les Caves*. I knew of course quite well that you hated the idea of my doing it. So why did I begin? I really think at first it was

---

[1] Strachey's book was translated into French by F. Roger Cornaz.
[2] A character in *Les Caves du Vatican* (*Lafcadio's Adventures*).
[3] 'I don't want to mar *my* (!) text.'

out of a disinterested regard for your reputation. Woman or no I shall make a better job of it than your man Mr. Rhys – certainly better than an ordinary hack translator – But the American publisher (American! God save us!) will no doubt think it too close to the text – as I expect very likely it will be – from his point of view.

This perhaps is all very selfish and vain. Really and truly if Llona[4] can find another translator whose work is likely to be good *and* acceptable or if the publisher himself can provide one, I wouldn't for anything stand in the way – You know I wouldn't. And I should hate to think that you feel bound to stick to me out of friendship's sake – so, as it might be gênant for you to have another translation of mine on your hands which can't be disposed of – I won't go on with *Les Caves. No need to answer*. Or I will – *as you please*. Perhaps after all I had better have accepted Heinemann's offer. After seeing my translation of *La Porte Etroite* they refused *it*, but begged me urgently to translate *L'Epithalame*[5] (so it wasn't my translation they objected to.) Remembering Ch. du Bos' panegyric in the *N.R.F.* and rather tempted to commit an infidelity for once, I read the book. But no – not even to save you from my translation of *Les Caves* – could I undertake such dreary, low, vulgar, deadly stodge.

Ah! Proust! Though one didn't know him, one feels his departure like the loss of an intimate friend.[6] What an event he was in one's life! how grateful one must always be not to have missed him!

Even so among the monkeys one imagines one who must have astonished his fellows, foreshadowing the change from beast to man. I like to think sometimes that consciousness will take another step onwards of the same kind. The *extraordinary* nature of Proust's gifts makes it almost easy to believe.

You might have told me *what* you were dictating to that happy secretary. Good-bye, dear Gide. I am quite content, knowing you are too busy to write.

Yours
D.B.

I have been reading Rivière's novel![7] I can't imagine it's interesting you. But it would interest me to know what you think of it. And some day I will tell you what *I* do.

[4] Victor Llona, an agent for the English translations of Gide's works.
[5] Jacques Chardonne's novel, which won the Prix Goncourt for 1921.
[6] Proust died on 18 November.
[7] *Aimée*.

78. André Gide to Dorothy Bussy

Cuverville

30 Nov. 22

Dear friend,

Impossible to work well before having chatted a bit with you. What you say on the subject of translations, and of yours in particular, enchants me – and would convince me if I were not already convinced. As for the translation of *Les Caves*, I only mentioned it because the book's weaknesses and strengths seem so profoundly unfeminine to me. But it's all right so long as you are taking real pleasure in it. I had only one fear: that what I say may cause you to give it up!

I returned to Cuverville the day before yesterday – and for as long as possible – for as long as nothing urgent calls me back to Paris – or as long as I can bear, without rotting or growing soft, a life deprived of sun and warmth and so diminished that it seems Lethe is already draining its vigour. Will I at least manage to turn out some decent work? I'd like to think it will be all the better, as there will be few temptations to distract me from it . . . But the worst temptations don't always come from without. – Oh at times I'd like to take the place of my portrait![1]

Good news from Italy.[2] When I read what you say of your conversation with Vanden E.,[3] I feel how indifferent I shall be to the opinion and judgements of other people. I would not forgive myself for having caused someone's unhappiness if I had acted out of selfishness, interest – or merely out of thoughtless abandon – But to be able to fill with joy a being who calls out to you – and not to do it! . . . But wait, yes, it would be very painful to me to be misjudged by Zoum – As for you, it is entirely different – and you are well aware that in speaking of this, all the words I use seem hollow to me . . . Au revoir. Your friend

André Gide.

[1] In a letter dated 26 November, D.B. had told Gide that Simon's finished portrait of him hung in the sitting-room at La Souco, facing the armchair in which she usually sat.

[2] Elisabeth Van Rysselberghe was then in Rapallo.

[3] In the 26 November letter. Jean Vanden Eeckhoudt's indignation was not directed at Gide, since he did not suspect him of being the father of Elisabeth's child. D.B. comments that Vanden Eeckhoudt 'has always been anti-feminist' and that he cannot conceive of the equal responsibility of two individuals.

79. André Gide to Dorothy Bussy

Cuverville 23 Dec. 22

Dear friend,

Don't be afraid! No amenuensis: I am alone in the room; alone with you. It is a training . . . I don't know if it is the same for you but I find very deceitful and disagreable to see these ugly prints instead of the confident handwriting. Excuse me: I can't help to find a devilish pleasure in teasing you.

A fortnight! already . . .[1] *How time flies! And what is still more wonderful is the memory I keep of your letters which make them reappear to me as if they were received just yesterday.*[2]

Double difficulty; it definitely took too much time. – Maybe it's because I have received no letters from you that the work has gone less well this past week. (A visit from the charming Maurois tired me somewhat) – My nerves are terribly taut. I'm afraid I won't last here until spring. The news from Italy is as good as possible. I know Zoum spoke of a visit . . . I find that very moving. I hope she'll be able to go. For questions of nationalization, it is important that the event take place in France. I am strongly urging that the place chosen be Menton or thereabouts.

Don't ask what I think about the future – about <u>that</u> future. – I know nothing about it. I think my happiness is so great that I am ashamed of it . . . Oh let's not dwell on it, let's get back to work. I no longer dare be happy.

You cannot imagine the tranquillity and the evenness of life here. It has all the appearance of felicity – if calm is felicity. But what undercurrents, what whirlpools – . . . I can't wait to show you what I've done. Will it be at La Souco? Yes, probably. Who is this 'Martel'[3] who will be your host in January? – I'm ashamed to have to admit that I was unfamiliar with that marvellous sonnet.[4] Thanks also for the newspaper clipping; today I learn that they have finally entered the last chamber . . . – I finished reading *Cymbeline* with you – and

[1] Gide had not written to D.B. since 30 November, a fact she reminded him of on 19 December.

[2] The English paragraphs were composed on the typewriter; the remainder of the letter, in French, is written by hand.

[3] The painter Eugène Martel was Simon Bussy's old friend; they had studied together under Gustave Moreau.

[4] A sonnet by Louise Labé which D.B. had quoted. Gide included it in his *Anthologie de la poésie française* (1949).

now, what else? – Had my translation of Act One of *Hamlet* typed. Shall I send it or perhaps keep it until I can go over it with you? *As you like*. But would like <u>not</u> to send it to the printer before you have gone over it.

I think of you, of Vincent and Janie . . . How I should like to see them 20 years from now! . . .

Jean Sch[lumberger] returns this very day to Saint-Clair – where, it seems, Théo is calming down. – Is Simon working? Roger Martin du Gard is coming to spend a few days here – from the 5th to 10th of Jan. – I have been correcting the proofs of the terrible books . . . In the hall my wife is decorating a Christmas tree for 40 of the village children. Au revoir. Soon, almost. – If you say I only think of you while shaving, I'll let my beard grow. Addio.

André Gide

80. Dorothy Bussy to André Gide

29th December 1922

My dear Gide

I must say there *was* a sentence in your last letter – in spite of all my resolutions to never be surprised at anything you do or say – there *was* one sentence (I expected all the others) which staggered me! 'j'insiste beaucoup pour que le lieu choisi soit Menton ou les environs proches.'

Hypotheses: 1. Pure selfishness? because it would be convenient for you to be staying in a house near by which would give you a plausible alibi – and at the same time not be too unpleasant to yourself.

2. Pure 'inconscience?' With at the same time at the back of your mind an agreeable sensation of an economical 'emploi du temps'. Killing two birds with one stone.

3. No belief in the reality of my feelings? (And Elizabeth's? I know nothing of hers. I *suppose* they are not as ridiculous as mine – but Heaven knows I wouldn't take your word for it.)

4. Disregard of them? These two last make the horns of the dilemma you described to me at Pontigny one evening. Is there any escape from them? Any way out?

'Love will find out a way' says the English proverb and at last on the third day, I have found out mine.

Unworthy – all that is unworthy. You *must* have some other reason, some other thought. What can it be but that you want me to . . . How I could be there – so near – without going to see them? But how could I embrace Elizabeth and your child without a too visible emotion? And what would she think of me – an *interfering*, sentimental ridiculous old woman? What good would that do you?

But now that you have put the idea into my head. (No it had never once occurred to me as possible except in a dim and distant future when perhaps you would be dead) now that I have been looking at it and thinking of it for three days, it is beginning to seem the only thing in the world left that I really want. But aren't you afraid that if once I set my feet in this path of renunciation to which you are continually guiding me, I may take to it once for all? Can one renounce partially? And aren't you afraid that if I succeed in pulling out those evil passions which you hate I may pull out at the same time those others which are my only virtue?

No – extinction will more likely come from fatigue.

Yours
D.B.

Jan. 2nd
I either had to send this or never write again.

81. André Gide to Dorothy Bussy

Hotel Bristol
Rapallo

Tuesday [6 February 1923]
Epilogue to D.B.'s letters
and notes. Jan 1923.[1]

Dear friend,

Today the weather is splendid and I am feeling a bit better; I shall risk a letter – for you can imagine that the catch-all I wrote you the other day didn't satisfy me any more than it did you. – It hasn't been

[1] Written by D.B. At the end of 1922 she had sent Gide pages from her 'black notebook' (as he called it), pertinent to his visits and to their friendship. These pages were mentioned in letters exchanged in January 1923.

cheery. Insomnia, dullness, general funkiness – every nerve on edge in this horribly noisy grand hotel where I've had to put up. I have just covered the entire town: impossible to find lodgings, every place full and prohibitively expensive. I'm afraid that a change would only be worse. – Terrible thing, never to find in one place all the elements indispensable to one's happiness. That explains my anxiety and my *Wandervogel* aspect; part of me frets while the other is *in clover*.

I had hoped that in our conversation in the Luxembourg gardens the day I recited the *nightingales* to you, part of what I said allowed you to understand the meaning behind my silence in regard to you. – Reading you, I made all sorts of reflections. How can you persist in refusing to understand that it is nearly intolerable for me to grant, even to you, anything which I think she might be jealous of. Oh I know, I know what you are thinking – but mistakenly . . . for all the rest, important as it may be, is precisely what I couldn't, or didn't know how to give her. But what you asked of me is precisely what I devote, what I reserve, for her.

And never, as much as with Elisabeth – or you – have I felt how deep, jealous, religious, is my love for her. What is cruel is that you are the one to know this – and suffer from it – not her.

Au revoir. And please look for my feeling for you well beyond these words. Your friend

André Gide

[Written by D.B. in the margin of the second page:] Seven months later at Pontigny he had forgotten that he had written this letter. Pretended to have forgotten? No, I think he really had.

82. André Gide to Dorothy Bussy

Sunday evening
22 April 1923[1]

The railway station at Marseille –

Yes, I know, I'm a monster for not having written. Complete inhibition of the intellectual faculties. – Quick, this card before heading north. Letter will follow. I return directly to Cuverville,

[1] The date is written in D.B.'s hand. The number 17 is underlined three times. At the top of the postcard D.B. has written: 'How characteristic!' and at the bottom: 'The date is wrong!' Catherine Gide was born on the 18th.

where a letter from you would give me great pleasure. A little Catherine breathes since the 17th. Best to the three of you.

André Gide

83. André Gide to Dorothy Bussy

Cuverville

7 Nov. 1923

Dear friend,

Another envelope of disappointments! I know how it is, I get them from Cuverville . . .

For the past week, again at Cuverville, after two whirlwind weeks in Paris. Worked rather well, but my nerves are strung taut and I'm a bit frightened by the prospect of a whole winter ahead. Already beginning to cast sidelong glances towards Roquebrune . . .

Massis is starting up a fresh offensive in the *Revue universelle*; last spring's was a mere prelude.[1] Actually it's rather bracing. I know that Maurois is looking over Janie's translation.[2] I was able to talk with him before leaving Paris; he's charming.

Domi[3] is with us for a few days. Yes, we have pretty much matured since we spoke of him in Cambridge! – I have a whole store of smiles for Janie, but no longer dare send her any.

Best wishes to Simon – and for you everything else –

Your
A.G.

84. André Gide to Dorothy Bussy

Sunday [13 January 1924]

Dear friend,

Migraine, fatigue, tension, etc. – as ill-disposed as possible for writing to you – just a few words.

Yesterday saw Llona, who is to write to you himself. I gave him the sad task of dismissing the new translator who proposes himself for the Dost[oevsky]. Clearly I would accept, and so gladly, your

[1] In an article, 'André Gide et Dostoïevski', published in the November issue of the review, Massis condemned Gide's 'immoralism' and his transformation of Dostoevsky into a Gidean moralist.

[2] Of David Garnett's novel, *Lady into Fox*. The translation was published in 1924.

[3] Dominique Drouin, Gide's nephew.

collaboration in this too, if the translation of this new volume doesn't cause you to take a dislike to me. But in the meantime, another translator has come forward, whom Llona is to interview first. Were he to be very good, you would then turn your zeal to a different book ... He will write to us soon (Llona will) on this matter.

Worked quite well at Cuverville; my *F[aux]-M[onnayeurs]* is taking on extraordinary breadth. I like the idea that entering through a narrow fissure, the reader discovers as he proceeds a vast underground.

Ah! Speaking of underground: the word *Cellars* I don't particularly like for the book's title (*Caves du Vat*). It strikes me as totally without atmosphere and altogether bourgeois. You go down to the cellar with a candle and come up with a bottle of claret. What would you say to *recesses*, or ... *dungeon*, suggesting, in this case, the Castel Sant' Angelo. (This would be suitably stressed in the course of the story.) – In any case, think about it, and I appeal to Janie for help![1]

Lytton wrote me an exquisite letter and said he was sending *Nightmare Abbey* – evidently as a remembrance of Pontigny!!![2]

Been very tired the past few days, the nerves are breaking down. Excuse me for writing to you so poorly. Have been in Paris since the day before yesterday, here to remain for some time. (They are rehearsing *Amal* at the Vieux Colombier.) As for Marc, he lingers on in England, without a thought for his classes which resumed a week ago!

Quick, au revoir. Soon. Your

                                                                    A.G.

85. André Gide to Dorothy Bussy

                                                                    19 Feb. 24
Dear friend,

This time it's my turn ... at last.

Your letter,[1] which no doubt you thought charming, angered,

---

[1] As originally published in the United States in 1925, the translation bore the title *The Vatican Swindle*. This was changed for a later edition to *Lafcadio's Adventures*, under which title the book was published in England in 1928.

[2] This was not far from the truth. For Lytton at Pontigny, see Michael Holroyd's *Lytton Strachey* (New York, Holt, Rinehart and Winston, 1968), Vol. 2, pp. 470–1.

LETTER 85

[1] The letter was not found among the Gide–Bussy papers.

wounded, pained me deeply. I wanted to answer immediately, but would have answered so harshly that I now congratulate myself for having allowed the night to calm somewhat my irritation and distress. What do you mean by affecting to announce incidentally, almost as a postscript, the upsetting news (news which, from the core of my happiness – so you would convince yourself – I could only hear with indifference) of J. and V.'s break-up. Clearly, you don't in the least understand my affection. I speak to you as a friend; you seem to want to take me for a . . . (you will disclaim any word I might use.) I write to you that I have given up plans of going to Morocco in order to see you – which in friendly language means that I shall have two or three weeks to spend with you – and you ask me to grant you 'two full days'. Charming!

Apparently I understand nothing about women. – Now, quickly undo your cruelty by telling me of Janie. What has happened? Poor Janie! Poor children . . . Was it too awful? But good Lord! what am I to think? to suppose? . . . Can you to that point fail to recognize my friendship? Could you be to that extent unaware – or should I surmise from that 'be happy, my Gide' beside 'J. has broken off with V.' a kind of . . . no, I don't even want to express my thought; why hurt you in turn? Au revoir. I am not deserving of your scorn. Try to be more deserving, more simply deserving, of my friendship – which you have wounded. Your

A.G.

86. Dorothy Bussy to André Gide

La Souco

20th Feb. 24

Dear Gide

Don't be too cross with me. I was most desperately miserable when I wrote you that letter. I really and truly thought it was useless to tell you how unhappy – no it isn't that – I simply hadn't strength to write it all out to you – and yet I had to tell you.

Don't think I'm unhappy about Janie. Not so much. It's about Vincent. She says she doesn't love him – 'isn't *in love* with him' – she was once – she isn't now. She wrote & told him so. It was a bolt out of the blue to him – as to me – though . . .

He is the kind of boy who suffers agonies – and will always – so it seems to me. And he has nothing else in his life. He loved Janie. But it wasn't only Janie. He has lost with her every pleasure – every freedom – every other happiness. Our house – we – everything he found here was the breath of his life. He has been cut off from everything at once. It would have been infinitely less terrible for him if Janie had died. At any rate he could have come here to be comforted. I love him too, as much as I do Janie – he was a help, a support, a joy to me – He had the eyes of a little innocent child, happy & confiding and he has been murdered, and by Janie – and I don't know whether she realises what she has done – But she couldn't do anything else if she doesn't love him – and if she loved him she couldn't have done it –

His mother thinks that it is only a passing terror of marriage and that she will get over it. I pretend to think so too – but I don't. And he writes me long, long letters that make me weep. I'm weeping at this minute. Don't be unkind to me too – I know I'm horrid and stupid – you know it too – but you've promised to put up with me.

I should like to talk to you. I feel as if you could help – advise – It's difficult to know what to say – what is best – what will hurt him least.

Dear Gide – Forgive – and come – come for as long as you can. You will do us all good.

Votre amie
Dorothy Bussy

87. André Gide to Dorothy Bussy

2nd June 1924[1]
Monday

My dear friend,

Your letter, so simple, so trusting, came to me on a day when I was in great need of friendship. Since you left,[2] I have been through a period of dry days, struggling with a perfidious sadness that in my case quickly assumes the aspect of despair. Yes, really, you brought me something like the coolness of shade and rest . . .

[1] Date written by D.B.
[2] D.B. had stopped in Paris on her way to London.

I found Marc yesterday (I hadn't seen him in ten days) after having thought him lost, perhaps for ever.[3] I found him more exquisite than ever, and it dispersed into the realm of chimera the hideous phantoms my imagination had created. I was so busy these past days I hardly found time to think of my sadness; but it was a sort of basso continuo to all my occupations . . .

You speak of your mother in a way that brings to my eyes all the tears I had in my heart. Deeply touched by your saying that she still remembers me. – Au revoir. I feel I am getting maudlin . . . Oh certainly you can feel that I'm your friend. –

A.G.

88. André Gide to Dorothy Bussy

Cuverville

25 June 24

Dear friend,

You are probably waiting for a letter before writing again. You say to yourself: what good is it? He has forgotten me. Nothing I do or think or feel interests him, and if, out of kindness, he listens, his attention stops as soon as I have stopped talking. Etc.

Etc.

I searched for photos of Cuverville for you. I could only find this one, but have other negatives, taken by Martin du Gard, which I shall have printed for you. From this one, you will imagine Cuverville to be completely choked by trees. A wrong impression. Once past the avenue of beeches, there is the great plain, vast wheat fields. I hardly ever walk there, and remain indoors nearly all day long, attempting to push a bit further the millstone of my novel. It barely advances, but I'm rather pleased with the last chapters. The chapter in progress always seems the hardest to me . . . to the point of thinking I shall never get to the end of it.

Corydon emerged from its cage last Friday. No talk of it so far, but I know it is available. Not only have I sent it to no one, but even the book dealers will be sent it only on request – so that its dissemination

[3] Marc had been made secretary-general of a financial and artistic enterprise called the Soirées de Paris, directed by the comte de Beaumont. Gide feared the bad influence of the 'dubious, snobbish' milieu in which Marc was required to spend nearly all his time.

can only be very slow. I had written to de Traz[1] in reply to his proposal of a lecture tour in Egypt next winter – which in principle I accept – that he please notify me soon if the invitation still held despite the forthcoming appearance of a certain work which may cause me to be considered 'undesirable'. I handed the letter (which in any case I didn't send) to my wife, since I couldn't find the courage to speak to her. There was, on her part, no drawing back, no protest, no turning away . . . I would almost say: on the contrary. – I shall prolong my stay here until 8 July and try to return either in the course of the summer (but I somewhat dread the 'family') or just before the end of September. The news from Saint-Clair (Suzanne Schlumberger)[2] is very distressing. Everything else is fine. Au revoir. Friendly wishes to Simon and Janie – and, if your mother still remembers me, give her my very warmest best wishes. Your friend

André Gide

89. André Gide to Dorothy Bussy

Cuverville
4 August [1924]

Dear friend,

A long silence – which perhaps pains you . . . To be able to write to you again I need to forget I have been silent so long. For ten days I have been in Cuverville where life is always calm and tranquil. The disturbance lies well below the surface. At times one wonders whether in fact the trouble is not imaginary . . . but it's not. Sometimes a word, falling like a pebble into a chasm, will awaken painful echoes. My brother-in-law, back from Brazil, and my great-niece have come to join me; his wife and the second of my nephews arrive tomorrow. It's called 'family life'; I have avoided it these past years; I shall submit myself to it another week, then head off to Pontigny – where I'll probably be detained until the end of the month. Then, most likely, a visit to Colpach, then Cuverville again while awaiting the great departure, which will require a heap of preparations. I am no longer going to Dakar and Tombouctou, but much further. Marcel de Coppet, Martin du Gard's intimate friend, become my friend as

---

[1] Robert de Traz, director of the *Revue de Genève*, had proposed that Gide make the tour with Valéry and a third person who had not yet been chosen.

[2] Jean Schlumberger's wife, who was dying of cancer.

well, is to return to Chad, where he has already spent several years.[1] I have decided to visit him at Fort Lamy. You embark from Bordeaux for Matadi, twenty days (Belgian Congo), the Chargeurs Réunis's last port-of-call. From Matadi a train takes you to Stanley Pool in two days. You cross it to reach Brazzaville, from which place you set off. Twelve days to ascend the Congo, terribly uncomfortable and monotonous, it seems; then the Ubanghi as far as Bangui. From there, in two days' drive, you reach the Chari, which you descend (for it flows into the Chad) until you reach Fort Lamy – which takes about another twenty days. At Fort Lamy, you stretch, recover, catch your breath and you decide whether you will return via the Cameroun, after launching a spearhead in some direction or other. Fort Lamy in itself holds no interest; it's a point of arrival and departure. My first idea was to go as far (with Coppet who knows the country very well) as the English border at El Fasher, then Khartoum, but I'm afraid the voyage across the Libyan desert would be terribly trying, and I should like to be back by April, if only not to miss Simon's exhibition.

Corydon is on sale, but nearly no one knows it, for no promotion has been made either in the press or the bookstores. Curious to know if the English booksellers have ordered it. So far, very little comment. – You can probably find in London the American review *The New Republic* of 23 July in which there appeared a very good article on *Strait is the Gate*. '*The excellent translation of Mrs. Bussy . . . It so adequately reflects the sober charm of the French that it will be unnecessary to cite it as an excuse for whatever neglect may be the fate of Gide in America.*' –

Everything went very well in Coxyde; delighted to see little Catherine, not in the least fearful, run to meet the surf and not cry when she was knocked down by the waves.

Was Marc able to see you before being called to Eastbourne? He promised himself that he would.

Quick please, some news of you. The news from Saint-Clair is very saddening. Au revoir.

Are you still in London? I'm afraid you are having a very sad summer. Does Lady Strachey still remember the one who has such fond and faithful memories of her? Best to Simon and Janie. Look after my memory with those I met in England. Your friend

André Gide

[1] Coppet, who later married Martin du Gard's daughter Christiane, was a colonial administrator of the Chad.

90. André Gide to Dorothy Bussy

Cuverville

19 Nov. 24

Dear friend,

Again in Cuverville after a few days in Paris. Unexpectedly encountered Bréal[1] who was on his way to lunch at Berthelot Philippe's. Charming.

To think that today I was to be crossing the equator!! And what admirable weather we should have had for the boat trip! However my *Faux-monnayeurs* is progressing . . . oh, very slowly, but growing fatter all the same. I have decided to have the first part published in a review.[2] It will do me good to see it in print. And it will bolster publication of *Si le grain ne meurt* –. How stupid they are to persist in sending me the *Nouvelles Littéraires* to La Souco. Yet you say you've written to them . . .

Have you heard that at its last meeting the Royal Society of Literature 'unanimously' elected me to replace Anatole France?[3] Gosse presided, and he knew *Corydon*!! Did I tell you that after reading the book he wrote me a really perfect letter of the warmest cordiality.[4] America wants to bring it out in a 'deluxe edition' to avoid censorship. She is the first to pick it up. Who would have thought?[5]

In the meantime you will have seen that *Strait is the Gate* is coming out in England. At last! – As for *Les Caves du Vatican*, nothing new. But patience. Everything comes in time.

And Oxford University Press is bringing out the fragments of *Si le grain ne meurt* given in the *N.R.F.* as a school reader! (I think I've already told you.)

---

[1] Auguste Bréal was the mutual friend through whom Gide met the Bussys. He had known Simon Bussy since they were both students at the École des Beaux-Arts.

[2] The first part of the novel was published in five instalments (March–August, 1925) of the *N.R.F.*

[3] Gide's honorary fellowship was terminated in 1933, the period of his flirtation with Communism. In 1939, the Society invited him to speak as guest of honour; he refused.

[4] It was, however, a letter without disclosures. (*v.* Brugmans, *The Correspondence of André Gide and Edmund Gosse*, pp. 169–70.)

[5] There is no evidence of an American edition of *Corydon* before that published in 1950 by Farrar, Straus & Co. (trans. Hugh Gibb).

I am immersed in *L'Egoïste* (excellent translation)[6] with <u>exaspera-</u>
<u>tion.</u> I don't even find it very good.

Marc has just done very brilliantly on three political science exams.
I get on with him better and better. I've given him (for the Congo trip)
a movie camera (the latest model), and now he is busy making films.
Martin du Gard and I draft scenarios. It's very exciting.

I hold fast to my writing table and force myself not to think too
much of the south. Want to give the most possible time to her whom I
must leave for so long.

It's been too long since you have written; that's not normal. You
must be nourishing a heap of devouring monsters who persuade you
that I have no use for your letters! They lie. I am your very faithful
friend; say so to Simon and Janie. When shall we see each other? I
don't know yet. If I can make up your mind to come, it will be
suddenly. Work, work, work –

Yours,
André Gide

91. Dorothy Bussy to André Gide

La Souco

22 Dec. 1924

My dear Gide

The weather here is so miraculously lovely, the sunsets and sun-
rises so glorious, the sea and sky of such incomparable colours, the
air so soft and still that a little of the ice about my heart has melted –
enough at any rate to be able to wish you a happy new year. I imagine
you sitting wrapped in a Cimmerian fog 999/1000 of you wishing
yourself on the Congo. At any rate I hope you have been getting on
with the *Faux-Monnayeurs*. I shan't change my opinion, you know,
that you have no right to go away and enjoy yourself until you have
finished them.

No particular news here. I like having my nephew John.[1] He is an

[6] Meredith's novel, translated by Yvonne Canque, had just been published by
the N.R.F.

LETTER 91
[1] The son of Ralph Strachey, who had recently died.

engaging creature, 'beaucoup de charme' says Simon, a great many good points too, but oh! too soft, too fluid, too unresisting ever to be able to achieve anything I fear. Simon, who is the contrary of all that, has painted two tiny pictures since we got back in October. One, he painted five times over and succeeded the sixth time in satisfying himself. When I tell him such a passion for perfection leads to sterility, he laughs and says no. He seems perfectly calm & happy in his work – the most disinterested person I ever met and the most 'canalisé' – not a drop of energy is wasted anywhere. I admire him more and more. Janie too is well and cheerful and working diligently and very pleasant.

Zoum is coming to stay with us next month. She writes very happily from La Bastide – full of admiration of Elisabeth and charmed by Catherine. Janie, who at this moment is very flush of pocket money, has filled the house with modern novels by Soupault, Delteil etc. etc. I can't say I find much sustenance in them. I have returned to the ancients – the *moderns* among the ancients – and am reading neo-Greek & neo-Latin novels (with the help of cribs) with a great deal more amusement. The loves of *Cleitophon and Leucippe*[2] is the most adorable book I have read for ages. Character, psychology, poetry, passion, humour, adventure, tumbling over each other in profusion and the whole thing bathed in the most enchanting freshness and sweetness. But have you ever heard of *Clitophon & Leucippe* [*sic*]? I never had. All the fame – and very unjustly – has gone to Daphnis & Chloe. The luck, I suppose, of having found a good translator.

Well, I must stop now. Please give my remembrances to your wife and believe me

Yours sincerely
Dorothy Bussy

92. André Gide to Dorothy Bussy

Thursday
[8 January 1925]

Dear friend,

Received last night your good letter and the book on Milton. Thank you *so much*, but for the moment I can't tear myself away

[2] A Greek romance (c. AD 250) by Achilles Tatius.

from Gibbon's *Memoirs*, which give me the keenest pleasure. It was three years ago that you gave me the book. I'd been waiting for the propitious moment. ('La Souco, March 1921'). Oh, you very accurately saw the delight, the contentment of mind and heart that I would take from it.

I am enjoying it all the more, and by contrast, after finishing Ruskin's *Praeterita*, which I find still more exasperating close-up than from a distance.

I've been up and about for two days; expect to leave the clinic the day after tomorrow.[1] I would be very comfortable here without the constant flow of visitors, which leaves only too little time for meditating – I can't yet say: for work.

No, I don't know the Greek novel you mention (by title, yes, but have never read it) – in what translation? . . .

Yes, it's strange to feel one is *still alive*

and *still yours*
A.G.

93. Dorothy Bussy to André Gide

La Souco

Jan. 23, 1925

Dear Gide

I am sitting on the terrace typing out another copy of the *Caves* and it has suddenly occurred to me that it would be much more amusing to write you a little letter. I wonder where you are (you told me you were leaving the clinique, but not where you were going – so like you!) I wonder whether you are still feeling sick and miserable or whether you have begun to feel well again; I wonder all sorts of things, but I imagine – I *like* to imagine that you are at Cuverville, feeling on the whole rather happy and comfortable.

The weather here is unspeakably glorious, but by the time you come to see us (you are coming, aren't you? you couldn't not be coming!) I'm afraid it will all be used up. There! I suppose you will say that that is like *me*!

[1] Gide had just undergone an appendectomy.

I am very glad indeed that you liked the Gibbon. It isn't three years ago, but four years ago since I gave it you (March 1921) and I was beginning to think that you must have read it and not cared for it which would have been a disastrous fate for my first gift to you! Or very nearly my first!

Simon is busy getting ready for his exhibition and moaning and groaning over it a great deal – otherwise well. We have had a good many visitors and after each one has gone he invariably says 'The only person I *really* like staying in the house is Gide.'

There! what a splendid plan to write to you on a type-writer! Impossible to be sentimental! I shall always do it in future.

Yours ever
D. Bussy

P.S. Just a line with my own hand to say forgive this letter. It isn't the *real* one that I wrote parallèlement.

Your
D.B.

94. André Gide to Dorothy Bussy

29 January [1925]

Dear friend,

I copy out these lines from my journal for you:

'28 January

Finished Gibbon's *Memoirs*. I read that book with indescribable delight. I place it, to reread later, alongside the best. Great desire to immerse myself in *The Decline and Fall.* . .'

– Now my wife is delighting in it. I'd like to understand better the mysterious marginalia that you (?) have jotted in pencil throughout the whole book.

Work went so poorly here these past days, and I felt so undone, that I saw myself scudding along to Roquebrune where sun and friends would revive my animal spirits. But since yesterday a noticeable improvement. Anyway I have to be in Paris in three weeks.* After that, I'd like to take flight. – I felt a real nostalgia for La Souco.

Certain moments it strikes me as so strange to be still alive . . . I wonder if I should believe it.

> *Yours*
> A.G.

* for the cataloguing of my library which Champion is to auction off this spring, rue Drouot.[1]

95. Dorothy Bussy to André Gide

> La Souco
>
> 30 Mars. 1925

Dear Gide

Don't be alarmed. Just a note written in the broad light of noon. (My mistake is that I write to you generally later at night when all the world is in bed and I alone with my emotions. A more vicious and degrading habit than brandy – and very like the kind of idleness in which Boris indulged![1] *I know*.)

Simon went off yesterday.[2] I wonder whether you will see him in Paris. If you go, you might send me a little line. It is absurd to mind about the exhibition but I should like him to have a little – not so much success as encouragement. His effort has been so great and so serious; I can't but believe that it deserves to be taken seriously – considered attentively. I hope it will be – by some.

Who do you think is staying with us (i.e. Zoum, Janie and me left by ourselves in the house)? Valéry. He put off coming until the day Simon should have left for Paris. Simon stayed for one day with him but couldn't stay more. Valéry in the intervals of paying his court to Hanotaux (I must say there are a great many more intervals than court!) entertains us. At times inhuman, desiccating, terribly fatiguing and horribly depressing – at others touching and 'exquis'. Last night

[1] The sale of 405 books and manuscripts was held in April of 1925. Besides rare editions of his own books, Gide also sold those which certain of his friends had written and inscribed to him. According to Mme Théo, whose posthumously published *Cahiers de la Petite Dame* richly document Gide's life from 1918 until his death in 1951, the auction was very injurious to his reputation.

LETTER 95
[1] Masturbation was the habit indulged in by Boris, the boy who commits suicide in *The Coiners*. (*Les Faux-monnayeurs*).
[2] Simon was in Paris preparing for an exhibition of his work at the Galerie Druet.

he read us poetry and we were all very happy – Read us poetry and explained to us – humanly – why he couldn't write any more – chained to his own task. What is it? 'M'approcher de la vérité' and he made the gesture of a man bowing over his oar and rowing doggedly and painfully. Pauvre galérien!

I wonder how you are and how you are getting on. Forgive this untidy, dull, smudgy letter.

Yours ever,
D.B.

P.S. I am collecting a series of questions about *Les Faux-Monnayeurs*.

What do you think of our handwritings – mine an irrepressible slope *up* – yours *down*. Who would think that these are (so say the graphologists) conclusive signs of *optimism* and *pessimism*. True, I believe.

96. Dorothy Bussy to André Gide

51 Gordon Square
LONDON

5th. July 1926

Dear Gide

Yes; it is high time to talk business. Before I knew you were coming back,[1] I went to see Gallimard to ask how matters stood about the *Faux-Monnayeurs*. When I told him that you had asked me to translate it, he professed to be extremely astonished, as you had said not a word to him about the matter. (And I looked very foolish!) He also said that Mr. Waldo Frank[2] had applied for the permission to translate it and he thought you would probably like this arrangement, but that he was waiting for your return before giving an answer. As a matter of fact I have done about half of the translation – copied and all. I don't suppose I shall really be able to finish it before the end of the year. If you would prefer Waldo Frank's translation or if you think – or Knopf thinks – he could do it quicker, and that that would be a great advantage, please let me know at once. Don't worry about

[1] Gide and Marc Allégret had left France for Africa on 14 July 1925; they returned on 31 May 1926. From this period of about a year, only three letters survive from Gide to D.B., and none from her to him.

[2] The American writer Waldo Frank who was one of the founders of the review, *The Seven Arts*.

the translator's pay (as far as I am concerned). Knopf paid me quite handsomely for *Les Caves* (American rights). Since then there has been rather a muddle which has so far held up the appearance of the translation in England – the combined fault of Gallimard, my agent and Knopf himself. I hope this matter will be better arranged for the *Faux-Monnayeurs*.

I am looking forward to Pontigny immensely – I really do always enjoy it very much – in spite of the horrors! And this time, of course, I expect to enjoy it particularly.

Yours always affectionately
Dorothy Bussy

97. André Gide to Dorothy Bussy

17 July 27

Cuverville

Dear friend

An unprovoked message!!

I read yesterday, in the 'Short History of english Literature' (Saintsbury), about Lamb's Adventures of Ulysses:

'Which are admirable in a most dangerous kind.' What does that mean? Did you ever read this book? Of course! Why, dangerous? I particularly like dangerous books. Very anxious to know your opinion and explanation.

Stil languishing; perhaps a little less; and keen at work notwithstanding; wanting whirlwinds and catastrophes.

Nothing to say. But for ever yours

André Gide

98. Dorothy Bussy to André Gide

51 Gordon Square
W.C.1
20th July 27

Dear Gide

It was a great pleasure to get an unexpected letter from you. I'm afraid you would be disappointed in Lamb's *Adventures of Ulysses* if you are searching for dangerous literature. It is merely the story of the Odyssey told for children in the same way as the *Tales from Shakespeare*. I can only imagine that Saintsbury means that the *genre* is dangerous for the person who attempts it – as of course it is & very rarely successful. *Ulysses* is not nearly as successful (to my mind) as the *Tales* – though very pleasant reading. But Lamb didn't know Homer as he knew Shakespeare.

I am glad you languish less. To be wanting whirlwinds & catastrophes seems a good sign of spiritual revival.

Your English is *very* good. Only a slight nuance may be pointed out. Though you may sign 'Ever yours' to anybody you know fairly well without compromising yourself in the least, 'for ever yours' is practically equal to a declaration! I am afraid I can't give you the credit of knowing this. But I – fully aware, call myself

For ever yours
D.B.

99. André Gide to Dorothy Bussy

19 Nov. 27

Dear friend,

Too much trickery, too much treachery and nastiness of all kinds, too many lies . . . At times it literally takes away your taste for living, which age has already diminished. I have great need of your esteem and affection, dear friend.

The altars at which I sacrificed the most during my life are today more or less completely disaffected. The writer's virtues which seemed most precious to me: – integrity, constancy, probity – are cause for smiles. I have hoarded a heap of money that no longer has currency.

Etc.

Let us speak of more serious matters:

I am sending under separate cover clippings from the American press that console me a little for the raps on the knuckles and slaps in the face I receive in my own country. Mr. Bradley[1] (the Knopf representative whom I saw yesterday and who has just negotiated for

---

[1] The literary agent William Aspenwall Bradley.

the *Voyage au Congo* and *L'Immoraliste*,[2] which I reserve for you with greatest joy) tells me there are others (articles) which he promises to send. I have asked him to send you some of the little notices (I find them excellent), in case you would like to pass them along to friends . . .

Various considerations fasten me to Paris – and when I do manage to get away it will be to return to Cuverville, despite the rheumatic aches and pains that await me there – and all the beckonings of the south.

Au revoir all the same, but when? I can't say.

Much yours,
A.G.

100. Dorothy Bussy to André Gide

La Souco

30th Nov. [1927]

Beloved Gide, (but I often begin my letters like that – not to you, but to other friends!). It would be foolish no doubt to ask you to say that you were not hurt or disappointed or vexed by my last letter, but you might perhaps write me a little line to say that you are feeling better than when you last wrote – morally – and that you haven't got rheumatism, or at any rate not very badly.

I don't suppose you can imagine how much I sometimes want you – you who have never it seems to me, needed any person's presence to be happy. It comes upon me generally with a very violent pang after tea-time, when the day's stress is more or less over, and I am settled in my armchair – your armchair when you are here – for the evening. And there are minutes when the pang is so violent that I say to myself, 'He must be thinking of me now, at this very minute. It isn't possible I should feel him so if he weren't thinking of me.' But alas, I know very well that nothing is more possible and that my feeling is merely the symptom of my own longing. You *do* think of me sometimes though. I know you do. How extraordinary that is. I can't imagine it in the least little bit. I can imagine your thinking of Simon and Janie and the

[2] D.B.'s translations of *Voyage au Congo* and its sequel, *Le Retour du Tchad*, were published jointly in 1929 under the title *Travels in the Congo*. *The Immoralist* was published the following year.

house and my translating and the fire in the drawing room and all the things that surround me, but not of me. When I look into that part of your thought I can see nothing but a dark blank. In reality I suppose they are the same ordinary thoughts as all the others and that is what I refuse to accept. Well. You are thinking of me now as you read this. Smiling I hope. Half the things I write to you are because I like to think of you smiling. But then you have never told me – how often I have wanted to ask: what time you get your letters at Cuverville – in the morning or evening? Twice a day or once? I wish I knew.

Well if at this very minute you were here in the room with me (everyone has gone to bed) there are 999 chances to one that we should have nothing to say to each other. You would be disinclined to speak and I should be unable to. You would be busy explaining that you were sleepy or cold or nervous and I should be thinking . . . we won't say what. In fact it would all be very unpleasant. How much better it is now! I can say what I please. I am not frightened. I am free. If I choose I may do the most audacious things. Take your hand for instance in both of mine and put my cheek upon it and perhaps my lips. Good-night my dear.

Your faithful friend
Dorothy.

101. André Gide to Dorothy Bussy

Christmas Eve [1927]

Cuverville

Dear friend,

Do not remain too silent. I need to hear your voice before the end of the year, at least to see your handwriting. I think I am infinitely more sensitive or sentimental than you believe me. But I don't like to own it.

So that, for fear of showing myself to be too sensitive to your last so good letter, I'm afraid I wrote you a very unpleasant one. Why is it so hard for me to be natural with you? I am always in fear of setting off cataclysms if I don't stay on my guard. (I was well-advised to give up saying all this in English!) But tonight, and far away from you, I feel I can embrace you fondly.

Your friend – am I not?

André Gide

My hand is all paralysed with rheumatism and the cold.

102. André Gide to Dorothy Bussy

Cuverville

30 March 28

Dear friend,

I wish I could be certain that our meeting[1] has not left you too sad. Myself, I am still embarrassed by all the foolish nonsense I managed to talk – to some extent by your own fault, for I always say stupid things when I sense I am being listened to too closely, and when I sense that you expect feelings from me that I am incapable of providing and you seem somewhat to disdain those that come naturally to me – so that with you sometimes it's as though I were in a country where the money I have has no currency. I have always to 'change' it, even if it means losing in the exchange. And even the gestures you would like <u>force</u> me into a short translation full of misinterpretations, for those which seem to you the tenderest are the ones I instinctively draw back from, which my innermost being refuses to assent to.[2] But listen; I'm afraid you won't understand how fond of you I have to be to dare write to you this way.

I felt heavy-hearted for not running to your hotel the next morning to accompany you to the station, but it wasn't possible. And truly, the nonsense of the previous evening was sufficient . . .

At Cuverville all goes well; but I lead a really posthumous existence here. All of me is posthumous and I no longer do more than pretend to be alive. I believe that one can indeed survive pain of a certain intensity, but one is left numb forever afterwards. *Hush!* . . . all the same, very much your friend

André Gide

The crossing wasn't too awful?

[1] On 27 March, D.B. arrived in Paris for a two-day visit on her way to England.
[2] See Letters 165–70.

103. Dorothy Bussy to André Gide

3d April 1928

I do not think that if you had taken a stick and hit me on the head I should have been more astonished than I was by your letter.

I don't see how I could give you a friendship less obtrusive than mine has been since you came back from Africa. And even that night though I rejoiced in what I believed was real tenderness, I don't think I could have come to you with fewer expectations, have made fewer claims, fewer advances or even fewer acceptances.

The truth is that it is the very fact of your affection for me that makes my presence in your life intolerable to you.

You will never lie easily in that premature grave of yours till you have destroyed every trace of tenderness in your heart & mine.

I can't think of any better way of showing you my devotion than by acquiescing and trying to help you.

not sent[1]

104. Dorothy Bussy to André Gide

51 Gordon Square W.C.1

4th April 1928

My dear Gide

I have tried not to answer your letter till I could do it with some sanity, for really at first my world seemed to be crumbling, but I think I have more or less recovered my footing.

I am sorry you felt so about our meeting, but this time I think I understand you a little better than you seem to understand me. If it would be any relief to you for me to withdraw out of your life altogether I would and could do it. But surely there must be some better way than that. Surely we ought to be able after ten years to make our friendship a help and comfort to one another; we ought in our different ways to be able to avoid causing and feeling bitterness. I try, my dear Gide, I honestly try, though I know I often still fail. But

[1] Found among D.B.'s papers.

let *me* always be the one to fail. I expect *you* not to. I beg you to be merciful to us both.

I will write to you again soon about the translation.

Always faithfully & affectionately yours
Dorothy Bussy

105. André Gide to Dorothy Bussy

Monday [9 April 1928]

My friend,

I have caused you pain, I'm afraid . . . and not just my first letter, the second as well, in which I said I so liked your laugh – which is true, but at a time when you probably felt like crying. And all this when you need all your courage and when I want to give you nothing but confidence and serenity. I cannot convince myself that what I feel for you in my heart is not really better than what you are looking for – and stronger, more constant, more serious. Believe, feel, that I am as much and more than ever your friend

André Gide

106. Dorothy Bussy to André Gide

51 Gordon Square

Easter Monday [9 April] 1928

Dear Gide

This is going to be a long tiresome letter I am afraid. But I can't help it. I really must say what I think or everything will go wrong.

Your letter hurt me most horribly – not at all because you said in it that you could never give me . . . etc. etc. As if I didn't *know* it – as if I hadn't always known it – as if you didn't know that I knew it. But you said it that time as if you hated me. I think when you wrote that letter you really did hate me. You accused me in it of making you say insincere things because I expect and want them – of forcing you by my wishes to express a tenderness you do not, cannot feel. You repudiated – almost with disgust, an evening in which I had been very simply and innocently (like a sheep who doesn't know what is awaiting it) happy.

And now I will tell you the real thought I had when you put your arm round me and I rested my head on your shoulder. 'This is very peaceful & pleasant. It is a rest to feel him kind and affectionate – but how different from what I should have felt a few years ago! There is no rapture – no excitement – no longing. All that is dead and done.' Old age! I suppose so. But, my dear, I should like you to understand what I have been trying gently to tell you ever since you came back from Africa. I too died in a kind of way when you went away. I cannot feel joy & grief as I did before – not passionately. I *épuisé* my grief during that year you were away. Don't accuse me any more of wishing for what you cannot give. I *don't*. I never disguised it from you when I did. So now you may believe me! Not that I don't still wish for a great deal – a great deal more than I get, I willingly admit. But what I wish for is refused by Fate more than by you. To see you more, of course. I often long for you. I hate the idea that the world's tide is separating us, that your multifarious interests, duties, ties keep you away from me more & more, will end very likely by smothering your regard for me. I am jealous of them. I am not jealous of your deepest feelings. I stand aside with all the respect – the *awe* of which I am capable. I stand aside I do assure you very humbly. That you shouldn't understand this, which seems to me the very root, the meaning, the whole *effort* of my feeling for you, was most frightfully bitter to me. That you should say it to me so harshly I thought wrong and cruel of you. But you do understand. I know you do –

Oh! dear Gide, what a bother all this is, how tiresome & how stupid. But how can one help it?

I think the nicest thing you have ever said to me is that you like to laugh with me.

I kept your letter for six hours without daring to open it. But the next will be worse.

My life for the last ten days has been a nightmare. One of my nephews (I have sometimes told you about him) has gone mad and had to be taken to an asylum. I am not fond of him (it was impossible) but it is a horrid affair in every way.

Do you know what an English Sunday is like? This is the fourth we have had all in a row!

> Your affectionate
> Dorothy Bussy

Tuesday
P.S. Your second letter has just come this morning. I send you this as it is before reading yours. I am rather frightened.

107. Dorothy Bussy to André Gide

> 51 Gordon Square
> London W.C.1

> April 19th 1928

Dear Gide

I enclose a list of the chief difficulties in the *Voyage au Congo* and should be very grateful for help or suggestions. A further instalment will no doubt follow from the '*Retour*'.

Nothing much to say here. Jane Harrison died two or three days ago. I am very sorry for Hope Mirrlees, of whom I am fond – a curious young woman with a passionate & complicated inner life. As usual when I am staying in London I feel as if I were living in a charnel house – surrounded by ageing friends, illness, madness, operations, death. And this year I see very little youth to counteract the impressions.

I suppose my life at La Souco is a very selfish one. I seem to be able to abstract myself from 'mortality' – hide my head, I suppose, like an ostrich. And yet my visions there don't seem like those of a hole in the sand! After all there is a great deal to be said for the ostrich. He is perhaps more sympathique in his stupidity than the hare fleeing from hounds & hunters, though of course less pathetic.

Forgive nonsense.

Are you cold? I am horribly. Have you begun to déménager? I should think it very nice of you to note down all those things of Goethe which you asked me whether I had read & which I said I hadn't. There were at least four. Do you know Marianne von

Willemer?[1] I bet you don't. She is the only one of Goethe's passions I should have liked to be. She had a rotten time of it – but came out triumphantly. It was she who always used to sign her letters
    'Unverändert Ihre'[2]

Yours always affecly
Dorothy Bussy

108. Dorothy Bussy to André Gide

51 Gordon Square

June 15th 1928

Dear Gide

Mr. Chambrun de Tabibe[1] has just called on me. He certainly talks as if literature was ground out of a machine, so much an hour. I told him (strictly true) that all my translations so far have been paid for by Knopf quite independently of any arrangements with you and that Knopf gave me £1 or 5 dollars per thousand words. He seemed to think this rather expensive but not impossible. I told him I must have two months in which to do 25000 words. I don't know really whether I ought to delay the *Congo* by so long, but Knopf has said nothing whatever to me about any time limit for the translation of the *Congo*. Has he to you?

M. Chambrun didn't leave the M.S. of *L'École des Femmes* with me.[2] He said he was going to see you in Paris shortly and would let me know what was settled. He wanted to know how I worked? *Exactly* how many thousand words I did a day? and why couldn't I do 25000 words in 25 days? In his opinion that was plenty. Besides which he could certify that *L'École des Femmes* was very easy to translate.

Who do you think is coming to tea with me this afternoon? Marc

---

[1] The young woman with whom Goethe, at sixty-five, fell in love.
[2] 'Unchangedly yours'.

LETTER 108

[1] A literary agent.
[2] *The School for Wives* was eventually published in instalments in the American magazine *Forum* in 1929, and in volume by Knopf the same year.

& John.[3] I was very much surprised when the former rang me up two days ago . . . And until I got your letter I had been saying to myself that perhaps some day in June *you* would ring me up. Not that I care. I care for nothing any more.

Well, I hope that your hand is getting on all right

Yours affecly
Dorothy Bussy

We have all been very much amused by the Savidge case.[4] So characteristic of the worst & the best of my compatriots.

And T. S. Eliot has become an Anglo-Catholic! Do you know what kind of a fish that is?

109. André Gide to Dorothy Bussy

13 September 1928

Dear friend,

Here I am, called back rather abruptly to Cuverville. The mysteries of the 'dotal regime' under which I was married require a double signature in drawing up the bill of sale on the Villa, which the purchaser is clamouring for impatiently. I'm not very sorry I had to leave Saint-Clair, having caught a bad cold there and lived in a state of indolence and depression which made me perfectly incapable of work. The most I managed was to read Montaigne's *Essais* from end to end, and to correct the proofs of a new edition of *Si le grain ne meurt*. I'm going to write to Chambrun de Tabibe to please warn *Forum* not to count on *L'École des femmes* for the agreed date and to postpone publication of that masterpiece until next summer – which would allow author and translator time to catch their breath. Favourable decision, is it not?

How I love your letters, dear friend. Reading them, I rediscover a

---

[3] Probably John Reeves Ellerman to whom Marc had given French lessons in 1922 or 1923 when young Ellerman, then about thirteen years old, was visiting Paris with his parents. He was the younger brother of Winifred Ellerman (pseudonym Bryher) whose meeting with Gide, arranged by Marc Allégret, is related in her *The Heart to Artemis, A Writer's Memoirs* (New York, Harcourt, Brace and World, 1962), pp. 214–16.

[4] A case stemming from the arrest in April 1928 of a young woman (Miss Savidge) and Sir Leo Money for an indiscretion allegedly committed in Hyde Park. The affair brought about a Parliamentary inquiry into methods of police interrogation.

semblance of life – although I ill understand (feeling that I barely exist), how an encounter with my non-being could be a matter for dread or desire. Au revoir; I don't know when . . . I think I was much fonder of you than you ever dared believe – but I tell you this from beyond the grave.

Your
André Gide

110. Dorothy Bussy to André Gide

Savoy Hotel
Luxor[1]

8th December 1928

Dear Gide

Ouf! You can't imagine how delighted we are to be quit of Cairo. The journey was enchanting from the early start to the late arrival – thirteen hours in all – and before we had gone two hours the sand was an inch thick in our railway carriage and when we arrived we had almost to shovel our way out. Not that it mattered. We went by day to see the country. It was like and yet different from what one had imagined. It is the light and the colour of things that surprises one – accustomed as one is to think of them in photographs. For instance the pyramids (and there are not only three but shoals of them for an hour and a half out of Cairo) in the early morning are the rosiest, the palest, the most translucent, the most ether[e]al things you can imagine and the palm trees at their feet the lightest and brightest of greens. A great deal of the journey is very montonous, the flat tracts of cultivated land on either side of the Nile are enormously wide and edged east and west, but far in the distance, with a low ridge of cliff – the Arabian desert on one side and the Lybian on the other, but one can only guess at them. The native villages all along the line are wonderfully beautiful. Compact and low, built of golden brown earth, with hardly any openings in their plain walls, they look like miniature fortress cities with a huge grove

---

[1] The Bussys were spending six months in Egypt, where they had rented a house. Their return to France was made by way of Palmyra and Athens, precipitated towards the end by their general fatigue and by Simon's inability to work. They arrived at La Souco in late April 1929.

of palm trees growing out of the middle. And there is always a pool or a canal at their feet to reflect them. Then there was almost a continuous procession going along the embankments of the canals or the river in the single file – you know them – camels, donkeys, fellaheen, women, children – unendingly entertaining. And in the intervals one read Baedeker. OH! Here was St. Anthony's retreat. Here Plotinus was born. Here Nestorius exiled. This is the meeting place for the pilgrimages to Mecca. This where the caravans from Bagdad hold their first market u.s.w.

We arrived at Luxor late at night but when we got up the next morning how delicious it was to find ourselves in pure air – no trams, no streets, no horrors. Our hotel is in a large garden of palm-trees, rose trees, accacia trees in flower. It is on the shores of the Nile with a terrace where one can sit & watch the boats. The little village is absolutely unsophisticated: so far there are very few traces of Europeans, the two or three hotels are hidden in their gardens. One is really at last in an authentic country. And then three or four minutes walk away one comes upon the ruins of the Luxor temple. I can't attempt to describe them but we were all transported. No photograph gives any idea of their majesty. At last we felt rewarded for the journey. Simon really 'emballé' – not 'emballé' he said – 'ému'.[2]

We think of you a great deal – we wish you were here. Whenever there is a strange bird or flower or insect (& you may imagine that even we ignorant ones see heaps) we want you to tell us its name. We want you to point us out the things that in our ignorance we miss. To travel with you would be to have one's pleasures multiplied & heightened to the nth. But perhaps there would be drawbacks!

Talking of drawbacks there has been a rather serious one for the last two days and that is an absolutely *icy* wind, so that one shivers with cold indoors and out, in spite of the perennially blazing sun. And when there is wind there is sand.

To-day seems to be beginning rather more quietly and I leave you to go out.

I haven't see Karnak yet but the others have and came back bereft of words.

Au revoir, dear friend,
Yours affectionately
Dorothy Bussy

[2] Emballé = 'carried away'; ému = 'moved'.

111. Dorothy Bussy to André Gide

Savoy Hotel
Luxor

18th Dec. 1928
good for another month

Dear Gide

It seems such ages since I heard from you. I suppose that it is one of my delusions. And perhaps I shall have a letter from you to-morrow. I hope you are all right. I don't know how I should bear it if you weren't.

Perhaps by the time you get this you will have heard – or perhaps not – that my mother died a few days ago.[1] I have only had telegrams so far. They told me she was seriously ill with bronchitis for six or seven days and then died quietly in her sleep.

I am chiefly sorry I think that I wasn't there. Of course I knew I risked this when I came out here but still hoped it wouldn't happen while I was away. Because of my sister Pippa who is not well herself and has had the chief part of all the harrowing circumstances to bear – not by herself, for she has a good many devoted brothers & sisters, but without me, who I think would have been a help to her.

If you were here I could talk to you about it all but I can't write.

The weather since I last wrote to you – ten days ago – has been uninterruptedly, indescribably glorious (no wind, no cold.) You won't be shocked if I tell you I am enjoying it. I find the night long enough to be sad in. But when I am riding on a donkey through this extraordinary country which is so totally unlike what I expected, looking at temples and paintings, at natives, at boats, at trees, or even when I am sitting in the shade of a palm, translating *l'Immoraliste* (I have begun it) I forget everything but the present moment, which nine times out of ten is exceedingly pleasant. But what would it be like if Simon & Janie weren't there & well, and if I hadn't the consciousness of you as an ever present background in my heart? I am fully aware of the precariousness of my happiness – and Fate is always there ready to rap us over the knuckles. Good-bye, my dear, Yours affectionately

Dorothy Bussy

[1] Lady Strachey died on 14 December, aged 88.

112. André Gide to Dorothy Bussy

Paris, 13 November 1929

Dear friend,

Malraux, who is proving to be most perfectly zealous and dedicated, much concerned lest you misunderstand, begs me to inform you: resulting from the negligence of Allard – whom you know he has replaced at the N.R.F. (too late, alas!) – and from the appalling disorder in which Allard has left all matters he had taken in hand, Fosca's preface has been misplaced, in other words lost.[1] Malraux has had to notify Fosca to get him to agree to do it over. Hence an inevitable delay – of about a month, according to Malraux, who would be much grieved if you attributed the delay to his negligence. Hence this letter.

Madame Knopf informs me of her arrival in Paris, of her wish to see me '*as soon as possible*'. There will be dirty linen to wash. I shall relate the results of the laundering to you.

I am over my head in work and beginning to feel very tired. I long for Roquebrune as for the Promised Land, but if I come south, I shall necessarily have to stop at Saint-Clair first. My trip to Germany has been postponed until I don't know when. I'd really like to rest a bit before facing the solemn performance of *Saül* being planned there in celebration of my sixtieth birthday, for it seems that *Die Stunde André Gide ist in Deutschland gekommen!!*[2] Very tiring. I spend every day, with the help of the excellent Groethuysen,[3] reading over and completely recasting a translation of *Les Nourritures terrestres* that is very defective but which will be excellent, so much so, that if the book is to be translated into English (by you . . . ? I should like that!), the German text be consulted in cases where the French seems ambiguous, vague, or weak. These daily sessions, which are exhausting but exciting and extraordinarily instructive, most often begin directly after lunch and don't end much before midnight, interrupted only by tea at five and by dinner. You can see there is hardly time left

[1] The little book on Simon Bussy, with black and white reproductions and with text by François Fosca, was finally published in May 1930 by the N.R.F.

[2] 'André Gide's hour has come in Germany.'

[3] The philosopher Bernard Groethuysen. The translation in question (by Hans Prinzhorn) was published before the end of 1929 – twenty years before D.B.'s English translation.

for anything else, even for writing to you – at least as well as I'd like. We have already devoted ten days to this work; I expect we shall have to count at least as many to finish it. I'm fagged.

A thousand fine remembrances to Simon and Janie.

> Your faithful friend,
> André Gide

113. André Gide to Dorothy Bussy

Paris, 18 November 1929

Dear friend,

Just a word on receipt of your letter.[1] The translation sessions continue daily, often beginning right after lunch and extending very nearly to midnight. If only it were for an English translation, I'd make a better showing! But this huge effort in German is less instructive than it is revealing of my ignorance. If only twenty years earlier . . . The *Never more* haunts me, the awful feeling that it is now too late – and not just for German, alas. But as nothing is more discouraging, I go on and I try to forget that in two days I shall be 60.

I'll pass on to Malraux the part of your letter that concerns him. I'd like to be able to give you some reassurance now. I do think he told me he had the rest, or that it was already in the hands of the reproducer.

I am to see Madame Knopf this afternoon at 4. Tea is enough, I shrank from the prospect of dinner. I dare her to prove to me that your translations are bad;[2] the various reviews I receive from America are on the contrary so laudatory of you that I doubt she will risk a fresh attack. In any case, I am told that the company's zealous representative, who was so dead set against you, has been dismissed.

I'm sending you under separate cover a number of the *Yale* [*Review*] in which was published, quite unexpectedly, (and I do think against my wishes – I'll search through my correspondence to make certain) a translation of *L'Enfant prodigue*.[3] This is merely to encourage you

---

[1] The letter has been lost.

[2] From the beginning, the Knopf company and its agents had maintained that D.B.'s translations were poor, and had encouraged Gide to entrust his work to other translators.

[3] The translation in the summer 1929 issue of the *Yale Review* (vol. 18, pp. 684–98) was unsigned. D.B.'s translation of the short piece was not published until 1953.

in the new endeavour you mention, and which gladdens me, since it allows me once again to occupy your thoughts. I even believe an adaptation (modernized!) was recently staged in America by some student or amateur group or other. I was dismayed and angered by the presentation in the *Yale*, which reduces my poor *Enfant prodigue* to the semblance of a decorative piece or humoristic little fantasy. Assailed on all sides by often extremely pressing requests, it is exceedingly difficult not to be caught unawares sometimes, and I can't say that I have always responded with sufficient resistance. I have however no memory, nor has my secretary, of ever having granted any precise authorization on the subject of this American translation, which, in any case, could not legally be published in Great Britain.

I'll speak no more of this today as I have a terrible lot to do and am beginning to feel tired. Your friend,

André Gide

P.S. The visit to Madame Knopf actually yielded nothing – if not that, despite what I may have said earlier, I desired the translation of the *Supplément à L'École des femmes* to be entrusted to you, if for your part, this were equally desirable. You will kindly reply on this matter. You are free to refuse if you judge that, given the particular tone of the piece, a masculine voice would be more suitable. I complained a good deal, on your behalf, of their neglect to send proofs. Mme Knopf promptly replied that:

1. it was not customary to send fresh proofs when corrected ones were used, to which anyone could refer. I objected that in the case of *L'École des femmes* this neglect had prevented you from remedying certain errors made in *Forum*, and requested very strongly that in any case proofs be sent you from now on, which you would pass for press.

2. the typescript sent by you was unusually covered with erasures, emendations, etc., in a word, submitted in such condition as to give undue work to the compositor. To this I responded with such astonishment that in the end Mme Knopf admitted that she only knew of it through M. Block, the person in charge of proof-reading your text.

I also countered with the sharpest astonishment the subject of the necessity of recasting certain of your sentences into grammatical conformity, and said I could see nothing more in this claim than the need to Americanize English. In the end, Mme Knopf conceded that your latest translations were 'better' than the earlier ones. The whole skirmish carried off with great onslaughts of smiles, cakes, cigarettes, and watered with cups of tea.

It appears that German novels are at a premium in America these days (Thomas Mann in particular), and that there is no translation of a German work (published by the Knopf company) that does not sell ten times better even than my *Faux-monnayeurs*.

Upon leaving Mme Knopf, and taking advantage of the rare day off – since Groethuysen also had business and we began our work together only after dinner – I went to call upon, in the most sumptuous of hotels, Siegfried Sassoon, passing through Paris, who said he would so much like to see me, and whom Lady Ottoline insisted I should meet. A most likeable gentleman to whom I could smile with unfeigned cordiality. In the room adjoining the private salon where he received me, lay a very young and very charming (too charming!) Englishman,[4] indisposed, who has just undergone a pneumothorax operation and whom Sassoon is accompanying, he tells me, to Sicily where his friend hopes to complete his recovery. He wanted to keep me to dinner, but Groethuysen was expecting me and I asked that the agape be postponed until their return from Sicily. In the room of the sick young man, whose hand, at least, Sassoon wanted me to shake, was an admirable, sumptuous parrot, loose, with which, it seems, he always travels. Spoke of Lytton, Duncan Grant, Edmund Gosse, Sickert . . . and of you.

I leave you, in haste, to return to work.

A.G.

114. Dorothy Bussy to André Gide

1er octobre 1930[1]

It is such a long time since you asked me to write to you but tonight you *almost* did, and so why shouldn't I try and ease my heart that aches always so dreadfully after I have said good-bye to you.

---

[4] This was undoubtedly the painter Stephen Tennant, who kept pet parrots and reptiles. See letter of Lytton Strachey to George ('Dadie') Rylands, quoted in Michael Holroyd, *Lytton Strachey*, Vol. 2, pp. 645–6.

LETTER 114

[1] The date is written in Gide's hand. The letter was written during the night of 30 September–1 October.

Dear and beloved, it is so sweet for me to think that I know you so well and so secretly. Nobody could possibly imagine our incongruous friendship, and if there are any people who guess at the feelings I have for you they don't dream of my rewards, I am sure.

And yet sometimes I think, yes still think – and in spite of all my experience of life can't be sure I am wrong – still think that I would have given them all – yes friendship and esteem and mutual confidence and all the other sweetnesses – just to have given you . . . well, five minutes common pleasure. Don't be shocked at me, dear Gide, that if desire is dead – as indeed it is – regret is not.

Did you notice I kissed the lapel of your coat? It was a greater pleasure to me – oh much – than kissing your face. And I daresay that in reality that's a symbol of my whole attitude – But oh I like watching your face. I know it so well. I have such a collection of its expressions. There is one missing. I deeply, horribly regret it . . . But don't let me become like Youra![2]

How sweet it was of you to come. It was all very unsatisfactory, but it was sweet to me all the same. I believe, I believe, oh, with a transport of joy that you *like* me to love you. (Ah, my dear you shall be indulged.) But indeed I am only *just, just* beginning to believe it, you mustn't think I am too sure of it.

I hope you will sleep tonight.

Your affectionate
Dorothy

Shall I dare send this?

115. Dorothy Bussy to André Gide

Grand Hotel
Rue de la République
Avignon

1st October [1930][1]

Dear Gide

What can have possessed me to write you that senseless letter yesterday at two o'clock in the morning? But there – you told me not

---

[2] The pianist Youra Guller was an admirer of Gide's. She was the wife of his friend and sometime publisher Jacques Schiffrin.

LETTER 115
[1] The year is written in pencil, in Gide's hand.

to be afraid – and then it doesn't matter, we shall both have forgotten all about it before we meet again.

I like writing to you though and I have been terribly abstemious about it lately. How was I to know that you like me to, unless you say so *some*times? (But thank goodness you have given up calling my letters 'exquises'!) And now perhaps, you won't want me to any more. How can I help being afraid of making you feel uncomfortable, or irritating or offending you in a hundred different ways? And if I write I can only write what pleases me – only it never does for more than a minute – and not what I think will please you. I write generally things that I madly want to say to you and afterwards they seem to me fatally foolish and injudicious. I can see now that I have always been injudicious with you. But I had to be. I should have hated myself more if I had been calculating. And besides one always says to oneself: I am like that, if he doesn't like me so, tant pis. And after all it hasn't turned out so badly . . .

But what I want to repeat tonight is that I am happy now because I have at last, I think, – but only since barely a year ago – come to believe that my love is in some kind of strange way important to you – that whatever happens it has been – no I can't say yet that I believe it always will be – no I can't believe that – but that it has been, that it is important. That is enough to save me from that horrible bitterness that pursued me for so long that it was all wasted – that all my efforts and tears had been utterly unproductive of any sort of good either to you or me, had been mere empty lashing of empty air. Thank goodness I don't feel that now. I feel not that you wanted my efforts and tears, but that you wanted the thing that could only be born of them – or if not wanted – glad at least to have it – glad in spite of yourself – for I never forget that what you really want is the desert.

I am writing this in the hotel bedroom at Avignon. Incoherent and distracted.

There were such heaps of things I wanted to ask you yesterday. There was no time. It was too distracting.

I am thinking of your new friend at Avignon[2] – suspiciously. Good night.

Your friend – your old friend –
Dorothy Bussy

---

[2] Probably Yvonne Davet who was to become Gide's secretary.

116. André Gide to Dorothy Bussy

3 October 30

My dear friend,

You have written me a frightful letter . . . but how grateful I am to you for writing me thus. Shall I in turn risk an avowal?: what you say does not surprise me. Dare I say I thought as much . . . ?

But what's more, what I was absolutely certain of, as soon as I'd read it, was that I would receive a second letter from you, chasing after the first, that tried to undo its effect a little. It came. And I made an immense effort to keep from laughing – a bit the way, in certain countries, to applaud they hiss instead of clap their hands.

No, have no fear at all; I shall not feel uneasy when I see you . . . since, precisely, the first letter reveals nothing to me . . . or very little. And what I have just said explains, on the contrary, why, sometimes, I felt ill at ease in your company.

I embrace you all the same . . . as though nothing were amiss. And am, as much as ever, yours,

André Gide

117. Dorothy Bussy to André Gide

25th Nov. 1930

Dear Sir

I beg to acknowledge the receipt of your cheque for 8725 fr. in half payment of my translation of *Si le Grain ne Meurt*.

Yrs. faithfully
Dorothy Bussy

I really think, my dear Sir, that this is all you deserve in the way of a letter.[1]

---

[1] Gide had not written since 6 October.

118. André Gide to Dorothy Bussy

Grand Hôtel
Grasse, A.M.

18/3/31

Dear friend,

I finished *Clarissa* this morning and my soul is grieving. It really is an extraordinary book. I am so grateful to you for urging me to read it. But finally, it relates very little to what I was lead, from your insinuations, to expect. One cannot, without misrepresenting Richardson, imagine that he is playing a double game. No no, he is not, as Blake says of Milton, 'on Satan's side without knowing it.' *Clarissa* is a moral book, an intentionally moralizing book. I believe Richardson to be perfectly sincere when he writes in his Postscript (but does this Postscript figure in your edition?) that . . . '*the story was to be principally looked upon as the vehicle to the instruction*'. And I have myself suffered too much from false interpretations not to take his declaration literally. I'll go further: independently of the work's literary value and of its psychological interest, it is morally, yes morally, that it moves me, and probably more deeply than any work of fiction had [*sic*] yet done. Lovelace's defeat, his moral downfall, in spite of (or even because of) his material triumph is of truly epic stature, and the triumphant apotheosis of Clarissa's virtue. We are free to see that virtue as gratuitous, to see everything she relies upon as illusory; that doesn't at all diminish the value, at least the aesthetic value, of this mainspring for a drama which, without that extraordinary 'petition of principles', would not exist. I may, with Flaubert, find Virginie's[1] (feminine?) modesty ridiculous when she prefers to drown rather than undress in front of Paul. (Although Bernardin suggests that this modesty is born of her love for Paul and of the Christian education she has just had in France – which is extremely cunning of him.) I cannot laugh at Clarissa's virtue.

What I do grant is that the child's pious respect for parents who are sometimes (and particularly in the present instance) far from deserving of it, that the submission of the woman vis-à-vis the man (submission against which Emma protests very eloquently), finds

---

[1] The heroine of Bernardin de Saint-Pierre's novel, *Paul et Virginie* (1788).

[*sic*] in this book much less support than resistance: but it is especially that which dates the book, and one imagines that the second part would still be possible, but the first not at all. In any case, I'm sure we would agree if we talked about it.

My letters never <u>reply</u> to yours. Nothing to be done about it. Too bad. But I am fond of you all the same; and much more than you are willing to believe.

André Gide

When does Simon leave?[2] I shall see him perhaps in Marseille. But I think I'll remain in Grasse until the 26th or 7th.

Have I thanked you for sending the linen!? Tiresome parcel to have to make up, I'm sure – but your sending it was all the more appreciated.

119. Dorothy Bussy to André Gide

19 Mars 1931

Dear Gide,

You completely misunderstood what I said about Richardson if you thought I ever doubted for a single second the sincerity of his piety, his morality, his constant preoccupation with preaching, re-forming, instructing, etc. '*Double jeu*!' Good Heavens no! No, what I think singular in his case is that living the narrow bourgeois life he apparently did, he should have had such a knowledge of evil, inside and out, and been able to draw Lovelace with such profound psychology. What seems to me difficult to believe (but I daresay I am wrong and in any case it is of very little interest) is that such comprehension of life should be acquired without experience – first-hand experience. As for the moral effect of the book, I remember writing to you – but it was really to Lytton I wrote about *Clarissa* – that it had made me think more about *virtue* and believe more in its essence and reality than any other book I had ever read, and that that virtue should be attached to a thing for which I profess very little

---

[2] Simon had already left for Morocco.

value doesn't take away from the interest of the book, on the contrary, I am glad it should be so attached. It is a kind of sublime proof of the intrinsic virtue of virtue. And that idea had never come to me before reading *Clarissa* and it was one of the reasons I wanted you to read it.

But I am eternally grateful to that extremely unsympathetic, pompous, moralising, conventional, conforming old fellow that he resisted the temptation to convert Lovelace on his deathbed and refused to be persuaded by all his lady readers to let Clarissa recover. Yes, you are quite right, the moral defeat of Lovelace is admirably done. But to the end it is a brave, a gallant collapse. Don't think I don't see the horror of Lovelace. But I admire him too. He is worthy of Clarissa. Just as Antony is worthy of Cleopatra.

The beginning of the book, Clarissa's submission to her parents etc. doesn't trouble me much. And it is pretty clear here that Richardson is *not* on the side of this convention, is in fact attacking it as subversively as possible. But the whole portrait of that colossal family in its realism and fantastic proportions seems to me of the same calibre as Goneril and Regan.

Roger[1] has written me a very nice amusing sweet letter, but to my mind utterly absurd. It is a very solemn warning to me as to my disastrous influence on you, and in my opinion shows a complete misconception of you in particular and literature u.s.w. in general.

As for my poor miserable influence . . . !!

But I must answer his letter and defend myself and then if you care to see them I will send them to you. It was *horrid* of you not to show me your second letter to him.

Ray has gone.[2] I gave her all your messages.

I told you in my last letter a week ago that Simon had left and even made a little speech about it. I have good news of him.

I *imagine* Marc & Pomme[3] have joined you at Grasse. But will you ever tell me? Not you! For ever wrapped in your mysteries!

I am battling with a wave of horrible depression. The weary, stale, flat and unprofitable feeling. I am depressed about the translation . . . and about everything. 'Rien à faire à cela' as you say. I feel as if I had swallowed 100 kgs. of *sand* since you left.

Yours etc.
Dorothy Bussy

[1] Roger Martin du Gard.
[2] Ray Strachey.
[3] Nickname of Mme de Trévise, Vicomtesse de Lestrange, Marc's intimate friend.

120. Dorothy Bussy to André Gide

March 22d. [1931]

Dear Gide

It's quite true that your visit[1] this year and above all your departure was one of those disappointments from which one *never* recovers. You have provided me with not a few of them in the course of our acquaintance and you *think* I have recovered, but not at all! I suppose one ought to be pleased – a sign one is not yet dead to hope – a sign that one is in a situation in which hope – even though forlorn – is still possible. (And I'll admit it wasn't as bad as Toblach[2] and some others – oh! not nearly.) But this time it was all for what? If it had been any good, I could have borne it better. But no – just to stick a knife into your 'charmante amie's' heart and go ten miles off to bore yourself unutterably, and wear out your eyes and read *Clarissa* and do no work. How can one possibly avoid saying to oneself – 'it's simply *me* he doesn't like?' But I don't. I don't exactly. And then I reflect. Very solemnly – I say to myself:

It is all of a piece. It is the result of a long life of struggle. Finding himself defeated in his battle with the senses, he had to prove to himself that it was not through weakness, that he could conquer his affections, which after all were stronger and more difficult to subdue and more dangerous. So in proportion as he gave way to the former, so much the more did he maltreat and punish the latter – until at last perhaps he smothered them out of existence altogether? And now, if he is kind and generous and devoted – as he always is – it is from a love of virtue and not from any love for A. B. or C. and this is a gain perhaps he thinks? But isn't that as much a superstition as the vow of chastity? And should not a man be complete and at least as indulgent to his heart as to his body? As for the mind, it is that that would have kept him straight, but he mistrusted that too.

Well, I daresay this is all very unfair and untrue and that I am leaving out the clue; or that is what you think; maybe you are right.

Or perhaps this time, it has simply been the complicated drama of Marseilles that has been tugging you, I suppose that is really the most likely . . . Jealous? Why not? I have every right to be. And you who

[1] Gide had spent a week at Roquebrune early in March.
[2] In September of 1921, D.B. had invited Gide to join the Bussys at Toblach; after a number of false starts, Gide at last did not go.

don't know the passion, remember that it is not simply grudging the other person's happiness and wishing to destroy it, but despair that one is no longer able to contribute to it in any – or all of the ways in which love longs to expend itself . . . But I daresay you will always like talking to me a little about English literature!

Well this isn't at all what I meant to write. And if you hadn't been at Marseilles, I should have written you something quite different.

Yours etc.

Dorothy Bussy

121. Dorothy Bussy to André Gide

La Souco

Sept. 29th 1931

Dear Gide,

I was very glad to get your letter and a little news of you, but the news that your 'gratte' has begun again distresses me very much. I had a presentiment that it had.

It is very nice of you to recommend La Souco so warmly to your cousins.[1] Your letter is a chef-d'oeuvre – another of your many! We think you ought to set up as a house agent! As a matter of fact our financial prospects and situation are very bad and if we don't sell La Souco I don't know what we shall do. We were foolish enough not to change our English money this summer. And all Simon's recent earnings (also poor Janie's little gains from her Exhibition) are in London. Our only investment, inherited from my mother, is of course in English War Loan. All that, however, wouldn't so much matter (as we have always more or less lived on our current earnings) if there were any prospect of earning in the future. A considerable source of our income was English boarders and pupils. But there is no chance of that now – translations – but I don't imagine English or American publishers will be taking any more – and the pay will be diminished by a quarter. And who will buy pictures? And of course all our English friends and relations are extremely hard hit. In the mean time as a measure of economy we have sent away Mathilde (she will easily get a better place than ours) but are keeping Thérèse who is the most faithful soul, and no servant of ancient days could be

---

[1] Inès Jung, wife of the playwright Charles Lafaurie, was a distant cousin of Madeleine Gide.

a more devoted friend. I hope too that perhaps we may get some
French p.g.'s for the winter. If we had two at really moderate prices
(compared to hotels) it would practically keep us going, and I thought
of writing to some of our French friends to ask them to recommend
La Souco as a pension. Desjardins perhaps? We shouldn't be rivals
during the winter months.

But if we could sell La Souco it would be far less anxious work.
The price we have told the agents here is 800,000 fr. This was before
the English slump and we don't mean to come down from this if we
can possibly help it – at any rate not this year. But that is for this year.
But that is for the *whole*. If the buyers consented to our keeping the
end of the garden and building there, we would take 650,000. I think
in reality these are *fair* prices in comparison with the other places
about here. Not exaggeratedly high or low. Our neighbourhood is
certainly becoming more and more aristocratic. Princess Ottoboni
has bought the Hanotaux' 'Olivette' and Chanel has transferred
Cocteau's cottage to the Duchesse de Gramont! Hightime we de-
parted.

No other news. Roger's play[2] sounds very interesting but I expect
– I'm afraid it wouldn't do for the English stage. So glad Marc's film[3]
is a success. We have seen a little of Zoum and François[4] who give a
glowing account of Beth's happiness.[5]

Love from Simon & Janie.

Your affectionate,
Dorothy Bussy

P.S. We were very much amused by the 'pamplemousses'!

122. Dorothy Bussy to André Gide

[November 1931]

Dearest Gide,

I have today given up the hope of a telegram from you announcing
your arrival – or rather I have pinned, as you say, that hope to a later
date. In the meantime I try to console myself with the translation of
Corydon. It is a pleasure having even the smallest thing to do for you,

---

[2] *Un Taciturne*, a play on a homosexual theme.
[3] Most likely *Mam'zelle Nitouche*, one of two films directed by Marc Allégret
in 1931.
[4] Zoum had married François Walter in September 1928.
[5] Elisabeth had married Pierre Herbart (1904–74), the novelist and journalist.

but I wish I could give you a more satisfactory opinion – at any rate it is not an uncertain one. The translation is utterly, hopelessly, impossibly, bad. The translator doesn't know the rudiments of either French or English. He doesn't understand the commonest French idioms: on a beau, tout au plus, il y a de quoi, faire le jeu de, faire grâce de, savoir gré à qq., tenir à qq., etc. etc.

He confuses: se tuer and se taire, atteindre à et attendre, jouir et jouer, réseau et réserve, rétaquer and réfuter with disastrous results to the sense. Translates *factice* several times over by *facetious*.

He fails utterly to follow the argument and constantly puts the vital clause in the negative when it ought to be in the affirmative and vice versa.

He has no idea of the value and very little of the meaning of particles and conjunctions such as en effet, pourtant, enfin, etc. etc. Dozens of his sentences mean either the contrary of the French, or have no meaning at all, or are incomprehensible unless compared with the original.

His English is no better. His use of auxiliaries is the strangest I have ever seen: will, shall, can, may used as in no English or American I have ever met. His prepositions are fantastic. As for elegance, subtlety, distinction, Heavens!

I have underlined in pencil some of the grossest mistakes, so that you may see for yourself I am not exaggerating. It is so often my fate to give an adverse opinion about translations that I am afraid of being thought malicious and uncharitable.

If you think my pencil comments in the margin are too crushing you must get your secretary to rub them out.

But it is incomprehensible to me why a man who understands a book so little should *want* to translate it or how a man who knows so little of a language should think he is *capable* of translating it. Mysteries!

Your last letter was from Cuverville. I wonder whether you are back in Paris. I wonder how you are. I hate to think of you wearing yourself out for . . . what? Even a good performance of Oedipe[1] is not so important as your health.

Love from us all.

> Your affectionate,
> Dorothy Bussy

[1] *Oedipe* was given its première performance on 10 December in Antwerp; the play opened in Paris on 18 February of the following year.

123. Dorothy Bussy to André Gide

La Souco

17th Dec. 1931

Dear Gide

This letter is not going to be a cheerful one. We are terribly anxious about Lytton. He was taken ill about a fortnight ago – a rather mysterious typhoid or paratyphoid, they think, with very high fever, I have letters every day, but they always say 'no better.' Pippa is with them[1] at his house in the country and her letter received tonight is very alarming. I know she is always pessimistic. But hasn't she always been right to be so? The days are very long waiting for the post.

Don't answer this. It's no good. I'll write again.

Your affectionate,
Dorothy Bussy

124. Dorothy Bussy to André Gide

La Souco

19th Dec. 31

Dear Gide

The news of Lytton this morning is a little bit more hopeful. Since Pippa wrote that despairing letter that I got on the 17th – the day I wrote to you – there has been a little turn for the better. There was the alarming symptom of haemorrhage on the day she wrote, but this is not necessarily fatal. The specialist, though pronouncing the word dangerous did not say hopeless. Since then the fever has begun to go down a little, his heart is very good and his calm and placidity (in spite of 40° temp.) surprises everyone.

Yesterday, I spent a horrible day jumping at every sound lest it should be the fatal telegram. Today I tell myself it is foolish to be too much reassured. There must be many more days of waiting.

[1] The household consisted of Lytton, Dora Carrington, and Ralph Partridge whom she had married in 1921.

If I hadn't got Jean Schlumberger's translation to do it would be much harder to get through the time.[1]

> Your affectionate,
> Dorothy Bussy

125. Dorothy Bussy to André Gide

Jan. 23, 1932

Dear Gide,

As I suppose you have seen in the papers, the blow has fallen.[1] It seemed particularly cruel because the very morning of the day on which I got the telegram announcing the relapse (it wasn't till 24 hours later that he died) there had been letters full of hope – the best since the beginning of his illness.

It is a dreadful and such an unexpected gap in our lives. He was the centre and the pivot of so much in our private family life as well as in his larger circle. He was our most beloved brother long before he was a famous man. And all the salt and all the zest of life seemed to come from him. I can't take a step in my mind (not to speak of my affections) without meeting his figure – and one other's – in all the dearest corners. I shall never be able to read Shakespeare again or Racine without a pang. I think of him too as a little boy when I had so much to do with looking after him, nursed him in his illnesses, took him to the sea-side, read to him, told him stories.[2] I remember the day I told him the story of Bluebeard and his excitement. He was the first child I ever loved. Affectionate, witty, happy, responsive creature. He never changed.

Poor Pippa. To have struggled so hard and to have failed at last. Everybody else will recover but she won't. I hope she will come and rest with us here, but I don't think she will.

Thank your for your letter. Don't let your good resolutions of leading a sensible life with a servant au sixième die away. But if there are people who sometimes fail to catch what you want to express of admiration and affection, it is not always and entirely because they

---

[1]   *Saint-Saturnin*, which was published in 1932 by Dodd, Mead & Co., New York.

LETTER 125

[1]   Lytton Strachey had died on the 21st.
[2]   D.B. was fourteen years older than Lytton.

are deaf, but also because there is such a thing as too low a voice. This for your uncle Charles Gide.

Your friend,
Dorothy Bussy

126. André Gide to Dorothy Bussy

Monday [25 January 1932]

Poor dear dear friend,

I had begun to hope again, to think you would be spared this awful sorrow. This morning I received your letter telling me that you too were taking hope again . . . My heart and thoughts are with you. And I think of poor Pippa . . . But I'm not only sad because of your sadness. Little as I knew Lytton, I feel now how keen my affection for him was.

I can't – nor want to – say anything else today – and I can't think of anything else. I embrace you fondly.

Yours,
André Gide

I went back to see my uncle[1] who grows weaker every day, but without pain. (His two children are with him.) But he at least was at the end of his life.

127. Dorothy Bussy to André Gide

Jan 26th 1932

My dear Gide,

I have just thought that there will probably be a notice of Lytton in the *N.R.F.* If so I should rather have Jacques Heurgon do it than anyone else.[1] I hope you will convey this to the proper quarters – though maybe it is too late.

Also, the *Revue des Deux Mondes* is going to publish his essay on

[1] The economist Charles Gide; he died on 12 March 1932, at the age of 85.

LETTER 127
[1] Heurgon, who had known Strachey since the Pontigny *décade* of 1923, had already translated one of the chapters of *Eminent Victorians*. See Letter 2, note 4.

Gordon (mutilated by Doumic of course) the *Revue Hebdomadaire*, Florence Nightingale.[2] Don't you think the *N.R.F.* might take the Cardinal Manning which I think the best of his essays, but a little bit too satirical for either of those 'bien pensant' reviews. This would not I imagine be an objection to the *N.R.F.* and I can't think that the essay would lower the tone, the reputation or the interest of any number it appeared in.

Gallimard has promised Jacques to publish the collected volume of *Eminent Victorians*, though he still appears to be undecided about when. Bad times etc. I gather it does not interfere with the sale of a volume if a portion of it appears in the review before hand. It has always been rather a thorn to me that the *N.R.F.* should never have published any work of an author who seems to me eminently fitted to please their public.

I hope you are pretty well and sleeping better.

Yours affec'y,
Dorothy Bussy

128. Dorothy Bussy to André Gide

Feb. 2, 1932

Dearest Gide,

Yes, I know, I do believe in your tender friendship.

I find it harder to write to you than to anybody, I can somehow detach myself when I write to other people – I have written a great many letters in the last few days – and write as if I was somebody else. But with you I am nearly always wholly engaged. And just now I shrink from being that. Pippa is coming to stay here. We are expecting her the day after tomorrow. I want her to come and yet I am dreading it horribly. I know I have never really imagined the pain of it all and now I shall have to – and I feel cowardly. I am afraid it was all worse than they let me know at the time. Of course, it must have been.

I wish you could sleep. I go to bed late but then I'm very tired and sleep well.

Dear Gide, you don't know that I simply hate being pathetic – and

---

[2] The first part of the chapter on Florence Nightingale, translated by Heurgon ('Jacques Dombale') and prefaced by an article on Strachey written by Francis Birrell, appeared in the *Revue Hebdomadaire* of 23 July 1932 (pp. 395–410).

what's more I haven't the smallest right to be. There are a good many
people who feel Lytton's death more than I do. I think, I know, it is
the worst grief of the kind I have ever had. But the springs of life are
still intact in me. I still care to have a letter from you.

> Your affectionate,
> Dorothy Bussy

129. Dorothy Bussy to André Gide

March 18th, 1932

Dear Gide,

I suppose you have been going through that melancholy business
of a funeral. I am sorry your uncle has left a world that badly needed
him. It was one of the encouragements of life to feel one's vague
and ignorant 'opinions' upheld by such knowledge and clarity and
reasoning. One of the last things of his I read was something that
astonished me but which I thought admirable – a defence of coloni-
sation! (how infinitely more sympathetic I thought his short, clear, to
the point, little articles, with such weight behind them of practical
knowledge, to those of Alain for instance!) But I don't know why I'm
saying this.

We have been going through another tragedy. But it is so difficult
to write about and explain. The 'amie' Lytton had lived with in the
country for years – and her husband was a devoted friend of his –
shot herself *accidentally* about a week ago and died two or three
hours later.[1] All the circumstances were particularly painful. She was
a curious and fascinating personality, greatly loved by a whole circle
of friends and amongst them by Janie, who has been very much
shaken. At least six of our most intimate friends have received the
most shattering blow of their lives by this double disappearance. It is
as if an island of gaiety and charms and reasonable pleasures, where
so many of us went for refreshment, had been suddenly swallowed
up by an earthquake. This is a very brief account of what has been
filling our hearts and thought for some time past. I write to you
because I like you to be *au courant* more or less with what is
happening to me. But in reality it's a useless effort, for what I have

---

[1] Carrington, who had lived with Strachey since December 1917, had attempted to
asphyxiate herself the day he died.

written has got only the most superficial connection with the reality.

And you? I imagine you went to Nimes. And from Nimes, very likely to Marseilles? And then to Saint Clair? And I know as little about your reality as you about mine!

I am very busy with *Saint Saturnin* and have begun to correct the proofs of *S. le G.N.M.* I felt rather enraged with M. Paulhan[2] for inviting me to contribute to a number which was already full. It made me waste a deal of valuable time!

The *Revue des Deux Mondes* is publishing *fragments* of Lytton's essay on Gordon, but *refuses* to print a note saying the text is not complete. M. Doumic has taken great trouble to make the *raccords* unnoticeable! *The Yale Review* out done![3] And I had thought that this at any rate was a civilized country.

Well, Stoisy[4] won't have to take her sleeping draught just *yet*, *which is a mercy.*

Pippa was called away by the telegram announcing the accident. She was beginning to get a little better.

Excuse these disconnected jottings.

Yr.
D.B.

130. Dorothy Bussy to André Gide

Le Souco

5th April [1932]

Dearest, dearest Gide

How miserable you sound, with all those horrible things being done to you![1] I can't help being anxious about you. Let me know when the wretches stop tormenting you. I sometimes have frightful flashes of what the world would be like without you. But I shut my eyes very quickly and very tight. And I say to myself it is very good for

---

[2] Jean Paulhan had replaced Jacques Rivière as editor of the *N.R.F.*
[3] See Letter 113.
[4] The nickname of Thea Sternheim, wife of the playwright. Her revision of the German translation of Gide's play *Saül* was performed in Berlin later in 1932.

LETTER 130
[1] Gide was in a clinic in Switzerland.

you to be locked up in a room and not allowed to stir, with nothing but Vicki Baum to read![2] You will come out regenerated body & soul. Your handwriting at any rate doesn't seem to have suffered. Even its downward slope though pretty pronounced is not so bad as I have often seen it, and I have never seen it clearer, firmer, more elegant.

We have got my sister Marjorie staying with us, who as usual can't open her mouth without making us all laugh – something of a clown. Stimulating, however, though sometimes to the point of exhausting her public. Then in a week or so my youngest brother James and his wife[3] are to pay us a visit. Poor James is rather a tragic character – left more lonely than ever by Lytton's death.

Private. I didn't at all like Heurgon's note in the *N.R.F.*[4] Yes, he sent it to me to look at and I told him what I thought of it. He seems to me, on pretext of saying nothing that was not essential, to have left the essential out – even to have misunderstood it. In writing history, Lytton's point of view was not '*anti-victorianism*' a grotesque word, which I greatly object to, it was *human character*. The singularities of human beings was what interested him first, and second the art of language. To have written even three lines about Lytton without saying he was a poet and a critic seems to me quite incomprehensible! As far as I could gather Heurgon was answering some un-named or perhaps imaginary opponents, and so led off into a side-issue. He was also trying, I think, to fall with what appears to me the lamentable style of the *N.R.F.* critic notes, and their no less lamentable reactions to literature. They never have a clean direct emotion. It has always got to be made metaphysically subtle. Oh, what a relief to read what you say about Goethe after the other soulless, heartless, desiccated hair-splitting! But I must say, Curtius's was by far the worst! Trying to prove that Goethe was a Christian and that he believed in angels because he uses the word in his poetry! The fact is 99 people out of a hundred haven't the faintest conception of what poetry is. But *you* have, dear Gide, and so, proudly I say it, have I.

I am just finishing *Saint-Saturnin*, and correcting the proofs of *Si le Grain ne Meurt*. I have read nothing lately but Colette's *Ces Plaisirs* . . . with ravishment.

[2] He was reading *Grand Hotel* 'with amusement'.
[3] See Letter 58, note 1.
[4] Under the rubric '*Lettres étrangères*' in the April 1932 issue of the *N.R.F.* (pp. 762–5).

Simon is still reading *Saint-Simon* (he says it is as exciting as *Clarissa*!!) and Janie the 2nd part of *Faust*.

Au revoir, dearest of friends. I am just the same as usual – stabbed at irregular intervals by a piercing desire to see you.

D.B.

131. André Gide to Dorothy Bussy

Sunday [17 April 1932]

Dear friend,

You do have at Roquebrune, haven't you, the text of that strange play you gave me to read two or three years ago?[1] If my memory is right, it seems to me that one might make quite a stunning film scenario from it. Been tormented by this idea for the past few days. If you have your text near at hand, be so kind as to send it to me so that I can reread it. Just last night I saw a German film (a great success at home): *Mädchen in Uniform*,[2] which is set in the same ambiance and shows that a good deal can be ventured. Very impatient to reread you. Already I picture Marc filming you – and it makes my head spin. Send the manuscript, quick!

Yours,
A.G.

A letter from Darmstadt informs me that my *Oedipe* will be performed April 30th. A great surprise, since I thought the project had been scrapped.

132. André Gide to Dorothy Bussy

Vittel

23 June 33

Do I dare tell you, now that your letter (just received) prompts me, that I very nearly invited you to come help me bear the tedium of the

---

[1] A three-act play entitled *Miss Stock* which D.B. had written before meeting Gide in 1918. Nothing came of Gide's idea to make a film of it, or of a much later effort (1950s) to bring a translation of it to the French stage.
[2] The film by Carl Froelich and Leontine Sagan (1931).

cure (which, with you here would no longer be in the least tedious), 'engaging' you as a secretary to whom I should have nothing to dictate. But no, I had best endure this maceration and meet you anywhere rather than in this seaside hole where one lives, vegetates, with folded wings – but doubtless preparing for flight. Because I am completely taken up by the cure, and besotted by it, it has not been possible to make any progress on the *Hamlet* translation. No alternative but to acquiesce and do nothing. No matter! I frequently receive *ghostly* visits from you. It's raining. It's cold. Life is slipping away. I no longer feel I have any talent. I admire everything I read (very bad sign) and say to myself: Well thought! Not at all badly written! You'd be incapable of doing as well, etc. And then I read! I read from morning to night. I read the way a cow grazes, the way I did at twenty, but how profitably then! At times I do still catch sight of things that might be said, but ideas seem so heavy to lift . . . or more exactly: so bushy that my courage and patience are powerless to reduce them to twigs. I should never have written anything but dialogues and novels, never expressed ideas directly. But now it's done, and I can no longer disengage myself from what I have begun to take on, from this position I have taken.

Where did I see this maxim of La Rochefoucauld criticized the other day?: 'L'esprit est souvent la dupe du coeur'. Certainly by someone who had not understood it. Myself, I understand it only too well. I shall all the same communicate to Gallimard the bit (translated) of your letter concerning the bibliographic service and the information relating to the Andersen biography. (But I'm afraid a *Vie d'Andersen* has already appeared in our collection.)[1]

By the way . . . are you still in touch with the bookstore (Norton??) you recommended to me?[2] I haven't written to them in a long time. I must still have a small reserve of credit in my account with them. If you see them, would you find out and would you order for me a complete Shakespeare in that charming little edition (a volume per play) that you have at Roquebrune – if it is still in print. If not, in one volume (a very recent edition) on very thin paper – that should be sent to me at Cuverville (marked: HOLD).

Pontigny? . . . I'm trying to decide whether I feel like going. The other years I was sure not, but this year I'm not so sure. Roger is to be there . . .

[1] D.B. had proposed herself to Gallimard (N.R.F.) as 'English reader' of current books, selecting those suitable for publication in France.

[2] The bookshop in question was owned by Francis Birrell and David Garnett.

In any case I have a vague premonition that I shall see you before autumn ... but with me that doesn't mean much; for, unlike you, I'm taken with all the options at the same time, yet don't very much bemoan giving them up one after another ...

Excuse these ramblings. An effect of the cure. I send this off quickly without rereading it ... Your

A.G.

133. André Gide to Dorothy Bussy

Paris

24 July 33

Dear friend,

I rack my brain to try and remember what I can have written in my last letter that would pain you and make you close like a sea anemone when a nasty old cloud passes between it and the sun ...[1] I tell myself it must be my fault, that the cloud between us is never of your doing. But if I suffer a little from it, it's because I know you are suffering a good deal more. Myself, I can't take these grey clouds seriously, as I do your sadness – since it, I know, is real.

Yesterday and the day before, I saw Ida R[ubenstein] and Stravinsky. My work is finished, delivered. Performance cannot be given before March or April.[2] I told Ida that I couldn't assure her I would still be in France then. – I think I am better (I have to go back to the doctor's this afternoon) but shall not really be well until I have taken something up again and submitted myself to a new obligation. It will require an enormous effort to get back to work, and I doubt whether I'll still be capable of it. To make it possible (this effort) a propitious setting and atmosphere would be necessary ... I'm not sure where to look for them. I would also need to imagine you are smiling ... and that you understand that I am still

your friend,
André Gide.

---

[1] D.B. had written him a brief, terse note on 21 July.

[2] *Perséphone*, a ballet in three tableaux with chorus and dialogue, was a stage version of an early work of Gide's *Proserpine, fragments*, which had appeared in the December 1899 issue of *Pays de France*. It was first performed on 30 April 1934 (directed by Jacques Copeau).

134. Dorothy Bussy to André Gide

Dec. 5th 1933

Dearest Gide

Somehow I can't resist the impulse to write to you tonight.

When the weather gets cold, I get anxious about you. Every day I say to myself, supposing he has got penumonia!

I wonder where you are. You have left Lausanne, I suppose. I hope the *Caves* went off well. Or perhaps you are still there. I think I would rather you were there than in Paris. But perhaps you are at Cuverville. Not that it matters. Wherever you are, you are too busy to think of me. But I don't care a scrap.

Not a sign from Mr. P. I can't help being afraid it's a bad case. His letter sounded to me as if he had spent the money forwarded by the Americans and that now he has got nothing to pay the printers with. I will let you know at once as soon as I get the proofs – if I get them.[1]

Dear Gide. I must stop this minute or I shall get too affectionate. It sometimes comes upon me in such violent waves that it's almost impossible to resist. But I will.

Yrs.
D.B.

Janie wants to know Stoisy's address.

P.S. A <u>deadly</u> secret. I have written a book![2] A very short one but I'm dying to show it to you. No one else in the world knows nor probably ever will. I didn't mean to say this when I started this letter. Indeed I had forgotten all about it. But when I have finished typing it I shall send it to you. For whether you will or no you have to bear a part in all I think and feel and do.

Oh! these postscripts. How dangerous!

Don't allude to this secret if you write to me ever again. Tell me rather about Geneviève.[3]

But I know what you will really say in your next letter. Ticket taken. Departure for . . . ? on such a day. I am quite prepared. What does it matter to me?

[1] J. B. Pouterman had undertaken for Random House to have *If it Die* printed in France. After considerable delay, the book was brought out in 1935.
[2] *Olivia*.
[3] *Geneviève*, which Gide was then writing.

135. André Gide to Dorothy Bussy

Lausanne

11 December 33

My very dear friend,

I think of you (and so tenderly) but no longer even find time to write to you. Completely submerged! I'm feeling well again, and even manage to keep myself quite suitably disposed for writing, if only so many importunate people would leave me a little leisure! I'm staying in Lausanne for another few days; it would be loathsome of me to abandon these students before the first performance of *Les Caves*, which is scheduled for the 15th.[1] (Already a premature performance took place the day before yesterday at Montreux. Nothing was yet ready.)

Directly afterwards, I return to Paris where innumerable cares await me – then a few days in Cuverville – after which I should like to fly off somewhere far away – out of reach – perhaps to Dahomey where the Marcel de Coppets are expecting me. In Paris, I'll find out what news there is of the printing of your translation. Mr. P.'s letter, which I passed on to you, didn't reassure me very much. The tone of that letter hardly pleased me . . . We shall see.

DEADLY anxious about your Post-script!! – Stop.

Yours,
A.G.

Stoisy has moved and I don't have her new address. Will make inquiries when I return . . . and write to you –

136. Dorothy Bussy to André Gide

Dec. 30th 1933

Dear Gide

I am sending you my M.S.[1] by this post. I am absolutely disgusted with it – poor, meagre, inadequate thing. I think at the last minute I

[1] The stage version of *Les Caves du Vatican* performed in Lausanne by students was later revised and presented in December 1950 at the Comédie Française. See Letter 260.

LETTER 136

[1] Of *Olivia*.

wouldn't have sent it, if it wouldn't have seemed making too much of a fuss.

Another reason is that when I was half-way through it suddenly occurred to me I might be encroaching on an early adventure of Geneviève's. I don't really think so, but I must have 'le couer net' about it.

I really began writing it in the vague hope of making a little money! But it amused me.

I am afraid you may think it indecent of me to send it to you of all people in the world. Mais nous n'en sommes pas là!

At any rate, it isn't long and won't take you half an hour to read. For heaven's sake, don't think it necessary to write to me about it. Drop it into that friendly, comfortable gulf of silence and oblivion that swallows up all my letters. It is less important.

I hope your lumbago is cured. I hope you are well . . . and perhaps escaped from Paris and working.

Best wishes for 1934 and also, if I may, give them from me to your wife.

> Yours affec'y
> Dorothy Bussy

Strictly anonymous

137. André Gide to Dorothy Bussy

> Cuverville
>
> 15 January 34

My dear friend,

Yes, it was with a very keen emotion that I read Olivia's story, in the evening, by the fireside, alone in the large bedroom I have made my study. Three evenings I delved into those pathetic reminiscences. How few are the ashes that even today cover so much flame! and how easily the breath of my attention rekindles them . . . And constantly, as I read, yours was the voice I heard.

Must I return these pages to you? I'd like to bring them to you, but don't yet know where to direct my uncertainty. I am in great need of solitude. Everything ceaselessly distracts me . . . Do you know I have just come back from Berlin? Accompanied by André Malraux, I had gone to take Goebbels an urgent request, in consequence of the Reich's verdict, for the liberation of Dimitrov. It seems that our efforts were quite useless, for although he was acquitted by the verdict, Dimitrov has still not been released – no more than the other two Bulgarians.[1] I wait for news every day, and am keeping all plans in suspension.

I am well, even very well – better than I have been in a long time. I'd like to devote this renewed vigour to work, like to escape I don't know where and find a little tranquillity. I'm besieged on all sides. I no longer belong to myself, can no longer do anything of any worth . . .

Do you sometimes feel how tenderly I think of you?

Your friend,
André Gide

138. Dorothy Bussy to André Gide

5th Feb. 1934

Dear Gide

I was wondering what postmark I should see on your next letter. I am glad you had a pleasant meeting with Roger[1] – with others too perhaps – and who, I should like to know, is with you now, at Syracuse? Such are my still jealous thoughts. I expect I shall know someday, not from you, which I shouldn't so much mind, but from public rumour which in vain I try and stop my ears to.

Roger's new translator is rather a remarkable find – not because he cracked up my rendering of the few sentences from *Les Nourritures* (which was very likely just flattery) but because at last we have found someone who really knows French, who can write excellent English, who is very intelligent and highly cultivated. (If you want *Corydon*

---

[1] Gide and Malraux had left for Germany on 4 January. A vast international campaign resulted in the liberation of Dimitrov and his friends, accused of instigating the burning of the Reichstag.

LETTER 138

[1] Gide had seen Martin du Gard in Marseille before setting off for Sicily.

translated nobody could do it better.) When I started reading the translation of the *Thibault* I thought at first he was one of the usual young men, but very soon discovered he was something far superior. Since then, I have had a little correspondence with him. He was at Oxford and then in the Indian Civil Service – 17 years in Burma. Now he lives in Paris and has written a book expounding *Ulysses*, which I have read with enormous interest and admiration.[2] The only thing I have read which really gives one an idea of what Joyce is at. But to expound Joyce one has to be, it would seem, almost as universally erudite as Joyce himself. I am amazed at both of them. It's a rather strange thing that such a man should be translating Roger. He got the job from an agency. I suppose he is hard up. I should like him to translate *Corydon* but not *Les Nourritures*. Yes, I feel I could do *Les Nourritures* better myself.[3] I always told you that I could do *Les Nourritures* better than *Si le Grain ne Meurt* (*nothing* from Poutermann) which I always told you I couldn't do. But it was all too clear that you didn't want me to do *Les Nourritures*, else I might have spent the last two winters more profitably and not wasted a good deal of my time – and even a little of yours – in producing an ineffectual 'elucubration.'

Thank you for your little emendation.[4] I hope you didn't think the whole of my story *true*. A good deal of it was, but still more wasn't. But of course you saw through it all. I don't know whether you will believe me, but I think it is true to say that I sent it you grudgingly, reluctantly, even painfully, but as a matter of conscience. Why I should have thought it my duty, I can't tell, but I did.

Well, I hope you will work in your retreat and to your own satisfaction. I am glad you have escaped from Paris.

Good-bye, my kind, benevolent friend

Yours affectionately,
Dorothy Bussy

Are you in the hotel of the Latomie? We stayed there once.

[2] Stuart Gilbert, whose translation of Martin du Gard's novel, *Les Thibault*, was published by J. Lane in 1933, later became an important translator of Malraux, Sartre, and Camus.

[3] D.B. did translate this work and its sequel *Les Nouvelles nourritures*. *The Fruits of the Earth* was not published, however, until 1949, when Gide had become a Nobel laureate.

[4] Gide had pointed out the ambiguity of a fragment of French dialogue in chapter ten of *Olivia*.

139. André Gide to Dorothy Bussy

Cuverville

12 September 34

My dear friend,

I am very much affected by news of Roger Fry's death,[1] which I read in yesterday's *Echo de Paris* (so far the only French newspaper to speak of it). It grieves you as well, I'm sure. How many memories are associated with him!

Oh, please don't misinterpret my silence. Here the days flow by in such an even course one hardly notices their passing, and I give the best of my time to my work. As for plans . . . I force myself to give no thought to the future and continue to be quite undecided about what I shall do this winter. It goes without saying that Roquebrune, in this gloom, casts a bright beacon, but after this terribly long period of literary inactivity, I cannot but subordinate everything to the completion of the work I have undertaken – which is still too formless for me to tell you about it.[2] I am better than I've been in a long time and want to take advantage of it. Doubtless the effect of the cure at Karlsbad; suddenly, while still in the south, I felt in a good mood, and without plan or design I began to write, letting my pen run, bits of dialogue that will have some place, if possible, in the comedy (or tragedy) I am presently attempting to construct. For a while I am denying myself anything that might distract me from it, reading, correspondence, etc. . . . repeating constantly to myself: 'now or never'.

The house is full up; we are twelve at table, and have been fourteen – a brother-in-law (Marcel Drouin), two sisters-in-law, three nephews, three nieces, and their children. Fortunately there is perfect cordiality and the possibility of being alone. I forget as best I can everything that could call me back to Paris, where I don't expect to return until the 10th of October. (And directly, I will badger Pouterman . . . but why doesn't the American publisher spur him along? . . .) All this doesn't in the least prevent me from thinking of you very often. Completely at Simon's disposal to facilitate his work

[1] Roger Fry had died on 9 September as the result of an apparently inconsequential fall.
[2] Gide was working on a play he had promised to Louis Jouvet, *Robert, ou l'Intérêt général*.

at the Vincennes Zoo, if I can (it won't be difficult, it seems to me).
I picture him now at the London Zoo and am happy to know he is
fully recovered and back to work. When we meet you will tell me of
your visit to Hamspray[3] and you will quickly see that I can be moved
by what touches you. Probably I shall be in Paris at the time of Janie's
exhibition . . . but can assure you of nothing – except of my very
faithful friendship –

Yours *ever*
André Gide

I am putting off reading Lady Bessborough's letters until
Roquebrune![4]

140. Dorothy Bussy to André Gide

51 Gordon Square

12th Sept. 1934

Dearest Gide

I wonder where you are and what you are doing and whether you
are well enough to be enjoying this lovely weather. Not even the flash
of your name in the papers have I seen for ages.

We are now settled again in London for another month or so.
Simon very well – as well, he says, as he ever felt, and working again
at the Zoo, but only in the mornings.

We have been extremely agitated and grieved by poor Roger Fry's
sudden death. He had just come back from his cure in France,
particularly well and cheerful. Then just a week ago to-day, he
walked across his room, slipped and broke his femur. He was taken
to the hospital and died after two or three days – from internal
injuries – or complications.

It has been most distressing. He was a very very old friend of ours
and of all our circle as you know. It is a shattering loss for a great
many people – amongst whom particularly my poor Pippa, who was
enjoying her month's holiday in Italy and who had to hear of it by
telegram – lest she should see it accidentally in the papers. I have

[3] The Bussys had spent a week at Hamspray in August, their first visit since
Lytton's death.
[4] D.B. had just read the two volumes of letters to Lord Granville and recommended
them to Gide.

sometimes imagined that she perhaps liked him as much as – for instance – I like you. (Private!)

Anyway he was an intimate friend. Pippa has always been unlucky in her affections.

Well, it was impossible to know Roger without being fond of him and he was the great enlivening centre of all our set. He had been very affectionate to Simon during his illness. We shall miss him dreadfully.

I have lately been unfaithful to you and translated *Veronicana* (if one can call it being unfaithful!) I don't suppose any English publisher will look at it. A real labour of love![1]

But I am going to show it to T. S. Eliot – who doesn't know Jouhandeau at all. By the way I have not yet asked J's permission. I shall apply to you for a recommendation if it comes to anything.

Love from us all.

Yr.
D.

P.S. I have just seen Pamela Fry, who asked me to write to you and tell you there has been a 'post mortem' and they say Roger couldn't in any case have lived much longer or at least it would have probably been in misery – so that we mustn't look on this accident as a premature and unnecessary end.

141. André Gide to Dorothy Bussy

1 bis, rue Vaneau, VIIe
Littré 57.19

13 Jan. 35

Very dear friend,

I interrupt for a moment, to embrace you, my bothersome task: 700 signatures to affix to the first sheets of the 700 copies of *If it Die*. I have another 200 to go. All I have actually are these first sheets which Pouterman is to come and collect tomorrow. At last it's done! The book is printed. What an 'Ouf!' you must have uttered when you sent back the last proofs . . .

---

[1] D.B.'s translation of Marcel Jouhandeau's novel was never published.

I have just returned from Italy (Rome) where I went for 10 days – question of a change of air to try to cure my catarrh – and to distract myself a bit from my play[1] and my thoughts. I'm not satisfied (not at all) with that play. A little later I shall look at it and see whether it is worth reworking for a few good scenes, or whether I had best drop it altogether. For the moment, I don't want to think about it any more.

I had the great joy, in Rome, of finding Ernst Robert Curtius – more affectionate than ever, despite a divergence of opinion. Political passions warp every relationship here. One no longer meets anyone but fanatics or perplexed sceptics. My own mind is all wound in coils by the recent events in Russia.

Happy to meet at last (in you) someone who likes Valéry's discourse on the *Prix de Vertu*. I must admit that I found it lamentable. Great sadness (and for the 2nd time – the first was his interminable '*Idée fixe*') at being totally unable to admire it. That bantering tone strikes me as . . . senile. And Valéry should not allow himself that kind of improvisational amplitude.

If the weather permits (for I continue to have this bad cold) I'll spend a few days in Cuverville. After that, the unknown.

Dear friend, dear friends, I embrace you fondly

André Gide.

142. Dorothy Bussy to André Gide

April 3d 1935

Dear Gide

No particular news but just a line of friendship. Two or three days ago Roger came over from Nice to meet Charlie and Zézette[1] at La Souco. Charlie was as wonderful as ever and Roger (after C. had gone) like a draught of oxygen to gasping lungs. Nevertheless, as we all agreed, one has a feeling of *veneration* for Charlie! He is writing a book on the Brownings – 'the most marvellous and perfect example

---

[1] *Robert, ou l'Intérêt général.*

LETTER 142

[1] Charles Du Bos and his wife.

of the love relationship ever known in the world of poetry.' This is what he is immersed in and ma foi, says some very interesting things about Browning's poetry. But can one think of Browning's poetry just now? As a matter of fact I can and Charlie's attenuated silk spinning sent me back to the old, worn, falling to pieces volume. There was a time, I remember, many years ago, when you used to quote to me – at least you did two or three times – a verse beginning '. . . No, No, That will never do.

There was a good deal of talk about you, Charlie of course being the one who said the most amiable and sympathetic things. Roger said – which was more interesting to me – that you had gone to Spain. So perhaps this letter will never reach you. If it does, and if you come back via the South East of France and visit your friends, we shall have a room free from April 17th. And this you will see at a glance is the real reason of my letter.

I am corresponding with Miss Pell the lady who is writing a thesis on *L'Evolution de l'Idée religieuse chez André Gide.*[2] She is rather amusing. When she undertook this job she hadn't the faintest idea or vaguest conception of what she was letting herself in for. Her eyes have been gradually opened – very very gradually. I think they are open now and in spite of her extreme agony she is holding on to . . . not so much admiration of you as to a furious revolt against the spirit of the Faculté de Grenoble. A plucky woman.

Good-bye, my dear.

Your ever faithful
D.B.

We shall be staying here I expect till the end of May.

143. André Gide to Dorothy Bussy

Fez

10 April 35   2 p.m.

Dear friend,

Owing either to error or neglect, my post was left some time without being forwarded. I spent two weeks without any news at all

---

[2] Elsie Pell's thesis was published by Didier in 1936.

(which allowed me to work as I had not been able to do for months). Then, all at once, in four packets, eighty letters, none of which was upsetting, but there was none from you – which amounts to nearly the same thing. Well, good lord, if you don't write I am well aware that I have only myself to blame for your silence, and that you always answer my letters very faithfully. And then I think: how long must it be since I have written to her to receive nothing in return? . . . Then suddenly I picture you making a kind of wisdom of indifference and of detachment from me, persuading yourself that I have forgotten you and that I have not even noticed that you've been silent a very long time . . . *Nonsense.*

I leave Fez in three or four days, after three weeks here. If only I were a bit happier with my work – or at least with the results! An unproductive life no longer has any savour for me. I've tried hard to take hold of my play again, to improve it and finish it. I'm afraid there is in it – as there is in my unfinished novel[1] – an essential fault that dooms it. And what's worse, I fear it will be the same from now on with everything I attempt to give birth to. The reasons for these successive miscarriages you will discover to some extent in the *Journal* pages that were just published in the April issue of the *N.R.F.* And if I were at least perfectly satisfied with those pages! So you can judge for yourself whether I feel like writing letters – even though it be to you! For I don't at all like to complain; but with you at least I can't playact at being happy.

4 p.m.

The afternoon post (I was unaware there was an afternoon post) has brought me your very good letter. It dispels all the clouds from my heart and thoughts. I am ashamed of what I wrote to you earlier. Dear, very dear friend, when I think of your smile . . . And I am overcome with an intense desire to see you. If only I were not hindered by the 3000 kilometre Spanish Railway ticket which – in order to save a great sum – I bought when I left and which encourages me in a very compelling way to return via Spain. These circular or 'round trip' tickets are very poorly suited to my temperament.*

Vedremo. In any case, do not doubt my very constant affection.

André Gide

* No, of course not. That's nothing, and you know very well I would

[1] *Geneviève*, published the following year.

disregard it. The question for me is to know whether I shall have the heart to prolong my absence from Cuverville.

These letters from Miss Pell may amuse you. I expect to leave Fez next Monday.

144. André Gide to Dorothy and Simon Bussy

Fez 16 April 35

Dear friend, dear friends,

I have wired, giving La Souco as the address for the consignment of proofs – which, most likely, will precede me by a bit . . . if I come. It all depends on the Tangier–Marseille boat service, which I am told is rather irregular. I can only get information at Tangier itself. I was to have left yesterday; everything was in order and the crossing certain – then suddenly, on the eve of departure, the catarrh of the rear nasal passages which I have suffered from for the past three months – and for which I had myself thermocauterized before leaving Paris – developed into otitis. The pain becoming very acute, I went to consult a very good local doctor; today, thanks no doubt to his treatment, it is a bit better; but yesterday I had a fever and could neither eat nor sleep. I can't consider travelling in this condition, sweating, shaking, shivering, etc. I shall consider myself very fortunate if I can leave Fez the day after tomorrow. And what enrages me is that these days of indisposition are stolen from you – I mean from the time I wanted to give you.

I feel rather cowardly writing to you like this and, because I feel poorly, seeking some bit of comfort by complaining.

Soon, all the same, I hope.

I embrace you all and am

yours,
André Gide

145. Dorothy Bussy to André Gide

April 25th [1935]

Dear Gide

The fact is I am horribly anxious about you and hardly know how to get through the days, haunted by all sorts of horrid imaginations.

It seems a little bit of a relief to write to you and imagine, by way of a change, that you will read this in Paris, the journey over and the pain abated.

···················· [D.B.'s line of dots] ····················

I never answered your first letter from Fez, thinking that I should see you before my answer could arrive. Not that there was anything to answer – only to say that, after a dreary spell, I was glad to be in communication with you again.

I return you Miss Pell's letters. She is a queer creature and seems to have taken the disease pretty badly. There is something rather attractive about her – a strange mixture of innocence & passion. She seems to be doing a lot of propaganda in America and all her friends, according to her, have suddenly discovered you. But on second thoughts I enclose a letter from her to *me* which I got yesterday. It may amuse you as you won't have to answer it. I assure you I didn't give her any information about your religious evolution, but tell her she would be making a great mistake if she thought, as at one moment she did, that you had no sense of humour!

I returned the proofs yesterday having read them very quickly in rather a turmoil. I took the liberty of correcting three or four English misprints and enclosed a slip with queries about other things.

Dear Gide, I am so sick with anxiety – foolish I hope – that I wrote to Malraux this morning asking him to give me news of you.

Love from the others.

Yrs.
D.B.

146. Dorothy Bussy to André Gide

La Souco

Jan. 7th 1936

Dear Gide

You certainly are the kindest person who ever breathed. Though I know it is *not* entirely for kindness sake you take such trouble but a good deal for the honour of the house. Any way I am full of gratitude and admiration and will tell Ray.[1] But one can't help wondering

---

[1] Gallimard was to have published the translation of Ray Strachey's *Religious Fanaticism; extracts from the papers of Hannah Whitall Smith* (Faber & Gwyer Ltd., 1928), an edition of a text written by her grandmother. The translation was not published, despite Gide's efforts.

what happens to people who haven't got such an influential, persistent and active friend as you.

I have been reading great wads (what is a wad? I have just looked it up in the dictionary: a lump of soft material like cotton wool, used for stuffing — I hadn't realized I had chosen such an appropriate word) of Jules Romains — a very intelligent man with encyclopaedic information and ingenious imagination — a super-journalist something like Wells, but much vainer, and as far removed from being an artist as is possible to be. I like him best when he is comic. Terribly shocked by his attitude to women. In this huge work which sets out to give a complete panorama of life — at any rate of Parisian life — at a certain epoch (I have read five volumes of it) he doesn't portray a single woman who isn't a 'poule' or an absolutely frivolous mondaine, with just a scornful allusion to the étudiante class — plain and asexed — which of course puts them outside the pale of humanity. But this blindness to such a large part of the modern world does seem to me to show a shocking want of real understanding.

Poor Roger (who is almost as bad as regards women) is terribly alarmed by Jules Romains' performance, afraid he has taken or is going to take the wind out of his sails. I feel sure he needn't be. Roger has got the artist's conscience in every sense. I believe it to be more important than any of J.R.'s gifts.

Forgive this long screed. Just working off a little steam — and you happen to be there. But oh! I am grateful for Geneviève. I wish you would go on with her.

I have to thank you too for Vol. IX of the O.C.[2] Here you have caught up the time when you came into my life. And here *parallèlement* I write you a letter which shall not be sent.

Yours affectionately
D.B.

147. Dorothy Bussy to André Gide

51 Gordon Square

9th Sept. 1936

Dear Gide

Your very red envelope made us laugh. Used, I suppose, for correspondence with Russia. I must say I should like to know what

---

[2] *Oeuvres complètes*; the standard edition of Gide's works, published by Gallimard.

you think about that obscure country.[1] I hope I shall some day.

Poor, unhappy Miss Pell. I have always thought her rather cracked but not as bad as that. I am afraid she has got that awful disease of persecution mania. Her letter indeed is quite unmistakably mad. I am afraid she thinks *I* am one of her 'enemies' too, poor thing, because I simply *cannot* answer all her letters. She really writes too many. But as a matter of fact I quite like her and think she is very clever in a way. And when I do write to her I try to be as kind and friendly as possible. Oh dear, oh dear. She certainly ought to be psycho-analysed. I wish you would advise her to be.

Thank you for sending the communication from Random House. I had received a similar one. It wasn't much of a surprise to me. And I expect as a matter of fact they are quite right, at any rate from a money point of view.[2]

We have recently made the acquaintance of Ackerley, the author of *Hindoo Holiday*. He was very much interested and gratified to hear that it was you who had recommended it for translation. He is now the editor of the *Listener* a weekly review which is very well spoken of. He is evidently intelligent and not much afraid of anything in the way of ideas. I know that he is very anxious to get an occasional contribution from you and says he wrote once and asked you but didn't get a reply. I said I thought you might perhaps give him a page or so of Journal if you are doing any more of it for the *N.R.F.* – or something of that kind. A nice, serious, rather good-looking man. Not very young. But he doesn't seem to understand much French, though no doubt he reads it.

The world is indeed a dark place just now.

I am glad you are back in France. It seems nearer. Though of course distance is merely an idea. It is only absence that counts – and sometimes the next room – or the same – is as far as Moscow. Oh well, I am accustomed to it by now and sometimes even see its advantages. If you were here now, or I there, I daresay I should be cross and you absent still. It wouldn't be a bit better than it is at this minute when I am near – as near as I *choose* to be. Though that's not much.

Yrs. as usual

D.B.

---

[1] Gide had returned on 22 August from a two-month trip to the USSR.

[2] Random House, which had published *If it Die*, had just refused the translation of *Les Nourritures terrestres*, claiming that the book would have little commercial success. See Letter 138, note 3.

P.S. I will return you Miss Pell's letters when I get a large enough envelope!

148. Dorothy Bussy to André Gide

Nov. 4th 1936

Dear Gide

Thank you for the proofs received last night.[1] Janie and I would like very much to translate the book. We hope that some steps are being taken to find an English publisher and get the book out in English *very shortly* after it appears in French. This would no doubt *enormously* help the success of the translation. So do tell Gallimard to *busy himself* about this and *not miss the bus*. Also let us know if there is a hurry and send us the text quickly. I think this is an occasion when one ought to *bustle*. Though I don't think bustle is much in Gallimard's line. I have reread this and underlined every other word, like Queen Victoria.

Yrs. D.B.

149. Dorothy Bussy to André Gide

La Souco

Nov. 20th 1936

Dear Gide

Your three volumes[1] brought by the postman a few moments ago were a little delayed by having been sent in the first place to London, where Gallimard must have thought we still were. Janie flung herself with avidity on – well, you can guess which, just to see, without cutting the pages, whether you had toned it down at all. She tells me she thinks not – perhaps the contrary. We imagine that it is perhaps at this moment that it is being read 'somewhere near Oslo'. It is

---

[1] Of *Retour de l'U.R.S.S.*, published that month by Gallimard. D.B.'s translations, *Return from the U.S.S.R.* and *Afterthoughts: A Sequel to Back from the U.S.S.R.* were both published in 1937.

LETTER 149
[1] *Geneviève*, Volume XI of the *Oeuvres complètes*, and *Retour de l'U.R.S.S.*, all three published that autumn.

impossible for me to think of that great exile[2] without emotion, admiration – gratitude.

I wonder what you are doing. I heard from Jean Schlumberger two or three days ago who said, among other things, that you were *not* going to Spain, but I had never heard that you *were*. There was another nice little sentence in his letter about you which pleased me.

I was meaning to write to you this morning in any case about a private concern of our own. We have actually bought (made possible by the devaluation of the franc and the increased value of English pounds) a small apartment at Nice. We calculate that we shall be able to live in it very much more economically and easily than here – (though that's serious enough), Janie is evidently anxious for the change. Amongst other things, it will put a fresh and varied range of landscape within her reach. Such [a] multitude of cars radiate from Nice. And Simon will profit by that too, though I think he is the one who will miss La Souco most, the view, the garden, the walks. As for me – well, I don't intend to be sentimental about it. What *I* shall miss most is that our tiny little guest's room at Nice and its rather cramped life will not be nearly so pleasant to offer to our friends and we shall certainly not see so many of them. Unless we let La Souco for this winter, which we are trying to do, we shall not make the move until after Easter. In any case we don't intend to sell La Souco but to let it furnished or unfurnished.

The Martin du Gards (English plural) have been most kind, encouraging, advising and sympathising. They also supplied us with an extremely competent house agent.

This will perhaps reach you on your birthday.[3] Last year you spent it with us – and I gave you a kiss and a book. This year merely a thought.

Love from all and thanks for
the books.

Your

D.

P.S. I have just written a review for an English weekly of Roger Fry's translations of Mallarmé. Ugh![4]

PPS Our new abode is called Palais Semiramis!!!!!

---

[2] Trotsky.

[3] His 67th.

[4] We have been unable to find D.B.'s review of *Poems*, translated by Roger Fry. With commentaries by Charles Mauron, edited by C. Mauron and Quentin Bell (London, Chatto & Windus, 1936).

150. André Gide to Dorothy Bussy

Hôtel Beau-Séjour
Gryon

1 January 37

Dear friend,

I do believe these have been the dreariest days of my life. Another fifty-two hours (I've been counting them) of purgatory before returning to Paris. I have done nothing, been able to do nothing here, not written one article, not one letter; my mind is sluggish to the point of imbecility, old, demonetized, obsolete. . . It's what they call 'going to Switzerland for a rest'. I brought along Catherine who proved to be unbearable. I excuse her when I consider her own boredom. Because I set about too late to reserve rooms in a place where she might have found companions, we were stranded at the hideous 'palace' of Caux, the only hotel where lodgings were still to be found. After a week of it (we had engaged rooms for no shorter period), I could bear it no longer, and by telephoning left and right we managed to find a modest pension where Catherine had the delightful surprise of finding her schoolmistress and daughter – a friend of her own age with whom at least she can go off skiing. Ouf!

I read with keen interest *I Search for Truth in Russia*[1] by Sir Walter Citrine, who reaches the same conclusions as I, while remaining a bit more optimistic. And I finished *A Passage to India*.[2] And I think of you, much and often – of you who are thinking 'He forgets me'. And if I haven't written to you sooner, it's because I found only dreary things to say – which is why I'll stop, after wishing you all a Happy New Year.

Indefectibly yours,
A.G.

'Lieutenant' Jef[3] is back at last – on a two-month leave. To Holland first, he is to come and see me in Paris on the 8th.

---

[1] Published six months before Gide's *Retour de l'U.R.S.S.*
[2] E. M. Forster's novel (1924).
[3] The Dutch writer Jef Last had been in Spain. His book on the Civil War was published in England under the title *The Spanish Tragedy* (G. Routledge & Sons, 1939).

151. Dorothy Bussy to André Gide

La Souco

3d Jan. 1937

Dearest Gide

I was very glad to get your letter. Even a 'morne' letter is better than none at all. I suppose you are going through a period of reaction after a violent effort. I daresay when the salmon has leapt up his waterfall and lies exhausted in the first sheltered pool, he feels pretty dull. But he will soon be out again still swimming up stream and frisking among the eddies. I think I'm sorrier for Catherine in this Xmas holiday than for you.

But it's a fact that you didn't say one single thing of the many I should have liked you to say in your letter – excepting only that you did give us news of Jeff, about whom we had been feeling very anxious. Give him our love when you see him in Paris and tell him that his presence in the fighting line gives an extra acuity to our feelings about Madrid and that we constantly think of him.

To tell you the truth, dear Gide, my feelings have been rather hurt that you did not answer, at any rate by a word, my last letter to you (about Nov. 20th) – even though I try to make allowances for you, maternally, if I may say so, as you for Catherine. I think it deserved a little answer. I do my best to realise of what microscopic insignificance the little events of our life are among the world's catastrophes, still it would be absurd to pretend that the step we are taking won't make a very considerable change in our private existence and I had taken for granted that it would a little affect or at any rate interest even you. But you don't so much as allude to it. It will be difficult for me, however, to correspond with you without alluding to it.

Well, that's for one thing.

The second is that I really should like to know whether you or Gallimard are taking any steps about the translation of the U.R.R.S. book. You sent me the introduction to translate 'en attendant le reste' you said. I did translate it and sent you the copy. Since when complete silence. I make suppositions! Gallimard thinks the English translation might interfere with the sale of the French edition in England? He has persuaded you that I am a very bad translator and you don't like to tell me so? Simple fatigue on your part? (I do really sympathise with this.) Or the usual negligence on his? I think it's a pity we didn't get that introduction at any rate into *The Listener* when it was *inédit*. It would have greatly pleased Ackerley, been a *very* good advertisement for the book in England and incidentally brought in a little money. But really and truly I should like to know something definite about the prospects of the translation. I have some other work possibly offered and I ought to see about it, though of course I would prefer doing yours.

Roger, (they are both in Rome at the present moment) who is extraordinarily kind and attentive, keeps me supplied with press cuttings about the book and we have seen with our own eyes that it has reached the *150 mille*. But we should like so much to know how the French Communists have taken it, how your young friends among the French and Belgian workers have re-acted. Whether or rather what you hear from foreign countries. All that must wait till we meet.

Stoisy was spending the afternoon with us yesterday and had been saying that she had seen you not so long ago, that you were 'splendide', 'glorieux', in the best possible form. She was here when your 'morne' letter came. I ran upstairs for a minute to read it in private but said nothing about it to Pippa. She was as charming as usual.

My sisters Pippa and Pernel have been paying us a short visit and leave tomorrow. They are beginning to look a little battered by the waves of life.

Janie says 'it's a pity he should read Citrine instead of Trotsky.'[1] But perhaps you have read both.

Simon was pleased by getting a small order for a decoration for the 'salle des oiseaux' for the 1937 Exn. But it is impossible to extract from any authority any necessary detail as to size, place, time, etc. And it will probably end in disillusion like most other things.

I haven't thanked you for Vol. XI which stirred (between the lines) many memories, best left unstirred. But I very nearly wrote you, and I daresay I shall some day, a disquisition about the scansion of German and English poetry in answer to something you say in your *Pages de Journal*.[2]

Yours ever
Dorothy Bussy

[1] *The Revolution Betrayed*, 1937.
[2] Volume XI of the *Oeuvres complètes* which Gide had sent D.B. the previous November contained the *Journal* for 1922–3. The passage D.B. objects to is most likely that of 29 June 1923 in which Gide speaks of what he considers to be the laxness of English prosody.

152. André Gide to Dorothy Bussy

12 Jan. 37

Dear friend,

Returned last night from Belgium (I had gone to greet Jef – to Brussels. Away two days.) I begin by writing to you, before reading my mail. Thirty-four letters – one of them from you. If I begin to read them, I'm lost . . . to you. There is always something urgent. It's the same every day. And from day to day I put off what is most important, most pleasant. By evening I am exhausted, yet feel I have done nothing. And if you could see my work-table – tables. An inextricable tangle of papers. Which perhaps explains that . . .

Yes, of course I received your letter of – November I think, which spoke of your decision. Yes, certainly I was upset by it. My sadness over La Souco is in a way too selfish for me to dare talk about it very much. No matter; I spoke of it all the same, and it was, on the contrary, you who didn't receive my letter. I don't much believe in 'lost letters'. The postal service is quite efficient. I shall most likely find the letter in the thick alluvium – thicker each day – which covers my desk. It was probably a mistake not to put it directly into an envelope. It has happened to me before. I need a zealous secretary who could cope with the impersonal trifles and leave me a free mind for the rest. Of every five letters I write (usually refusals) four might be written by him. It's true! at times I no longer know which way to turn. As for my play (three days' quiet work would suffice to make something quite good of it) there is no longer any question of it . . . no more than for any other piece of personal work. Yet it would be urgent, indispensable, that I affirm my position in order to cut short the perfidious accusations that my silence has sanctioned. I am implored to declare myself unequivocally (on the Spanish question) and not allow it to be said or thought that I have disavowed, denied, betrayed . . .

I read your letter of the 8th; that little swallow of pure friendship refreshes my soul. And I think the little piece you sent me from the *New Statesman* is excellent.[1] Thank you.

Jef has never been better – or more exquisite. I gave him your best wishes. But he wants to return to Spain in a few days. He won't return, you'll see. – In Brussels I saw Victor Serge.[2] Yes of course I've

---

[1] This enclosure was not found among the letters.

[2] It was Serge's translation of Trotsky (*La Révolution trahie*) that Gide had read.

read Trotsky's book! Also read, during the New Year 'holiday' the *Passage to India* . . . which I don't like very much – while considering it to be a very remarkable book.

I am being called to the phone. A quick but very fond hug.

Yours, A.G.

153. Dorothy Bussy to André Gide

La Souco

Jan. 13th [1937]

Dear Gide

It is dreadful that your correspondence should reduce you to such a state and prevent you from doing important work. Quite lamentable. But how often we have talked over this! And instead of getting better, it gets worse. What it is to have a conscience!

Three or four days to finish your play! Why don't you put it in your suit-case and bring it along here? Your room as usual will be available for at least another month. You would read it aloud to us and have nothing else to distract you. No answer is required to this – only a wire the day before if the fancy seized you.

The Spanish affair gets more ghastly every day. I can't help feeling bitter resentment against the English govern.t who, it seem to me, are disgracing themselves. As indeed they have done on every single occasion since they came into power and since Sir John Simon destroyed the league and almost all hope of better things by giving away Manchuria. The origin of all this horror, including Abyssinia lies there. They are a dastardly and despicable lot, and of course they really want Franco to win, though they don't actually dare say so.

I rather imagine you are right about *A Passage to India*. There is a strain about Forster which is slightly antipathetic to me.

Dear Gide, why not think seriously about coming here for the last time? But I'm not sentimental about it. I don't think I really care about *things* in that way. Not even much about memories, in connection, I mean, with things and places. Graves are not sacred to me.

Goodnight. It's queer that the only letter of mine (almost) that I have really expected you to answer is the one the answer to which never reached me. I shan't expect one again for another twenty years (almost).

Your

D.

154. Dorothy Bussy to André Gide

40 Rue Verdi
Nice

17th Mar. 1937

Dear Gide

As my last letter from La Souco was addressed to you, so shall be my first from here – our new abode. And almost the first we have received here is from you, a very sweet one which gave us all a great deal of pleasure. It was forwarded from La Souco to which we said good-bye yesterday morning. But we were all far too busy packing up and settling a thousand details to have any time for sentimental regrets, and we are even more busy here unpacking and arranging a thousand other details. Like Proust and his grand-mother, regrets will no doubt come upon us later and unexpectedly, when we are putting on our shoes or something equivalent.

We all rather like the new apartment and think it quite 'sympathique.' We expect to settle down in it quite pleasantly. I shan't describe it because some day you will come and see it. There is a room for you – really not so bad. So close too to Cabris[1] and to Roger that you couldn't altogether avoid us – even if you wanted to! (This is meant as a tease and to make you say 'How like her!').

Dear Gide, every one of our books are [sic] on the floor in the sitting-room in a huge pile, the Littrés[2] sitting on the top of the tiniest. But you know what its like. The 'petite dame' has just peeped in, kindly laden, our second visitor, the first being Hélène R.M.G. come to help. Every body is *very* kind, and Mme Hanotaux actually wept when we left! I was very much touched.

[1] The home of Elisabeth Van Rysselberghe Herbart.
[2] Gide had made her a gift of the Littré dictionary in 1927.

I hope you are well and working. How I wish Jeff Last were out of it! How horrid the riots in Paris![3]

I must stop. I am very tired and have got a migraine and a carpenter is hammering nails into my head.

Yours as ever
D.B.

Janie sends her love and anticipatory thanks. Her book will no doubt turn up to-morrow.

155. Dorothy Bussy to André Gide

40 Rue Verdi

8th May [1937]

Dear Gide

Thank you for your note and 1st batch of type script, both of which I was very glad to get. I don't think it will be tedious to translate – even this first part, so full of figures.[1] The difficulties you present to the translator are always so great that he never has any chance of getting bored. His job is a perpetual wrestle, in which he is invariably defeated. (Perhaps I ought to say 'she'.)

How different when it is other people's prose. Guilloux now I manage much better.[2] I don't the least mind being 'free' with him. I don't feel that scruples are in the least necessary. I can dash along quite easily, keep his sense, find equivalent idioms, give the impression, with the sacrifice of hardly any subtleties. But with you when a word is altered, when the order is disarranged by a hair's breadth, the whole spirit of the thing seems to vanish. And yet the unhappy translator *must* alter words and disarrange order. But though you have often told me (very politely) that you don't think I am 'free' enough, I still believe that I am least unsuccessful when I stick the

[3] A demonstration by the rightest Croix de Feu provoked a leftist counter-demonstration on 16 March which resulted in several deaths and casualties.

LETTER 155

[1] This was *Retouches à mon Retour d l'U.R.S.S.*, which was published later that year by Knopf and Secker & Warburg as *Afterthoughts: A Sequel to Back from the U.S.S.R.*

[2] D.B. translated two texts of Louis Guilloux; the one alluded to here is 'The "Paradise"', which appeared in the summer and autumn issues, 1937, of *Life and Letters*.

closest to your text. This perhaps is only true with writers of your calibre – unless you get a translator who himself is so fine a writer that you read him as a text and not as a translation – and let the real meaning & spirit of the author go to blazes. Not the case here.

I suppose you have received the Knopf edition of *Retour de l'U.R.R.S.* Strange to say even Janie has failed to detect a single misprint in it! So I must apologize as far as that goes. But I am annoyed that he should have wantonly altered my title *Back from the U.S.S.R.* which exactly keeps the innuendo of *Retour de l'U.R.R.S.* into *Return from the U.S.S.R.* which means absolutely nothing but that you paid a visit to the U.S.S.R. and returned. Back from = *away from*, into an earlier position. (cf. O.E.D.) But Knopf, of course knows neither French nor English. I shall never, you know, get over having been forced to use the hideous hybrid counterfeiters instead of *Coiners*. A sore point in my professional career.

The English publisher[3] of course has kept the title *Back from the U.S.S.R.*

As for real American technical words I don't the least object to them in an American edition. One or two changes of that kind have been made in this version, perfectly justifiably – i.e. subway for tube, checkers (I didn't know this) for draughts.

Enough.

What are your friends the anarchists up to in Barcelona? It is all too horrible. And sometimes I think, often I think, the cost is too heavy. Let us knuckle under to Hitler, Mussolini, Stalin and the rest. Let us save our young men's bodies and let their souls perish – since that seems to be the frightful choice.

Yr.
D.B.

156. André Gide to Dorothy Bussy

16th evening [December 1937]

My very dear friend,

A Huge Hindignation toward you sends me lunging for my pen. Your last letter is the cause: the way you compare the letters I receive from you with the ones, so overabundant, that I get from importunate

[3] Secker & Warburg Ltd.

people! Stop right there! Your letters (and Roger's) are always a rest for me, a relaxation, an oasis; time stops, or rather, I stop it; and when I cannot, as was the case with your last – for I have just returned to Paris and was at once swept away by a flood of tasks – I put it in my pocket (where from time to time in the bustle of activity, I feel it, touch it, caress it, and say to myself: soon . . .) and I wait for a moment in the evening when I can be quietly alone with you. It is then that I have the sense of becoming once again myself and of making contact once more with reality.

I have known, these past days, other oases: I've been preparing, for the Pléiade collection, an anthology of French poetry,[1] and this important task greatly interests and delights me. Nearly every day I have managed to devote one or two hours to it, dipping at times into La Fontaine or Chénier, at others into Hugo, and most recently into Ronsard. I am to write for the anthology (of 1000 to 1200 pages) a long preface, explaining and justifying my selection, and that also interests me enormously. My trip to French West Africa will interrupt everything, but no matter; the poets will still be there when I return.

I have just spent four days at Cuverville where I worked admirably well. Calm days, happy days even – which will allow me to leave without too much anguish . . . In any case, I don't expect my trip will last more than three months. You know I am going with Pierre Herbart. We shall probably not be ready for the ship which leaves on 24th December, but will embark most likely on the 4th of January. You still have time to write to me before then – and when I leave, I shall feel your thoughts are coming along with me.

I received the Trotsky *Verbatim Report*[2] which I won't have time to read until boarding ship; much moved by what you say about it.

18th December

Unable all day yesterday to find a moment in which to finish this letter. It was to have been much longer! I go on chatting with you, even though 'recessing' . . .

Tanto vostro,
A.G.

---

[1] The anthology was not published until 1949. See Letter 252.
[2] 'The Closing Speech at the Hearings of the Preliminary Commission of Inquiry into the Charges Made Against Leon Trotsky in the Moscow Trials, Held April 10 to 17, 1937, at Coyoacan, Mexico.'

157. Dorothy Bussy to André Gide

40 Rue Verdi

17 March 1938

Dear Gide

In the middle of all this frantic turmoil a private disappointment has come upon us which I tell you about at once because it concerns Simon and I know you like to share what affects him. I think I told you that the Beaux Arts invited him to exhibit in this year's Bi-ennial International Ex.[n] at Venice. They offered him 'une petite salle' to himself with '12 metres de cimaise' and said they hoped he would send 25 gouaches or aquarelles. Simon was pleased at this first small sign of public attention and also because he thought this would be an opportunity of exhibiting an *ensemble* of his oil pictures which you know he has never shown anywhere so far. He accepted, not saying that it was *oils* he would send and not pastels or water colours. He did not think this could make any difference, as the sizes and subjects of the pictures are identical, the sizes being as you know very small. He worked very hard all the winter, preparing, choosing and framing the pictures, experimented with arranging and hanging them and finally decided that 35 small birds, fishes and butterflies could be spaciously placed on a 12 metres cimaise and make a good *ensemble*. The pictures were sent off to Paris.

Yesterday he heard from M. Hautecoeur who makes the following objections:

The pictures are oils and the particular room they are destined to has been *traditionally* reserved for drawings and water colours. The Italians might object to a change. Nevertheless he proposes to keep *ten* of the oils and asks S. to send 15 pastels to make up the number. This he thinks would 'break the monotony' and be 'advantageous to Simon's own interest.' As for 'breaking the monotony' it is absurd, as to all intents and purposes the pastels (of which he has only at his disposal some that have already been exhibited and left over) are identical in size, colour and subject. And if the Italians don't object to 10 oils in the room, why should they object to more? M. Hautecoeur also says that he asked for 25 and Simon has sent 35. But 25 of Simon's size would be too few in a 12 metres cimaise.

The fact is only too obvious. M. Hautecoeur *doesn't like* Simon's work and wants to have as little of it as possible.

Poor Simon! I am really rather heartbroken about it. We were all so pleased at what seemed a little recognition, and a little opportunity. He declares now that he doesn't care. They may do as they please, and shrugs his shoulders. But it is obvious that it's another and *he* says 'the *final*' disappointment.

I write you all this because my heart is full, not that I think you can do anything about it, though I know you would if you could.

And even though Hitler marches into Vienna and England is too frightened and too selfish and too stupid to stir, one still feels the 'spurns that patient merit of the unworthy takes.'

Adieu, dear Gide.

Yours ever
D.B.

158. Dorothy Bussy to André Gide

40 Rue Verdi

10th April 1938

Dear Gide

The other day, hunting through a pile of books left at La Souco, I came across the first three volumes of Florio's Montaigne (Dent) (The other two I am afraid are missing). I have been comparing it word for word with the original, out of curiosity, not with any practical views – for I think that affair is dead and buried. However it may amuse you to hear my impressions. In the first place, I am positively astounded at the accuracy and conscientiousness of the translation. Not a word is omitted, very occasionally one is added, as a little kind of flourish. The meaning is very accurately rendered. Sometimes his version is illuminating to me; sometimes, not often, it seems to me a contre-sens, and sometimes of course – not nearly as often as I expected – the subtleness, the raciness, the idiom of the original is impossibly out of reach. Sometimes, on the other hand it seems to me actually as good as the original! In our XVIth century everybody (even Italians!) seems to possess the Heaven born gift of writing – men and women, high and low, professional and amateurs, ignorant and learned, clerics and lay men, they have only to lay pen to paper and out flows the juiciest, the directest, the most passionate, the most magnificent language. By Milton's generation, it was already becoming too self-conscious, or, as in Bunyan's case, too much over shadowed by the glories of the Authorised Version (1603). But in Elizabeth's days, the humblest private letter, the most protocolaire dedication, the Queen's own public utterances – all are superb. And Florio has caught the infection.

I cannot imagine such a translation now-a-days. And hasn't a translation more chance of being successful if it is contemporary with the original? Other things being equal, it seems to me that the 'air' of the epoch is an essential element in any great work. And this *must be sacrificed in a later translation*, as it can only be re-produced later as a pastiche – than which nothing is more irritating.

Florio amuses me sometimes by simply taking the French word and spelling it as if it were English – and for all I know it may have been at that time. It always sounds well. But could *I* dare to do such a thing?

It would falsify the whole style.

Forgive this little essay. To whom else can I write – what I am thinking of?

And so we pursue our clerical vocations amidst the wreckage of the world.

Au revoir, dear Gide.

Your affectionate
D.B.

159. André Gide to Dorothy Bussy

Easter Monday [18 April 1938]
Cuverville

Dear friend,

You may already know of the sad event that has brought confusion into my life. I had left to make room for the Drouins who have come for the Easter holidays. It was at Chitré, at Madame de Lestrange's[1] where I had gone to spend a few days, sensing her to be very sad and

---

[1] See Letter 119, note 3.

alone, that a phone call, yesterday morning, summoned me quickly back to Cuverville. At about three o'clock Easter morning, my wife, taken with heart seizure, had called to her sister and niece; she stopped living after a very short struggle. She had told me that she hoped I would not be present at her death, and in any case, she was unable to speak. The few days I had just spent with her had been profoundly serene.

If Madame Théo is still in Nice, tell her please. I haven't the heart to write to her, or to Roger or Hélène.

I shall probably return to Madame de Lestrange's for a few days after the lugubrious ceremony which takes place Wednesday. And then . . . I don't know. The idea of seeing people in Paris terrifies me.

Tell Simon and Janie I think of them – and you, dear friend, I embrace you.

André Gide

Ask the American publishers[2] whether they have perhaps heard of a certain Emerson who wrote one of his best books on *Representative Men*. Wasn't Montaigne one of those seven? What you say about Florio's translation interests me a great deal. Wouldn't it suffice to have my essay preceded by a short biographical note that would somewhat inform the unenlightened reader?

160. André Gide to Dorothy Bussy

Cuverville

23 April 38

Very dear friend,

Yes, I can see the little room in Nice. I know it awaits me – and with it, your warm affection . . . Thank you for telling me again.

Tomorrow I leave Cuverville where I have been busy these last few days – and am busy still – with numerous details. My wife used to help a number of indigent families whom I cannot leave without support. She has left the property (terribly burdensome) to Dominique Drouin; I must help him bear the expense of maintaining it. All that

---

[2] Longmans, Green and Co., who published Gide's selection from Montaigne in 1939. Assuming Montaigne to be unknown to American readers, the publisher requested that Gide add biographical information to his prefatory essay.

had distracted me until now. But afterwards . . . Neither plans nor inclinations nor desires. Were death to beckon, I would give in without the least resistance.

If I didn't prefer solitude to all else, at least for the time being, your presence, I feel, I should like more than any other. I'll write to you again when I can see more clearly what lies ahead.

I embrace the three of you. Your faithful friend,

André Gide

If you see Hélène Martin du Gard would you kindly tell her how moved I was by her affectionate telegram.

161. Dorothy Bussy to André Gide

Tel. Eus. 1526   51 Gordon Square W.C.1

2d July 38

Dear Gide

I was glad to get your letter this morning. I was beginning to think you had completely forgotten my existence and was wondering how long I should wait before reminding you of it.

I give you the assurance now and before seeing it that however frightful & horrible I think your Montaigne I will undertake to translate it. I am leading a very idle existence & am longing for a little work, besides which I can't bear the idea of anybody else translating you. And besides believe that anybody who is *likely* to translate you is *unlikely* to do it as well as I. So that my conscience is at rest.

Do you still intend that I should collaborate in the choice of the extracts? If so, it is essential I should know whether they are to be in French or English, and to what length they are to run. I should immensely like to see another volume of the same series, which I believe Mr. Mendel promised to send you.

You don't say anything about Miss Starkie and her proposal.[1] I am assured she is English and there is every sign of this in her book. Her Rimbaud is profoundly interesting – more, no doubt, because of the subject than because of her treatment of it. But her treatment is extremely respectable and that her actual writing is very bad is, on

[1] Enid Starkie's only book on Gide is the short study *André Gide* (60 pages) published in 1953 by Bowes & Bowes in the Studies in Modern European Literature and Thought series.

the whole, an advantage and a relief. There is no showing off in it at all. I was not at all well up in the matter but I gather she has discovered a good deal of fresh material – though it didn't need that to make the story the most terrific I have ever read. (I don't think this is an exaggeration.) *But* I am not at all sure that this kind of treatment – psychological criticism of a man's works and life based on actual documents – is at all suitable to a *living* author. In the first place, however much the author is himself willing, it is impossible to get at the actual and crucial documents and no amount of auto-biography is sufficient. Her book upon you would have to be different to her books on Baudelaire and Rimbaud. How difficult to draw the line between legitimate psychological research and impertinent curiosity. But Miss Starkie is not at all impertinent. She might make a very good introduction to you in England and America and leave a helpful contribution to the life of you that will be written fifty years hence. I should like to know her. Perhaps, if you accept her offer, you might give me an introduction to her?

Another question: The English publisher of the U.R.R.S. books is thinking of reprinting the two together in a single volume. This would not however be long enough and he would like some other short work or fragment of yours that would fit in with the two Russian books. It seems to me that a selection from *Pages de Journal* is *indiqué*. Would you agree? Have you any ideas about it? I have got none of them with me. Would Gallimard send me the two vols. of the *Journal* & possibly the May Number of the *N.R.F*? (I have passed on *Zuyder Zee*[2] to Secker's who seemed very anxious to take it, but I don't know whether they still will be when they have read it. Between ourselves, I think it a complete failure, an excellent subject utterly ruined by such a confused manner of telling it that it is almost impossible to understand the really interesting parts. (But of course I didn't say this to Secker's.) Very glad to hear from yr. letter to Pippa that poor Jeff was out of his gaol.

I am sorry that Marc's departure has fallen out at this moment & left you more lonely than usual.

England is in a more feverish state than I have ever known it. Militarism rampant. A.R.P. (air-raid precautions) bawling at you from every hoarding and unreasoning cowardice & selfishness installed in the government.

---

[2] Jef Last's novel, which was not published in English.

No personal news. We are all going on exactly as usual including myself who am

Yrs. faithfully
D.B.

162. Dorothy Bussy to André Gide

40 Rue Verdi

2nd Jan. 1939

Dearest Gide

Many thanks for the mandat (3500 fr.) which I received duly on the morning of the same day your letter came. I suppose you have as usual been more generous than just, but I hope that if Mendel-Longmans cheated you of your French rights the American ones were satisfactory.

Here comes the charming little copy of *Antoine et Cléopâtre*.[1] I feel very much honoured by receiving so rare an object, pleased at being included in your salutation to my country and touched by your special remembrances. I could add some more of my own. It was almost over your first translation of A. and C. that I really got to know you. We worked at it together for several evenings in the little back dining-room of 51 Gordon Square the year (how long ago!) you came to England one summer with M. and E.[2] But your head was so full of other things that I expect you have forgotten those queer conversations which were so upsetting to me. Perhaps you remember a little better when the summer before last you wrote my name in the blue edition at Victoria Station when I was seeing you off after that very odd visit to Russell Square Hotel. But no, I daresay not. Then too your head was full of other things (When, in fact, is it not?) But I remember it. It was in the station buffet where we took some coffee while waiting for the train. I watched your profile in a looking glass that was behind you as you wrote, and thought how far, how infinitely far you were from me. And then when I read your 'dedicace' – it was in English – behold, it was the nicest one you have ever

---

[1] A new edition of Gide's translation.
[2] In August 1920. See Letter 42 ff.

written in a book for me, almost, oh, perhaps quite, the nicest thing you have ever written to me at all. God! How I envy the women who have had love-letters! No. I didn't mean to say that. But there it is! Tant pis.

I am delighted you have made it up with Hélène. How much more comfortable for everyone. As for Roger, poor dear, I am afraid he must have found us all terribly boring during the one short visit he paid us when they were in Nice. Still I expect it will be delightful to be shaken up by him. We are quite looking forward to it. And I wish to goodness you weren't staying in the same hotel. I dislike excessively the idea of your even alluding to me in your conversations with him!

I think I had better stop now. It is late at night which is a dangerous time for me. I hope you will soon be quite well again.

Your affectionate
D.B.

(*Next morning*)

P.S. I like *albatros* much better than *cormoran*.[3] The whole thing in fact, read like that, forgetting the English, seems to me superb. Different points come out strangely – in spite of your perfect fidelity. There is a kind of unity too and swing and élan about it which seem to strike one more forcibly because we are less distracted by the marvels of Shakespeare's language which forces us at every moment to linger, to wonder, to interrupt the impetus and the flow in order to savour the poetry, or try and understand it.

I hope you won't think this insulting!

Perhaps if one didn't know the original, your poetry would have the same effect!

163. Dorothy Bussy to André Gide

40 Rue Verdi Nice

5th March 1939

Dear Gide

It was nice to get your letter, though I'm sorry to hear you are still not very well and still feverish. I think on the whole Egypt is an

---

[3] D.B. is referring to Gide's translation of the phrase from *Antony and Cleopatra*: 'like a doting mallard' (III. viii. 29).

unwholesome place.[1] Too much dust, too many flies etc. I had a horrid go of sinusitis myself, caught at Assouan (though not as bad as Mme Berthelot's) a most unpleasant complaint.

I am glad you sometimes weave thought of us into your reflexions on Egyptian art, though as a matter of fact Abydos is one of the places we didn't go to. Simon will enjoy discussing your impressions.

The Rogers dined with us the day before they started and he hadn't then had your letter. Unless he got it the next morning he will have started without it. He seemed delighted to be going and was very brisk. As for her she said she was dazed and looked it. Poor Hélène! Rather a 'poids lourd'.

This winter has been filled (for Simon especially, though we have by no means escaped) by the Matisses' conjugal drama, which has ended apparently in a final rupture. Mme. M, after having been a bed-ridden invalid for the last 20 years, five months ago suddenly sprang to her feet and has ever since shown the most terrific energy, physical and mental, in a continual and remorseless battle with M. who has spent all the time left him by these attacks in coming here and pouring out accounts of them to Simon, Janie and me. It is all terribly dull and I haven't a spark of sympathy for either of them. M. is selfish and ego-centric beyond belief and Mme. M. has resorted to the meanest and basest weapons. Enough! But really we have hardly seen anyone else this winter.

Both Ray and I wrote polite letters to Mme. Martin Chauffier offering assistance in the translation and expressing the wish to see proofs.[2] But since then not a sign or a word. Neither have any proofs arrived from our Mr. Mendel, who hurried us so to get the English text of Montaigne, without the smallest intention apparently of getting it printed. But all this will seem very dim and distant to you. What are you doing in your Garden besides meditating on Egyptian art? Not a word as to that. And though you say you are going to Alexandria towards the middle of the month, it never occurred to you of course that it would interest me to know where the boat would be taking you from there. You are incorrigible. But perhaps after all you are quite right. Perhaps after all it doesn't interest me as much as all that. I am now approaching the danger zone so will stop. Simon and Janie send their love. And I am as usual.

Your affect.e

D.B.

[1] Gide had left for Egypt on 24 January, and returned on 17 April.
[2] See Letter 146, note 1.

164. André Gide to Dorothy Bussy

Luxor

11 March [1939]

Dear friend,

I have absolutely nothing to tell you, merely to protest your accusation of mysteriousness concerning my immediate plans. (For I have just received your two good letters at the same time.) Didn't I tell you I was considering spending the Easter holiday in Greece with Robert Levesque? *Of course!* since you mention it immediately afterwards.

I am writing to you from the little terrace of the Savoy where I like to picture you, but which seems very empty without you. I come here nevertheless every day to attend the sunset. Today the sky is overcast. The heat is suffocating. I have just purchased a fly-swatter. Until today I attempted to convince myself I would grow accustomed to it – to the flies, but they are maddening. Tonight I dine at the charming Chevrier's.[1] The Savoy's little donkey, still the same, bids me send you his best regards, and so do the two monkeys. As for the crocodiles, impossible to catch their attention.

As I write, the sky as though by miracle has cleared. The air too seems less heavy. The surface of the Nile is slicker than I have ever seen it; not a breath; the big barges slide by in a kind of timeless tranquillity. The perfect décor of happiness. . . I feel it is impious of me to contemplate so much splendour with as much indifference. The sun has just set; the sky is still filled with its glory, but in a few moments I shall no longer be able to see enough to give you my fond regards.

Six o'clock. The fellahin are returning from work.

No, I have no prejudice against Lawrence and anticipate the great pleasure of reading his letters. The maladroit admiration of certain people, it is true, has somewhat exasperated me – but not exactly with <u>him</u>. I am quite convinced that he's a great and important figure – and what's more, I like his face . . . but keep in mind that thus far

---

[1] Henri Chevrier was the architect with the Services des Antiquités d'Egypte who was responsible for the reconstructions at Karnak.

all I have of his, sent by Bennett, is *The Virgin and the Gypsy* . . .*

I can't see any more. Au revoir.

Yours,
A.G.

I can't manage to feel sorry for Matisse. I greatly admire a number of his canvases (his latest exhibition in Paris showed some remarkable ones) but feel no sympathy for the man.

Work went rather well the first ten days. Then the Egyptian languor got the best of me. Engrossed myself in *Pickwick*, borrowed from the library, with no great pleasure. First finished Thomas Mann's enormous and tedious *Joseph in Egypt* (in translation). I find it more fruitful to reread Goethe's poems – or the poems given in the Pelican anthology which I have just bought here.

* [Jotted in the margin, in D.B.'s hand:] 'He has confused D. H. Lawrence with T. E. It was the latter I wrote to him about. D.B.'

165. Dorothy Bussy to André Gide

3 Mai 1939

I am terribly afraid you have done something irreparable, not to our friendship, which must still go on as best it can, not to *your* friendship for me, which I still believe in, but – what I never thought could happen to me – to my feeling for you. I am very unhappy.

I have written you other letters but not sent them. I cannot say like you 'la crainte de peiner est une des formes de la lâcheté à quoi tout mon être répugne.'[1]

T.V.

[1] Volume XV of Gide's works, published in the spring of 1939, contained the *Journal* for 1928. The entry of 30 March reads: 'T.V. would like love; I can only give her friendship. Great as this feeling is, the expectation I sense in her of a more affectionate state falsifies my actions and leads me to the brink of insincerity. I explain this tonight in a letter that will perhaps cause her pain and which it pains me to write. But the fear of causing pain is a form of cowardice which my whole being rebels against.' See Letter 102.

166. André Gide to Dorothy Bussy

1 bis, rue Vaneau

4 May 39

Very dear friend,

I returned this instant from Perpignan where I had hurried on Monday night in hopes of securing the liberation of some prisoners . . . to find your letter that sends a chill over me. What have I done? What can I have done?

I beg you to enlighten me a little. Your incomprehensible note leaves me greatly distressed and makes me feel how indispensable to me your friendship has become.

Incomprehensible – even the signature. What does 'T.V.' mean? Have I lost my mind?

Yours,
A.G.

167. André Gide to Dorothy Bussy

4 May – Midnight

Dear friend,

I understand! I understand!

But look at the date. We have come a long way since then. You know very well that I would not write those lines today – and that if I allowed them to be printed it is only because I assumed you knew that.

Yours,
A.G.

168. Dorothy Bussy to André Gide

5th May 39

V. Page 131 of Vol XV of your Oeuvres
30 Mars

Dear Gide

Is it possible to be so 'inconscient'? Is it possible to stab your friend in the heart and then *forget* you have done it?

I remember you showing me that entry years ago and what pain it gave me then. How unjust, how untrue I thought it. I remember putting my head down on my bureau and sobbing (I can only remember one other occasion in which I have cried in your presence) and you stood over me and patted me kindly on the shoulder, not understanding, I suppose, in the least what it was all about. But I told you then, though it was the least part of my complaint (it was the only part uttered), that I hated to think that you showed that paragraph about to everybody and anybody, that it *exposed* me, and then of course you declared you didn't, that you kept it quite private. And now you have *published* it! Nobody who knows us both can possibly fail to recognize the T.V. as me. Those absurd initials which barely altered from mine are the flimsiest disguise. I am afraid to let Simon see the book. If he took much interest in such things he would know at once. Even the long journey mentioned in the entry before makes it damning. As for Janie of course she recognized it. I *know* she did. Every one of the initials in your diary we discuss together and wonder and talk and laugh over. But *those* she didn't allude to, nor I either. I *couldn't*. I feel humiliated. I hate Roger to know my secret and Jean and the Van Rysselberghe. I hate to think that *that* is the light you put on our friendship, that I, by my 'attente', force you to 'fausser' your words and 'gestes' to the verge of insincerity. That is how I shall figure briefly in your life, and you and I know that it is not true. Your words and gestes, tenderer than those of friendship, (and there have been not a few) have never been expected by me – unless you think desire and expectation the same thing. They have always surprised me. Mirage, I say to myself. I have sternly trained myself not to believe them, but I have always believed, I still believe them sincere *at the moment*, and always feared and *felt* that you regretted them afterwards. And this was the bitterest of all for I thought it must be the explanation of what seemed a dreadful betrayal of confidence. In this way he has a perfect alibi, absolutely proof against any of his past indiscreet (perhaps) kindnesses and against any past or future indiscretions of mine. He has preserved his reputation for fidelity in the eyes of posterity – the only kind of fidelity he cared for at *my* expense. I can answer nothing.

I have been very desperately unhappy. I who thought I was going to end my life reconciled to my fate and at peace with you. Jealousy, which I have suffered is nothing, nothing to the pain of feeling I couldn't trust you. All the wounds you had a *right* to inflict on me were easy to bear, but not this.

Make me believe that it was out of carelessness that this entry crept in. That you forgot it was about me. That you overlooked it when you were correcting the proofs. And whether I succeed in believing it or not, I still love you, long for you, cannot face life without you.

Yr.
D.

Perhaps all this is an exaggeration, a trifle, a delusion. It must be, since it has left no impression on you. I would give almost anything to believe it. Yes, that is what I must believe, that sometimes you act like a child, unconscious of the deadly weapons he possesses, unaware, ignorant of their effect.

I have hesitated a long time – so it has seemed to me – before sending this. Perhaps I should have smothered it. But I cannot pretend to you. I cannot. And even if you say that it is true that you have often been 'insincere' with me, *why* should you tell the world, your and my friends?

169. André Gide to Dorothy Bussy

7 May 39

Dear friend,

In the meantime you will have received my second letter, written the night of the same day, but which I was unable to get into the post until the following day. You will tell me it doesn't change things very much. At least it will show you how much that note of yours, which at first seemed so mysterious, could worry and torment me. To tell the truth I didn't stop thinking about it all day. Your letter, received today, makes me feel like a monster, but you are right in thinking that thoughtlessness has a good deal to do with it. The extent to which I may have been cruel sometimes, without being aware of it . . . I can only explain to myself by the strength of the illusion which allowed me to believe that my intention would suffice, and that what had no importance in my eyes could not have much for the other person.

And even now, while telling you this, it strikes me that the only feeling that counts is the one I have for you today; and that feeling at the same time causes me to consider the past without any longer understanding it very well, and to forgive myself ill for having hurt you. I know only one thing – that I am nevertheless – and more than ever – your friend

A.G.

170. Dorothy Bussy to André Gide

8th May 1939

Yes, my dear, there's no doubt you're something of a monster. But after all I suppose that was why I liked you. Don't I know that certain things have to be bought with one's life's blood?

And that certain things are worth it.

D.B.

171. André Gide to Dorothy Bussy

18 June 39

Very dear friend,

You musn't be unpleasant with me. If you knew how well I can read between the lines of your letters! I sense you are trying to convince yourself that I am withdrawing from you and will withdraw more and more, that I don't need you . . . in a word, everything that might cause you to suffer a little – or a lot. But I don't like to chase after you; it makes me short of breath. I like to know you are there, to feel you are there, and that you hold back from me as little as I do from you . . .

Truly I have had, these past days, the wherewithal to slake a thirst for sadness. From everywhere (Czechoslovakia especially, or Hungary) I receive distress calls, cries from people who are drowning and whom I don't know how to help. Then this morning, to crown the whole sombre thing, a letter from Jef that is so lugubrious, so hopeless – from Jef whom I believed to be happily in Norway, from a poor hunted Jef expelled from Norway and no longer knowing what to do. The Communist Party is pursuing him with tenacious hatred and manages to shut him off from the newspapers and reviews he makes his living from.

With all this, I have a toothache, for the first time in my life.

In four days I get myself abducted by Mauriac and his son (with

whom I get on very well). I'm not sure what this country holiday *à
trois* will prove to be.[1] The prospect frightens me a bit. I'm afraid
Claude Mauriac expects me to support him against his father – who
has just written in *Le Figaro* a long article on Flaubert (whom he
annexes like a Czechoslovakia) on the theme of: He-has-too-many-
virtues-not-to-be-a-Christian![2] I feel a strong urge to reply, but too
many cares just now to collect my thoughts.

A visit from Matisse. I don't know if I uttered an unwise word, but
suddenly, sitting himself into an armchair, he mistook me for Simon
– for an entire hour (and I was terribly busy!)

Forced to interrupt, but I am still close to you – I hope you feel it to
be so.

Affectionate wishes to all 'yours' –

A.G.

172. André Gide to Dorothy Bussy

Hôtel Sarciron – Le Mont Dore

5 August 39
– but in a few days: Pontigny –

Dear friend,

Any letter I wrote you could only reflect the gloom of my inner
state. One small bright possibility can be discerned however: the
possibility of spending with you, in Cuverville, the second half of
September. Isn't that the time you would prepare to return to Nice?
Therefore a simple stop on your way south. After incredible difficulty,
I am given to understand – from a letter Marcel Drouin wrote me –
my sister-in-law has managed to find sufficient ancillary assistance
to restore Cuverville to its former hospitable possibilities. He invites
me to profit from it myself soon, but I can only do so towards the end
of the vacation, detained in the first place by the cure I am making
here, then by two successive 'décades' at Pontigny – the one being
organized (if I understand correctly) by the *T.L.S.* which is conscript-
ing a few important representatives of English criticism and that
Madame Desjardins has made me feel it my duty to attend – and the
preceding one, where discussion will centre on the agonizing refugee

[1] Claude Mauriac devotes nearly a hundred pages of his *Conversations with André
Gide* to this visit to the Mauriac family estate.
[2] The article was a review of Henri Guillemin's *Flaubert devant la vie et devant
Dieu* (*Le Figaro*, 10 June 1939, p. 5).

question which is particularly important to me. This takes me to the 5th of September. Then I have promised Catherine to spend a few days with her in the south. Even if my time were less taken, I should have lacked the *élan*, the vigour, the joyfulness to come and join you in England, as I had spoken of doing earlier; and this is why I have allowed my time to be taken up without too much regret. I have been a bit better the past few days; but the entire beginning of this summer I was like a piece of flotsam, incapable of work, meaningless and dull and limp and woeful. The state of the world is enough to take away your taste for life. Everywhere I see nothing but distress, absurdity, madness. Reading the *Epilogue* of the *Thibault*, the proofs of which Roger[1] asked me to correct, was no great comfort. It was exactly what was called for and nothing more. I expected better and couldn't hide my disappointment from him. He seems merely to have discharged a burdensome chore.

I'll write again when I have made a clear decision concerning Cuverville – Were you unable to go, I think I should most likely give up the idea of going myself . . . in the meantime I hold on to that hope as to some mooring to keep from sinking too far into non-existence. All the same, very much yours,

A.G.

173. Dorothy Bussy to André Gide

51 Gordon Square W.C.1
Address from to-morrow: Aug.
12th 1939
c/o Mrs. Rendel
Acton
Wittersham
Kent

Dear Gide

Your letter was very lamentable and I find it difficult to write. I hope Mont d'Or has done your health good. Horrid place! I know it well. We went there three years in succession for Janie's bronchitis when she was a small child. We were there for the last time in 1914 and left by the last train before the mobilisation. My memories of it are odious.

I hope Pontigny will cheer you up but it doesn't sound very likely.

[1] Martin du Gard was in Martinique.

As for plans for the latter half of September, I feel incapable of making them just yet. Janie and I would so much prefer your coming to see us in London rather than my going to Cuverville. Perhaps you don't realise how much *spiritual* endurance it requires for me to visit you at Cuverville. I would endure cheerfully if I really thought the help to you would be at all equivalent. But this I find difficult to believe. If you mean to work there, I fancy I should feel more or less derelict. If you intend to sacrifice some days of work it might just as well be in London. We could in all probability give you a bedroom (and latch-key) as well as meals and we would read and talk English, visit films, etc.

Simon starts for Paris to-morrow. I am glad to think of him as your guest. Janie and I are leaving the same day for my sister's, Elinor Rendel and hope to stay there till the end of August. After which we shall return to London.

Please give my kindest messages to any of my friends at Pontigny. Special souvenirs affectueux to M. and Mme. Desjardins. La petite dame and Jean [Schlumberger] in a category apart: Love from all.

D.B.

Poor Roger! I am sorry you wrote a severe, or disappointed letter. Why did you expect more?

Everyone knew it was a 'devoir-corvée'.

We have had such letters from him about Martinique that I felt quite sure your next move would be to join him there.

174. Dorothy Bussy to André Gide

Hôtel de Danube
Rue Jacob

25th Aug. 1939

Dearest Gide

I tried to telephone to you tonight from your own telephone Rue Vaneau. I thought I might reach you at Pontigny. But it was no good. It is perfectly horrible being in Paris in this dreadful state and with no you anywhere. England seemed to be no place for us, everybody terribly anxious and every hole and corner already allotted to people with their own work to do. So Janie and I left yesterday at a few hours notice. I can't say there was a panic in England but since the

Russian coup everyone seems to have no doubt whatever that the worst is going to happen.[1] The atmosphere in Paris seems quite different, Jean Schl. telephoning to Simon all about the English decade at Pontigny as if it was all going on as usual, but surely people have found out by now that there's not the smallest chance of an English decade. There isn't going to be any Munich this year. And what are you going to do? And Catherine? It doesn't seem possible you should leave her in Paris or Cabris. Will you take her to Cuverville?

As for us it has been arranged ever since last year that if Nice became uninhabitable we were to go to the Tertre.[2] Roger, Hélène and Christiane have been very kind about it and it seems the most sensible thing to do. When the crisis arose we were to settle things with Chauveau[3] who is going there too. But the crisis *has* arisen and there is no Chauveau to be found in Paris and we feel quite incapable of going to the Tertre without him.

Yet I think it would be madness to go back to Nice at the present juncture and if we delay in Paris we shall probably be caught there by the mobilisation, which will be very unpleasant from every point of view and ruinously expensive. So we are thinking of leaving – perhaps to-morrow for Gargilesse where the Walters are staying and where they say we can find rooms, and perhaps we shall eventually find our way to the Tertre from there.

Dear Gide, we have spent nearly the whole day with Simon at Rue Vaneau, I longing most dreadfully to see you. Do you think I ever shall again?

Yr.

D.

175. Dorothy Bussy to André Gide

Chez Mme Brigand
Gargilesse
(Indre)

1st Sept. 1939

Dear Gide

So in spite of all the blow has fallen – I suppose of all our

[1] The USSR had just signed two agreements with Germany: a trade agreement on 18 August and a non-aggression pact on the 23rd.
[2] The home of the Martin du Gards, in Bellême.
[3] The writer Leopold Chauveau was a close friend of Roger Martin du Gard.

generation you are the one who will feel it most. All the young men you are fond of – all the hopes you had of the future.

Let me know (when you can) where you are, what you are going to do. Marc? Catherine? If Italy betrays her friend – to follow the fashion – Catherine and we shall be able to go back to Nice. If not *we* shall try very hard to go to the Tertre. We are terribly cut off here in this inaccessible village very uncomfortable and very unwholesome. I suppose it doesn't matter. Nothing does.

The English when I left, seemed to me to be ferocious already.

I know very few young men. Most of my friends have country houses to which I suppose they will go. But Pippa and Ray will no doubt face the bombs in London, sticking to their job of organizing the women's Auxiliary forces.

No. I don't want to believe in God. I'm thankful I don't.

Simon has gone out this afternoon painting as usual. Janie and Zoum doing house work and looking awful. I incapable of anything and utterly useless.

Write to me, my dear one.

J and I left London on the 25th. I wrote to you from Paris and addressed to Pontigny on the 26th.

Yr. D.

1st Sept. 1939

Janie wants very much to have news of Stoisy and the Hardekopfs.[1]

Love to Mme Théo – Paulhan will have told you Simon had gone when he wrote about yr M.S.

Is Herbart mobilized?

176. Dorothy Bussy to André Gide

Sept. 6th 1939

Chez Mme Brigand

Gargilesse

(Indre)

Dearest Gide

Your letter of Aug. 31st dated from Pontigny has just reached me. We are very thankful to get it as we seemed to be completely out of touch with you which was very distressing. I hope by now you have got to Cabris, though perhaps travelling has been too difficult.

[1] Ferdinand Hardekopf, who had translated *Les Faux-monnayeurs*, *Si le Grain ne meurt*, and *Les Caves du Vatican* into German, and his wife, the actress Sita Staub.

Anyway it seems now pretty certain that Italy is going to have the sense to keep out of this mess – at any rate for the present. That being the case Catherine will no doubt be safer at Cabris than anywhere else, and we shall go back to our own flat at Nice – as quickly as we can, that is, as quickly as it is possible to travel. We are more uncomfortable and miserable here than is at all necessary. Zoum, François and their child, another young woman, whose husband is mobilised, and her little boy and we are all herded up together in very close quarters in this extremely remote and smelly village. The only radio in the village which a kind neighbour allowed us to listen to has now broken down and it seems impossible to get a paper, so that we seem cut off from all outside information and we are 14 kilometres from the nearest station with no means of getting to it. So heaven knows when we shall be able to leave. We *hope* to, however, and if ever we get to Nice we shall hope to see you.

Not knowing where you were I addressed a letter to you to Rue Vaneau 5 or 6 days ago. Is it possible that in the letter I sent you to Pontigny I didn't tell you we were going to Gargilesse to join the Walters? Perhaps I was too agitated. I too tried to telephone to you from Rue Vaneau, but failed.

Will Mme. Théo have gone back to Paris, now that the catastrophe has really occurred?

We were glad to have news of the Hardekopfs. Last time you mentioned Sita it was to say she was practically dead – or that Hardi said she was.

Good-bye, my dear, au revoir, I hope.

Love from us all.

Your
D.B.

177. André Gide to Dorothy Bussy

Cabris
(près Grasse)
Alpes-Maritimes

12 Sept. [1939]

My dear friend,

Word from you at last! (of 1st Sept., received yesterday p.m.) I immediately passed the news on to Madame Théo. It pains us to know you are so poorly lodged, poor friends! Let's hope that Gargilesse will be nothing more than a very brief purgatory. But I don't dare advise you to return to Nice until we know more about Italy's intentions. Better Le Tertre, if it's possible to get there. Let's wait.

Myself, I was able to reach Cabris by car, to the Herbarts where Madame Théo and Catherine are. The house was full up and couldn't accommodate me, but after five days in a miserable room at the crowded village inn, I found a place to lay my head in the new house that Madame Mayrisch has had built and which is not yet quite finished. Once again I feel shamelessly favoured. – Cuverville is full of in-laws. My two nephews have been conscripted. I'm very worried about Stoisy's fate, having received no reply to a letter I wrote her a week ago.[1]

Marc has been mobilized, but doesn't yet know for what destination.

The Hardekopfs came tumbling into Pontigny one fine morning, the day before war was declared. Two very pleasant rooms were found for them in the village and I did my best to try to spare them confinement in a concentration camp – which I think they are in no condition to endure.

If it were not for Catherine, Madame Théo and I would return to Paris. I don't dare make plans; I live in a state of expectancy – and think of you with all my old heart's strength.

> Your very faithful,
> André Gide

178. André Gide to Dorothy Bussy

> [Postcard dated 19-9-39 and addressed to 40, rue Verdi.]

Dear friend, dear friends,

With what emotion, what joy, we received your phone call! What a frightful journey you must have had! At last you are in safe harbour, and very near us . . . It is the torment of Tantalus for our

[1] Thea Sternheim was in a concentration camp in Gurs, where she remained until August 1940, at which time she took refuge at the Bussys' apartment, rue Verdi, Nice.

friendship, since communications are terribly difficult. – According to the information we have, it takes six hours to reach Nice by coach; in other words, one cannot make the round trip in a day. But they say things will settle down, straighten out, in a few days. And if they don't, I shall come all the same, *nevertheless and notwithstanding*, it goes without saying. What a joy to say: soon!

Madame Théo, Elisabeth, and Catherine bid me convey to you thousands and thousands of best wishes and fond welcomes to the south.

Pierre Herbart has been in Paris since the day before yesterday. He is to see, at the Ministry of the Interior, whether there is some useful employment for me – other than speaking on the radio. That I refuse to do!

Very much with you,
A.G.

I write on a postcard in the hope that it will reach you sooner.

179. André Gide to the Bussys

Tuesday 4th [June 1940)

Dear friends,

You understood I was too moved to embrace you when I left.[1] I need to write to you at once, although I'm slightly giddy from

[1] On 5 October 1939, Gide had moved in with the Bussys at Nice and remained with them until 7 May of the following year. The petite dame, who was staying not far off at Cabris with the Herbarts, visited him whenever possible. On 7 November 1939, she notes in her *Cahier*: 'I feel that he is very happy with the Bussys; their studious nature safeguards his freedom, and he has been working at English with zeal and determination.' Again, on 14 February 1940, while spending a week in Nice, she notes: 'I have seen Gide every day, usually at the hospitable home of the Bussys, where he appears to be really well, happy, completely himself.' But on 29 March: '... I wanted a chance to have lunch alone with him; I felt the need of a slight clarification; and wanted to point out to him that although I was comfortable, profoundly comfortable, at Pierre and Elisabeth's – to the point of not feeling in the least burdensome to them; and although I felt that he was equally comfortable with the Bussys, I was convinced, deep down, that this mode of living was merely provisional, dictated exclusively by present circumstance, and that I had every intention, if he felt as I did, of taking up our life in common once more . . .' (Since the spring of 1928, Gide and Mme Théo had lived in adjacent apartments in rue Vaneau.) On 7 May Gide left the Bussys to settle with Mme Théo in a hotel in Vence. With Italy arming for war, the Bussys thought it wise to leave Nice; on 16 May they, too, moved to Vence and set up in an apartment which the petite dame had found for them. It is to that address that Gide sends his letter.

fatigue, but having – all things considered – very well endured that enormous jaunt. We left Vence at 6.30; drove all night without taking a moment's rest,* then today, until 4 o'clock, with only a two-hour stop at Le Puy to have lunch and hear the 12.30 news. Dr. Cailleux and M. Vezal, the young Belgian,[2] relieved each other at the wheel. The doctor dropped us here at this old, slightly delapidated *château* which he owns and which already houses two valetudinary refugees and their puny scion; then went off to Châtel Guyon, 40 kilometres further, where he has business and where he will take us tomorrow. His extreme kindness has not slackened a single moment. I shall accept his invitation to remain here for a few days so that the post forwarded from Vence can reach me, and my friend Naville[3] come from Vichy to put my papers 'in suspension'. The caretaker's wife does a bit of cooking for the guests, and one 'settles' with her commensurately with what she is to prepare . . . or can prepare.

The place evidently has a number of rooms, sparsely furnished, but habitable, which he would gladly put at your disposal, he repeated to me once again. The house is large enough so that I can take my meals separately from the valetudinarians (but with the Belgian probably – who went to bed upon arriving). It would be the same for you, were you to decide to come, or could find nothing better. This is obviously more serious than a poet's proposal, but not very exciting all the same and, I'm afraid, terribly cool and humid once the sun, which now warms me, has gone down. I'll make my stay here as brief as possible.

We passed through the loveliest countryside! Weather so radiant as to make you doubt there was a war. But from 7 p.m., and even before reaching Grasse, until 4 in the morning – which is to say daybreak – we were constantly being stopped entering and leaving villages, or even in the middle of the mountains, to show our papers, answer interrogation, and were unable to forget the horror and menace that hang over the country.

In a moment I go down into the village, to the grocery store, to try to hear the 6.30 news, hoping with all my heart that it will reassure me of your fate. How can I not think, if I learn that Musso is showing his claws or his I don't know whats, that I should have remained near you! It's intolerable to think you may be in danger . . . The only thing

---

[2] Roland Cailleux (1908–80) had treated Gide earlier that year for colic. The Belgian refugee, in whose car the three made the journey, was also a patient of Dr Cailleux.

[3] Arnold Naville, who in 1949 published a *Bibliographie des écrits d'André Gide*.

that will console me for having left you is the certainty that there is no threat where you are, my dear friends for whom my affection grew from day to day all the long ineffably sweet time I spent with you.

7.30

I have just heard the news. Is Musso backing off? One doesn't dare believe it yet. But all the same, I feared worse, and this isn't at all what he said he would do.

The Belgian, who went to bed on arriving, asked to be allowed to sleep and did not wake for dinner. Alone I ate the last of the sandwiches we'd brought from Grasse, and two eggs. I am drunk with sleepiness. My head is spinning. And I wish you quickly a good night.

Wednesday 5th

Let's go ahead and burden with a few practical concerns a letter I should have preferred to be all affection – and also with this little note I don't dare commit to the post with such an incomplete address. It requires all the gravity of the situation for Madame Bourdet[4] (I don't even know her husband's Christian name) to excuse me for having chucked her invitation so cavalierly. (Josipovici style!)[5]

Were you given the note, in the doctor's handwriting, that I dictated while precipitously packing my trunk – since, having decided not to leave you, I had prepared nothing? I entrusted one of the hotel's chamber maids with the note. In it, I told you that I was leaving for you at the hotel:

1. <u>my</u> sugar.
2. two pots of jam and a few odds and ends (vial of iodine, etc.)
3. some books, including a dictionary and a French grammar intended for German refugees, passed on to me by Mme Bourdet and which I was unable to use. *La Mauvaise conscience* lent by Josipovici; *La Vie de Marianne* borrowed from the Girieus.[6] The rest to be discarded . . . or kept, *ad libitum*.

For the trousers which, on Thursday, are to return from Nice, and for some linen sent to be laundered, I shall give, as soon as I have

---

[4] The wife of Claude Bourdet whose father Edouard had been Administrator of the Comédie Française. Ida Bourdet later made a translation of D.B.'s play *Miss Stock*, which was never performed.

[5] Jean Josipovici is the author of *Lettre à Jean Giono* (Grasset, 1939).

[6] Friends of the Bussys'.

arrived in Capvern,[7] instructions for having them sent to me. Likewise for the typist, with whom I hadn't yet settled my bill. I'll write to her directly.

When you stop by the hotel for the books and miscellaneous articles . . . no, I'll write to the manager and have one mail delivery forwarded to the Poste Restante in Vichy.

That's where you may write to me once, if you don't delay – until further notice.

My heart and thoughts are still with you, and I embrace you fondly, all three.

André Gide
Château de la Tourette
Saint Genès
Puy de Dôme

* It was also because we wanted that same day to get out of the zone before it is militarized, for fear a sudden decision by the government would slow us down.

180. André Gide to the Bussys

Vichy

11 June 40

Dear friends,

It matters little that we expected it . . . Italy's declaration of war[1] gives the heart another little twist. I'm anxious to hear from you. With each mail delivery I go to the Poste Restante – so far to no avail. And I'm afraid communication with Cuverville will soon be cut off. I think continually of those I left there, and with such anguish! The day before yesterday, at least, I received a telegram, forwarded from Cabris, that reassured me on the subject of Dominique;[2] having escaped from Dunkerque, he is 'well' in England. Since May 10th, we had had no news of him. Perhaps a much-needed leave will allow him to see his parents. But can he still reach Cuverville? . . .

As for myself, I expect I am in Vichy for a long time. The certainty

[7] From Vichy, Gide intended to take a cure at Capvern in the Pyrenees.

LETTER 180
[1] On 10 June.
[2] Dominique Drouin, Gide's nephew.

of not finding lodgings in Capvern or nearby obliges me to give up my 'cure'. An excellent local doctor, very enthusiastically recommended by Cailleux and whom I have just consulted, will strain his ingenuity to find right here an approximate equivalent.

Arnold Naville (with wife and daughter) remains stuck in Vichy (like me), the Stock Exchange, as well as all banks, including his own, having moved here.

I am therefore writing to the Domaine de la Conque to have my post forwarded to: Hôtel Grande Bretagne
                                        Vichy – (Allier)
It would be kind of you to stop at the cleaner's (near the little fountain) and see that my un-gummed trousers get sent to that address.

Simon's little bird, which faces my table, keeps me company. I don't need him to think of you with all my heart.

Send news . . . out of pity for your

André Gide

181. André Gide to the Bussys

Alet-les-Bains,
near Carcassonne

20 June [1940]

Dear friends,

Will this letter reach you? Towards Bordeaux communications have been interrupted. Perhaps not in the direction of Marseille and beyond. We'll give it a try. I would think only of joining you (of trying to) if I weren't kept here by the treatment I have been advised to take and the 'necessity of which is making itself felt'. By miraculous chance, it happens that a tiny thermal station not far from here (Ginoles les Bains) seems to be a suitable substitute for the inaccessible Capvern. During the three-week treatment, the situation may perhaps improve – although I see only black ahead of us. At least I'll know whether it is still possible to reach Nice, and Vence – where I like to imagine you still are.

25 June –

This attempt at a letter lay collapsed, but this morning there comes the great comfort of your letter of the 20th and your telegram.[1] (I never received the others you mention, doubtless addressed to Vichy and in the process of being forwarded – but did get Janie's. Thank you!) Both were sent to me by the Hôtel du Commerce in Carcassonne, to Alet, a small village nearby where we found bearable lodging in the home of an exquisite old woman of the region, Madame Naville, her two daughters and I, as well as a few refugees. The great annoyance is not being able to isolate oneself. But in this dreadful ordeal one makes the best of everything. What cruel news since you last wrote to me![2] One can think of nothing else. And without news of anyone, save you. I have anguished thoughts of those in Cuverville . . . But how happy to know you are with Madame Bourdet and Dr. Cailleux! Give them my very best. Soon I shall do the impossible to join you; the train service, I hope, will be restored. Either at Cabris or Vence, but near you. Any news of Roger? of Jean S.?

If you have the means to telephone, give news of me to those in Cabris. I haven't the heart to write to them. I am:

c/o Madame Bourguet-
Alet-les-Bains (Aude)

Before leaving Carcassonne, I saw the group from the N.R.F. disembark. Gaston Gallimard, his wife, his aged mother; Paulhan, his wife, his mother, etc. They have no news of their mobilized sons.

I think of you with all my heart, very sadly –

André Gide

Awful weather. It rains almost continuously. One shivers.

182. André Gide to Dorothy Bussy

Cabris
23 July 1940
received the 30th[1]

My dear friend,

A telegram has come, addressed to you, forwarded from Vence.

---

[1] All but two of the letters which D.B. wrote to Gide in 1940 have been lost, including the two mentioned here.

[2] France had fallen; on 22 June the armistice with Germany was signed; on the 23rd, the Vichy government established; on the 24th Vichy's armistice with Italy.

LETTER 182

[1] In D.B.'s hand.

To save time we took the liberty of opening it so as to telephone the message to you immediately . . . and I am struck with dismay. How can I tell you the sad news? Your friend Ray succumbed following an operation. What must your sadness be if mine is already so great? . . . Isn't the war sufficient to fill our hearts with grief? . . . (A card from Jean informs us of the death of Blaise Desjardins,[2] killed at Lisieux the beginning of June!) Dear friend, I knew Ray well enough, and you spoke of her often enough, to share in your sorrow with all my heart; you know that, don't you.

I tremble lest my next letter bring you news of some other cause of grief – this time from Cuverville . . .

I embrace you very tenderly, very sadly.

André Gide.

183. Dorothy Bussy to André Gide

Nice

23rd Dec. 1940

Dear Gide

Thank you for the little envelope. You have a very good memory for trifles.

I am sending you two little Everyman volumes. One a Gray. There is a collection of his letters in it. Do you know them? They are amongst the most charming ever written and when you, or if you, ever have time would repay a glance.

Your verse from Collins's ode was perfectly correct except for a superfluous 'a' in the Nymph's name.[1] But there are a good many different readings in the text. That is, there are two texts equally authentic. The first appeared in 1746 and was followed by a reprint a year or two later. It has amused me to scribble the variants on the version given by the little book.

I believe, but I can't explain why, that 'brawling' was the original. Not nearly so good on first thoughts as 'solemn'. And yet?

Did you listen to Winston last night? I thought his sober passion very fine. And Amadis' little scheme for New Year's Day? Very

---

[2] The son of Paul Desjardins.

LETTER 183

[1] Gide had quoted the 'Ode to Evening' in his letter.

ingenious isn't it? I shall certainly particularly enjoy my siesta that day & feel patriotic without an effort.[2]

Roger and Hélène at Marseille. He really not well enough to travel. What news will he find there?

Mr. Fry[3] and lady friend delighted with you and their visit to Cabris. They had tea with us yesterday.

Farewell

Yr D.B.

184. André Gide to Dorothy Bussy

22 March [1941][1]

I feel like writing to you but have nothing to say. But I think of you, and not just of you, but of all your dear ones in England, some among the dearest, now gone; you must so often think of them.

How extraordinary it must be to feel one is from a country upon which we hang all our hopes, upon whose victory our fate, our civilization, the freedom of our future depend. And how much I like to remember that it is your country. The page you copied for me from your sister's letter goes straight to the heart. – I expect the nice Madame Boris has delivered the bar of soap she took you from Cabris.

I am deep in Buckle's *Civilisation of England*, and taking a very keen interest in it, especially in the long chapters he devotes to France, and should like to know what you think of him . . . and of Margaret Kennedy whose *Constant Nymph* I didn't like at first, but wasn't bored by – and now I have reached some less vulgar and hastily done pages. But so what? It doesn't seem to me one need make much fuss over the book . . .

Soon, I hope . . . yours,

A.G.

[2] In a radio broadcast, General de Gaulle asked the French to remain indoors on New Year's Day from 2 to 3 p.m. in the free zone and 3 to 4 p.m. in the occupied zone in silent protest at the presence of the enemy.

[3] Varian Fry, of the New York firm Editions de la Maison Française which published French books that for reasons of censorship or lack of paper could not be brought out in France.

LETTER 184
[1] All of D.B.'s letters to Gide for the year 1941 have been lost.

185. André Gide to Dorothy Bussy

Hotel Adriatic
Nice

10 October 41

Dear friend,

I am worried by the news of you that Mme C. Bourdet gave me yesterday on the phone. Her saying that you were 'much better, nearly recovered' didn't help . . . I'm not entirely reassured by it. Poisoned! . . . We run that risk these days, however little we may want to avoid ratatouille and tomatoes. For having yielded, more from hunger than gluttony, to the temptation of some cakes or other at the big pastry shop on the Avenue de la Victoire, the Petite Dame and Catherine were seized with violent vomiting, followed by a running diarrhoea. But they are both sturdy and you aren't. I'm hoping for your return to Nice, but at the same time, the queues at the market – before nearly bare shelves, so much privation . . . how I fear it for you!

To avoid speaking of nothing but eating: the Gallimard brothers, whom I saw in Grasse 10 days ago, told me that the authorities were going to prohibit the sale of all books translated from the English since . . . 1820! The very extravagance of these new 'measures' is reassuring.

Soon, though. Were something wrong, a sign from you and I would come running to Roquebrune.

Your faithful friend,
A.G.

186. Dorothy Bussy to André Gide

Wednesday evening[1]
[29 April 1942]

My very dear. I who have written you so many love letters thought I should never be able to write you one again, but here I am once more

[1] Written on the eve of Gide's departure for Tunisia. He did not return to France until 1945.

after so long an absence. I thought the only kind thing I could do for you was to keep away, to pretend indifference, to *achieve* indifference, since that I thought was what you wanted. It is only so that I can serve him, I thought. He shall not suffer pity or remorse for me. I will kill my love since it is a nuisance to him. And sometimes I thought I was very near succeeding. But I can't think any of that any more tonight. The sweetness came back to your voice and your eyes – sweeter, ah, than they have ever been before. But it is not happiness you can give me, not happiness that I want from you, something deeper, fiercer, more like anguish. It has to be bought – perhaps with anguish. I know, I know it can only come very rarely.

This morning you were very near to me, your cheek on mine, your lips so near to mine. But no, I did not dare. That must be reserved for dreams. They have sometimes come.

Good-night my very dear.

Tear this into a thousand pieces & drop them in the sea.

Yr. D.

187. Dorothy Bussy to André Gide

40 Rue Verdi
Nice

18th June 1942
Anniversary of the battle of Waterloo.
Oh for a Wellington!

Dear Gide,

We were glad to get your letter (dated June 12th) from Sidi Bou Saïd. Like those persons, however, you so often complain of, there was no address on it – though, like them too, you ṣay you are impatient for news! I suppose you are well enough known however for simple Sidi Bou Saïd to reach you. I have written to you once to your hotel, but there is no sign in your letter of today that you have received mine. There was nothing in it of any importance but in these days of accidents one likes to hear whether one's letters have reached their destination. What about Sidi Bou Saïd: It conveys nothing whatever to my imagination – except perhaps something rather dreary. And you don't tell me whether your Tunis masseuse really relieved your 'gratte'.

Here our heat wave has suddenly turned into a freezing wave. We are all shivering and have returned to our eiderdowns and woollies – too thankful that we are not yet at Peira Cava. Our food situation is worse than it has ever been. It is practically impossible to buy anything whatever in the market and we are living almost entirely on potatoes. We have luckily got a small stock of these. The population is getting very restive and our authorities very nervous.

I have had a letter from our friend Fry late of Marseilles. There is a message in it chiefly intended for you. He wants me to spread about the word that there is a French publishing house at New York anxious to publish works in French by authors who for lack of paper or other reasons find it difficult to get printed in France. 'Editions de la Maison Française.' He asks for M.S.S. to be addressed to him. *M? Varian Fry, 56 Irving Place, New York, N.Y.* I spoke about this publishing business to Jean Sch. (we had a very charming visit from him the other evening) and he said the syndicate of French publishers i.e. Gallimard ('Il a suffi' said Jean, 'que je lui en parle favorablement pour qu'il se mette du coup en opposition')[1] had decided to discourage this effort as being prejudicial to their interests. Though one would have thought there were many cases which could not possibly compete with Paris publishers and would appeal exclusively to the American public whom *they* cannot hope to reach. But perhaps there still exist some outsider writers who are not bound by contract to the Paris syndicate of publishers and might be glad of such an opportunity? Fry sends you his best regards and adds 'Do you suppose that you could persuade him to send me part of his Journal?' This I quite understand is out of the question.

Queues in the morning, sleep in the afternoon, reading in the evening – such is my life just now – hardly ever a friend and the dearest absent, distant, cut off.* Encouraged by you, I go on with my Latin and have now got a volume of Pliny's letters which are on the whole very easy and queerly modern. (pre-war!) I was amused by coming across a sentence quoted by you (via Ste. Beuve) in your little book on Montaigne. On the death of one of his friends: 'Vereor ne neglegentius vivam.'[2] I couldn't remember at first where I had seen it before but finally found the references. Nothing could be less like Tacitus, whose great friend he was, than the amiable Pliny. There is

[1] 'My speaking favourably of it was enough', said Jean, 'to set him immediately in opposition.'
[2] 'I'm afraid I am living in too careless a fashion.'

an amusing letter of his addressed to Tacitus of all people, comparing two styles of writing and speaking – the abundant, rich, full, all-embracing and the concise, brief, concentrated, and coming down decidedly and eloquently on the side of the former. He was no lover of '*litote*' but his defense of the opposite is by no means ill done. So I try to distract my thoughts from Tobrouk and Sebastopol.

Vale
Yours,
D.B.

* This is ungrateful for of course the two dearest are with me. They send you their love.

188. André Gide to Dorothy Bussy

Sidi Bou Saïd
Tunisia

26 June [1942]

Dear friend,

I had notified the post office, and 'Sidi Bou Saïd' would have been sufficient address; but your idea of addressing your letter* to Tournier[1] was excellent. He gave it to me last night at the American Consulate where we had both been invited to dine. The only ones there to receive us were two charming young 'attachés'; without formality, together with Boutelleau's (Chardonne's) son's wife, who is English. He (Chardonne's son) left Sidi Bou Saïd to spend a few days in Paris with his father (whose ideas he does not share), but remains stuck in Vichy since he hasn't managed to obtain his *Ausweig* to leave the zone.

Let there be no mistake, Sidi Bou Saïd isn't dreary. It is one of the most beautiful sites in the world. The architect Reymond's pretty house, where I am living (about as large as La Messuguière, expertly and comfortably furnished, almost outside the village) opens its terrace and windows on to the immense countryside above which it stands. To the left is the gulf; directly ahead, the spit of the Goulette; to the right, the lake of Tunis and the plain – and the whole of it edged by distant mountains that seem to evaporate into the blue.

---

[1] Jean Tournier, the book dealer who had encouraged Gide to come to Tunisia.

Hic purior aer, late hic prospectus in urbem.[2]

For ten days I have lived here completely alone. Next to the Reymond house is the Arab dwelling of the villa's caretaker. His wife comes every morning and brings me a mug of café au lait and two Arab cakes, then does a bit of housework. As for the other meals, I am obliged to take them some way off, and make use of the little train that takes me either to Tunis or Marra, where I can bathe. To return from the station to the Reymond villa, half a kilometre of steep climb in full sun – a bit tiring. The architect and his wife (who is an ophthalmologist) are kept in Tunis by their work and until now I have only seen them at weekends, but the day after tomorrow they come home on holiday – and have invited me to take meals with them. My tranquillity is guaranteed by the fact that they are both very much engaged in their work. Without their hospitality, I could not have found decent lodging anywhere in Tunisia; every hotel is full, with rooms reserved months in advance.

The food shortage is beginning to be felt here; but nothing comparable to what you tell me of the distressing situation in Nice. Unfortunately I am allowed to send nothing from here (there has been such abuse!) except two parcels a month to an officially recognized close relation. Even so, at the largest store here, I could only find very poor products to send to Catherine. My heart and stomach constrict when I think of you. (Roger writes that he has grown so thin he no longer recognizes his shadow.) And the news from the outside is hardly cause for comfort! What can I say about it that you haven't already thought, that we don't think together?

What can I tell you that will be a bit cheering? That I discovered in the Reymonds' little library the letters of Pliny the younger (which I had read a little in my childhood, and with delight). – I have them now on my table to read or reread with you. 'Amisi vitae meae testem.'[3] – But I haven't yet recovered from the fatigue of Tunis; I make vague attempts to work, but can hardly do more than doze all day long under a mosquito net that screens me from the flies. Oh, how time weighs on me! I think events would oppress me less if I could suffer them near you, with you . . .

Yours,
A.G.

* yes, I did receive the earlier one.

[2] 'Here the purer air, here the view into the city.'
[3] 'I have lost the witness to my life.'

189. Dorothy Bussy to André Gide

Chez Mme Walter
Peira Cava

8th July 1942

Dear Gide,

Thank you for your letter – a long one for you. It is a pleasure to know that you are in agreeable surroundings and that by now your hosts have arrived so that you no longer have to toil out for your meals and take an exhausting walk back after them.

We are now settled at Peira Cava and find it very pleasant, warm in the daytime and very cool at night. We are relieved of all housekeeping worries which now fall upon Zoum and though we don't have *very* much more to eat than at Nice, it is a great rest for Janie and me not to have to bother about it. The painters paint and I go out by myself carrying a little bag containing Gillet's *Joyce*, a copybook and a pencil.[1] I wander about in the woods, which are lovely, until I find a comfortable and moss-cushioned seat, head in the shade and feet in the sun, with a glimpse of pale misty mountains between the pines. Then I dawdle into my translation and the time goes very quickly. But this morning instead of Gillet I have taken a sheet of paper for you.

Catherine came to say good-bye before we left Nice. She was very charming and pretty, and told us that she hoped to go and stay with you in Tunisia. If she does I hope you will tell us. I very rarely write to the 'Scandinavians'[2] and shall never know if you don't. Perhaps it is unnecessary to say that I'm not particularly delighted at the idea. Jealous, you will think. I don't know. I don't think I have ever been really jealous of your serious loves. Of *Emmanuèle*[3] – oh no! Though sometimes jealous *for* her. Nor of Marc either. I was glad for you to be happy with him. Envious perhaps. Though not that either. How can one be really envious of something so impossibly different. But

---

[1] There is no evidence that this translation of Louis Gillet's *Stèle pour James Joyce* (Marseille, Sagitaire, 1941) was ever completed or published.

[2] The petite dame, Mme Mayrisch, and Elisabeth were living at the Pension Scandinave in Nice. D.B. is imitating Roger Martin du Gard's use of code names when speaking of friends during the war. Gide was 'l'Oncle Edouard'.

[3] The name Gide used when speaking of his wife Madeleine in the *Journal*.

your lighter loves. I have sometimes hated them and you too for, it seems to me, wasting yourself on them. I don't believe you and Catherine can do each other any good. Oh, if you had had the daughter I should have liked you to have, I don't think I should have been jealous.

I was greatly touched by your taking up Pliny because I was reading it. I don't mind your being so far away in Tunis. You seem to me a great deal nearer there than you did this winter at the Adriatic or last when you were at Cabris, when a black cloud hung between us, when there seemed nothing whatever we could say to each other, when we took no sort of pleasure in each other's society. Will the time ever come back when I felt, when I was confident, that you *liked* being with me? When we could be gay and serious with equal ease? To tell you the truth, I think that when such things go they very rarely come back. But I shall try and write to you sometimes, though even that is difficult now. I shall tell myself that it is not friendship-indulgence but that it is good for you too to know that my particular and peculiar brand of affection is still yours – not without its *exigences* though.

Yours,

D.B.

Ah! public affairs. Yes I know we feel together there as elsewhere.

190. André Gide to Dorothy Bussy

Sidi bou Saïd

15 July 42

Dear friend

 The avion which brought me your kind letter shall not go back to France without some messages for you. Glad to know that you breath easily at Peira-Cava, far from the harrowing cares for subsistence, in the kind society of the dear Walters (many greetings for them), wandering, meditating and translating, all beautiful summer-day long. So do I, in the calm Sidi bou Saïd. I resumed, at last, the translation of Hamlet *– at the request of Jean-Louis Barrault, whom*

I met in Marseille. He wishes my text for a reprise of Hamlet at the Comédie Française, and I am pleased by this tribute of regard, for Barrault is an excellent actor, a genius.

After some admirable scenes that I'm having the greatest pleasure copying over (and I am immoderately satisfied with my translation!) I get caught in painful passages that I don't know how to make the most of; in particular Hamlet's last words to Guildenstern and Rosencrantz immediately before the entrance of the players. They allude to customs we can no longer understand and I'm sorely tempted to skip over them. '*These are now the fashion, and berattle the common stage . . .*' etc. '*These are the fashion*' no more. And '*there has been much throwing about of brains . . .*' You're telling me!!

I have just sent to the *Figaro* 25 pages of reflections on the subject of interpreting the role of Phèdre, and am sketching others on that of Iphigénie. I expect the pages on Phèdre will greatly irritate certain readers. Not the slightest desire to speak of current events – and in any case it has become harder and harder to do so.

The people here (at least those I frequent, beginning with my hosts) couldn't be more sympathizing and *sympathetic*, and re-assuringly optimistic. On the whole, I find myself in a situation that is unexpectedly propitious for work – despite the annihilating heat we endured for ten days. 48 degrees in Tunis and over 40 right here, with sirocco. The fish in the lake all died. Every night we waited, hoped for a storm, fainted from the heat.

I understand only too well what you say about Catherine, and about yourself in relation to her, and her in relation to me. I am not bound to her, and at times feel detached from her – or her from me – completely. But it can't yet be said that 'the die is cast, the chips are down'. I sometimes think her capable of having great surprises in store for us. She has never yet <u>committed</u> herself, and has until now been content to amuse herself, be pleased and please others by being charming; I don't think she will be satisfied with that for long. If I went on writing I would miss the mail collection.

Perhaps I should have been able to write this whole letter in english. If I didn't, it is not in pride, but in shame to misuse your tongue, and fearing to make you blush for me. Notwithstanding, je vous embrasse bien fort.

André Gide

191. Dorothy Bussy to André Gide

Piera Cava

30th July 1942

Dearest Gide,

I don't mind your being 'fâché tout rouge'. I feel myself perfectly innocent. No, I shall never change because *you* will never change. I suppose no one will make you understand how baffling you are, how 'insaisissable', how you slip out of the hands that would hold you like an oiled Indian thief, how you always manage to be in some unassailable position, while your adversary – or fellow player – is left disarmed – by fair means or foul – by your charms or your disingenuities. Yes, the 'ingenuously disingenuous' is my secret description of you. I remember once your saying to me that Catherine had all the worst *feminine* failings and that you pitied anyone who should fall in love with her. You then proceeded to describe these failings. I hardly knew whether to weep or laugh in recognizing them so exactly, not as feminine, but as *Gidian*. The fact is in my relations with you it is not myself that I mistrust so much as you. Those virtues you possess so pre-eminently of generosity, fidelity and patience, it is under their cover that you persuade yourself you cannot sin against them. A dangerous persuasion. If I had not one day had a nervous break-down you would have gone off to Tunis perfectly content to leave me to perish (for all you knew . . . we are pretty near the end) in Siberian cold and Cimmerian darkness, saying to yourself cheerfully and I daresay half believing it, 'She understands.'

And then you know, you are adept at the art of dismissing us. Those who have seen you do this so gracefully must in such circumstances have an uneasy feeling that this art is being practised on themselves. Why not? During the whole of my life in my relations with other people I believe I have never been oversensitive, susceptible or suspicious. I can perfectly bear not being loved, bear it that is without any resentment – but there are certain kinds of torments I cannot bear –. And I have recently endured them. Enough!

To return to Hamlet. There can be no doubt whatever that a 'suit of sables' means *mourning*. Sable is *black* and not isabelle or anything else. It seems to me clear enough. 'Even though the devil wears black, that's not going to prevent me from doing so too.'

We are leaving Piera Cava sooner than we intended and shall be back at Rue Verdi on August 8th. The Walters have rented a furnished house at Figeac where, it seems, there is plenty to eat and they are going there almost immediately. I am going to spend the first fortnight of September with Christiane[1] and Janie with Zoum. We shall then seriously examine the food and heating situations of Figeac and consider the possibility of spending three or four months there, rather than another hellish winter at Nice. But how difficult it is to make plans. Who knows what is going to happen tomorrow or next day?

Dear Gide. Believe that your letters are a help and comfort to me even though you are 'fâché tout rouge.' Good news of Roger. *He* is the person I am *really* jealous of![2]

Ever your D.B.

192. Dorothy Bussy to André Gide

40 Rue Verdi

22nd August 1942

Dear Gide

Yes, of course. Your translation[1] is wonderfully good. The *tone* perfect. Polonius almost more amusing than in the original. The whole, like Goethe's flowers, *revived* by being put into the pure fresh water of translation. (You will remember the original.) However, you never like my compliments, so I will pass on to a few criticisms which I have ventured on. They are mostly verbal and trifling. There are one or two, however, to which I attach some importance. I expect you will tell me it is impossible to alter them!

The two poetical speeches couldn't be improved (I don't mean the rest could!) 'Pierrot lunaire' is a *trouvaille*. (Not Fr. Victor Hugo's, I hope.)[2]

[1] The Martin du Gards' daughter.
[2] Martin du Gard was spending a 'blissful' summer writing the *Journal de Maumort*.

LETTER 192
[1] Of the second act.
[2] Concerning the translation of the expression 'John-a-dreams' in Hamlet's soliloquy at the end of Act II. The *trouvaille* was Gide's. François-Victor Hugo had translated: 'Jeannot rêveur' (1865).

I posted you a little volume the other day, but not by air mail – too expensive. I hope you will get it all right.

We are not at all down-hearted by foreign news – in spite of everybody's frantic efforts to make us so. This, on the contrary, seems encouraging!

Have you heard from the young couple, friends of Robert Levesque, recently arrived from Athens? They came here hoping to find you. Alas! Nice young people with truly appalling tales of the condition of Greece.

Farewell for the present.

Your
D.B.

193. André Gide to Dorothy Bussy

18 September 42

Dear friend,

This morning the postman brought me your letter of the 11th. Remember there is no longer more than one mail plane a week, hence the great delay of certain letters, even those stamped for air. In your preceding letter, you say 'We leave Figeac Sept 15.' I thought it would be safer to address mail to Nice (especially since I couldn't find the Coppets' address). It goes without saying that I miscalculated, but you immediately accuse me of not reading your letters carefully . . . Shame! How mean! I read and reread your letters; there is even one (simply dated 'Wednesday evening')[1] that I always carry with me. But what's more vile still ('*worse remains behind*') is having to bear the accusation that I've had enough with hearing your remarks and corrections. I don't know what sentence of mine can have let you believe that. I am impatiently awaiting those that concern the re-maining acts; I demand them, amicably, urgently; <u>I cannot do with-out them.</u> You have seen that I've already taken note of all (*but one*, I believe) of the preceding, prepared as I am to correct and correct again with infinite patience. I shall continue to work at '*in the Beaten Way of friendship*', for I clearly see what you mean. As for 'farouche' I'm not sure . . . did you look up the word in Littré? It has so many different meanings . . .

[1] See Letter 186.

On a separate slip of paper (since the sheet, I admit, was already overcharged) I asked you kindly to <u>copy my corrections</u> in your handwriting, <u>on to the typescript.</u> I have much greater confidence in you than in Mme Fiquet for the intelligent effectuation of these slight changes.

Very impatient to know what you will think of the other acts, in particular the gravediggers' scene that caused me so much trouble but which I think is one of the most successful – and which differs most from earlier translations.

But these last acts will probably be a little late, since Mme F., overworked and exhausted, has had to go for a rest to Vence, Domaine de la Conque, for a couple of weeks.

And certain days, I feel that I can no longer bear it either. Reading no longer manages to distract me from the universal horror and distress (which is only aggravated by the 'inadequate' means which are being proposed for getting us out of it.) I feel terribly far away from you – rare beings with whom I can fraternize. I'm slipping into a dun mire of indifference and apathy. Everything you write concerning Catherine is only too true, and it contributes not a little to my sadness. However, and despite everything, I am full of hope . . . but God how tiring it is to be right! and how costly!! Understand that I need more than ever to feel your friendship, and that this is hardly the moment to be writing me these hellishly 'feminine' little sentences which seem to question what should be beyond questioning and that make me suffer much more than you seem to believe . . .

[no signature]

194. Dorothy Bussy to André Gide

40 Rue Verdi

20 Sept. '42

Dearest Gide,

I returned from Figeac on Sept. 17th and found the typescript of your Hamlet awaiting me.[1] First let me say that your translation seems to me absolutely *étourdissante* and shows your extraordinary mastery of language, especially triumphant where the text is especially

[1] Acts III and IV.

difficult. I have greatly enjoyed examining it word for word, as I have done, and it has left me with increased admiration and respect for you . . . *and* Shakespeare. Many things struck me afresh, or at any rate, as they had never done before. One of them – this will perhaps make you smile and here the admiration goes to Shakespeare rather than to you – is Ophelia. I had always rather despised and neglected her, not only as a character but as a creation. And now she seems to me the very acme of art. How did he manage to capture such simplicity, to convey such anguish with barely more than 'Oui, Monseigneur', 'Non, Monseigneur'? She surpasses Desdemona. I mean as a creation. Desdemona's tragedy is so much more obvious, so much easier to bring off. Ophelia's so subtle, so slight at first, so gradual, so infinitely more cruel. I don't know why I have gone off into this.

I sent you my annotations yesterday. They are most of them quite unimportant. But I am relentlessly conscientious and let nothing go by. There are only two or three that are really worth bothering about. At the same time this translation is so remarkable that I have ceased to consider it as merely an offering to M. Barrault, with a view to production on the stage. Therefore think it *is* worth while to make it also as accurate as possible. Have therefore changed my mind about '*cutting.*' Obviously the stage version must be cut (at least it always is) but let *your* version be complete – even to the passage which is so tiresome with its topical allusions to the players.[2] You have not yet given me any instructions as to what you wish me to do – if anything – about the alterations you have settled on in Act II. There are a good many typescript mistakes in Acts III and IV. Artistes instead of asticots was good, but the Manager Mercure runs it alone.[3]

Your telegram with change of address arrived yesterday.

I wish I could stop here but I must tell you that I have had another blow to my dearest affections. My doctor niece, my sister's Elinor Rendel's daughter, has just died of cancer. We had been anxious about her for several months, known that her case was hopeless for three. She was greatly beloved by us all – and more than beloved – for her profession had made her the intimate friend, counsellor, support of us all, always understanding, devoted, helpful and regardless of

[2] In Gide's version, this scene is abridged.
[3] 'Asticots' = maggots; the second phrase should have read: 'le messager (messenger) Mercure'.

self. She was really all that was left to my sister of her five children. Vincent and his eldest brother have their own families. But she had Ellie – it was enough.

And so farewell to another of my friends. Ray, Virginia [Woolf], Claude, and I don't forget Betty Balfour.[4] I don't think I ever talked to you about her. She was the first. She did not make part of my life like the others. She was in a different social and intellectual world from mine. Fortune threw us together when we were twelve years old and throughout our adolescence, until she married, we sharpened our wits and our intellects on each other and learnt the meaning and uses of friendship. She was always adorably kind to me as she was to everyone. A kind of saint with love streaming from her and joy and eagerness in living. Oh, what good friends I have had, how much they have taught me and given me, how grateful I am to them! But it is no use going on like this. There's no knowing what I might say next. You needn't think I am unhappy. I am amazed at the number of things I still enjoy in spite of the horror that surrounds us.

Ever Yours,
Dorothy Bussy

P.S. I liked your article on *Iphigénie* exceedingly. Let us have more of the same kind.

195. Dorothy Bussy to André Gide

40 Rue Verdi

9th Oct. 1942

Dearest Gide,

I enclose my annotations of Act V which Mme. Fiquet deposited here the day before yesterday. They look as if there were a lot of them, but they are nearly all quite trifling. However, I have done it conscientiously. Please excuse when I make suggestions in French. This is generally to make my meaning – my *shade* of meaning more clear. Sometimes this is difficult in writing. Why aren't you here, so that we could talk it over? So much easier. I was wondering this morning why

[4] D.B.'s childhood friend, Lady Elizabeth Balfour, was the daughter of Lord Lytton, Viceroy of India (and Lytton Strachey's godfather).

> 'Good-night, sweet prince,
> And flights of angels sing thee to thy rest!'

is so absolutely certainly a subjunctive that no English person can mistake it for a moment. The verb is absolutely identical with the Pres. Indic. What then? After some reflection I came to the conclusion that it is the word '*And*' that does it. 'Good-night' then becomes a wish, and *and* introduces a sentence that means '*May* flights of angels etc.'[1] I hope my writing is not too small for you to read. The nib of my fountain pen has been injured and I can neither replace it nor get it repaired so that I have the greatest difficulty in getting it to function at all and have to coax it with all sorts of manoeuvres extremely prejudicial to my handwriting. Now remains the latter of Act II which is not all 'throwing about of brains' in fact has some of H.'s most celebrated sayings, if I remember right. Then there is Act I which I suppose you will reprint with the rest of the new translation. May I do the same for that as for the others? I remember there were one or two objections I wanted to make to you about that, but didn't, as it was too late.

I have marked your emendations on the typescript. What next. Middleton Murry, who, whatever nonsense he talks about religion and philosophy, is sometimes a very good critic, makes a remark about Hamlet's last line which much struck me:

> 'And in this harsh wor*ld d*raw thy breath in pain'

It is impossible to say this without a great effort, without a pause which marks the struggle for breath of a dying man. Thinking no doubt of his own pain.

Dear Gide, your letter too was a very nice one. I don't think you realise, or have ever realised, what a difference it makes to me when you care to let me feel that you feel something – almost anything. What you don't realise either is my necessary diffidence vis-à-vis to you which makes you think that I have too little self-confidence and am absurdly susceptible and over-sensitive. I have been on intimate terms with many friends and one or two lovers, but not one of them ever wounded my feelings or found me susceptible to imaginary grievances. With you, it is different. There is nothing *equal* between us, as little in affection and my claim to affection as in everything else. This is not modesty but fact. And it is a situation which no doubt

---

[1] D.B. cites this verse in the course of an explanation of the English subjunctive in her *Fifty Nursery Rhymes* (p. 272).

does make me sensitive and susceptible. But it is true that very little of the *things I want* seem to be *assuré*. Certain others, yes. But without the former, I care no doubt too little for the latter. All this will seem perhaps very obscure to you or what Charlie [Du Bos] used to call 'Byzantine'. But believe I don't want to hurt you either – at any rate not today – sometimes a little too much like Hermione[2] – I do. Not today, my very dear, all I want is to . . . let us say, 'vous embrasser'.

Yours,
D.B.

Very glad to hear your doctoresse is progressing. Extremely glad to hear that Catherine's plan of going to Paris has been abandoned. I will ask Roger for the letter about *Iphigénie* when they come back to Nice – shortly, I hope.

Your later dated 25th Sept. reached me on Oct. 5th. Today is Oct. 9th.

I am glad you found Dover Wilson interesting.[3] I am in no hurry for it. How much I enjoy this working with you and Shakespeare, how much I admire both your Hamlets, it would be difficult to say.

Yr.
D.B.

196. André Gide to Dorothy Bussy

c/o Librairie Tournier
10, avenue de France
Tunis

30 March [1943]

Dear friend,

Quick, take advantage of this resumption of the post and send me news of yourself.[1] I continue to worry so about you. Here, food restrictions have become severe, but I'm afraid they are still worse in

---

[2] The character in Racine's *Andromaque*.
[3] Gide's *Hamlet* was well under way when D.B. sent him the John Dover Wilson edition (Cambridge University Press), whose introduction and notes he found none the less useful.

LETTER 196
[1] Mail service between Tunis and France had been cut off since mid-November of the previous year.

Nice and that you're suffering a great deal from it. It matters, however, that we hold out until we can see each other again. That constant thought sustains me. I think of you all the time. I am well and hanging on with growing optimism. Been working a little, reading a lot: presently immersed in Gibbon, with the liveliest interest, having buried Samuel J.[2] (two long readings that I'd been looking forward to for a long time – because of you and your brother.) Also read Kleist's *Penthesilea* (which you know, don't you) and a good deal of Lessing. Time can't hang more heavily on you than it does on me – who am very much alone here, despite the affectionate attentions that surround me. Oh, if I knew at least that the three of you were well and 'hanging on' . . .

I embrace you fondly, and remain faithfully, your steadfast

A.G.

I am sending a card to the Rogers and one to Mme Davet[3] – which probably won't arrive until quite a long time after this letter. In the meantime could you please give them affectionate best wishes.

197. Dorothy Bussy to André Gide

September 21st. '43

Dear,

We yesterday got your Red X message (dated July 22nd.) which said you thought you would shortly be seeing our relations. In hopes of this I am sending you some items of news which you may or may not receive through other means before this letter reaches you. In any case I feel I must make the attempt.

To begin with the saddest and what will grieve you most: Marcel Drouin is dead. I know no details. The bare fact was communicated to the 'petite dame' by Copeau. Sadder still, because more gratuitous, poor little Odile[1] has died too 'en couches'. I remember her so well during that extraordinary visit I paid in your home. She was very sweet and charming to me and I liked her very much. I know you

[2] Boswell's biography.
[3] Gide's secretary.

LETTER 197
[1] The daughter of Marcel Drouin.

were fond of her. I don't know what happened to the baby. There are no other catastrophes in your personal family that I know of. The whole of the 'Audides' party has migrated to Paris to the old familiar apartment.[2] The 'petite dame' was the last to go. She left yesterday all by herself with a great deal of luggage and was seen off by Roger, who reports that she was as brisk as ever. Beth, Pierre and Catherine are already settled in. Catherine, whom we have not seen much of since you left, came very dutifully to say good-bye before leaving for good. She was looking beautiful and radiant, with her father's dark eyes and her lovely golden locks – not her father's! She was in high spirits, looking forward to work at the Conservatoire and the promised help of Barrault and Mayenne.[3] She had already spent three weeks in Paris during the spring and found it enchantingly gay and delightful. This, however, is not the usual impression brought away from Paris by less youthful persons. Catherine, too was very enthusiastic about the art . . . is it an art? of acrobatics, which she says she is studying professionally and she talked with the greatest zest about the 'grand écart' and such like. Poor Elizabeth has passed a very hard winter and spring without any help at all, doing all the house-work, cooking, washing, gardening looking after rabbits and goats and cutting wood and grass. When we saw her last she was looking very well and handsome in spite of this, but decidedly thin. The accounts of Mme M.[ayrisch] are always the same, 'not well, no better'. Jean S. has left for his own home where he devotes himself to teaching his small grandson and to cultivating his garden. You have no doubt seen his last volume of Jalons which I liked better than the first. Roger, though thin too – but who isn't? looks to us well and is as charming as ever. He works, I gather, by 'fringales'. Hélène is not well and suffers from 'tension'. This has a very depressing effect upon Roger. When she went away for a month and enjoyed herself in the mountains, he was a different man.

'Le Comte Louis'[4] has become one of our most faithful habitués. In spite of his 'milieu', his heart is firmly fixed in the right place. But then his 'milieu' too has evolved.

I said at the beginning of this page that there had been no other catastrophes in your family, but as a matter of fact there was very

2   At 1 bis rue Vaneau.
3   Familiar name of Marie-Hélène Dasté, who was Jacques Copeau's daughter. She was a member of the Barrault troupe.
4   Louis Gautier-Vignal.

nearly one a little while ago when Marc's wife[5] was taken severely ill. She is now said to be out of danger, but poor Marc who was at Antibes while Nadine was in Paris went through a terribly anxious time.

Our young friend the 'attaché d'ambassade',[6] on his way home some months ago suddenly and unexpectedly found himself travelling in the opposite direction. We hear, however, that he is not uncomfortable. I am in correspondence with 'la petite D...t'. Some curious freak seized her last winter and she went off of her own free will to the place which gave its name to the Paris bridge that joins the Champ de Mars to the right bank of the Seine.[7] Her surroundings are less agreeable than those of the attaché. She regrets her folly and is not very happy. Her letters are very interesting (though there is a great deal about you in them!). I do my best to be kind.

A short while ago two young friends of Jef's suddenly turned up here with messages from Jef. They had taken a long journey and wanted to take a still longer one. I doubt whether they will succeed. They gave a very good account of Jef who was grossly libelled a little while ago. His conduct is all that is admirable and his character beyond reproach. The young men inspired us with confidence and evidently knew their Jef well. He has so far got into no serious trouble. I don't know whether these little details will give you any idea of the atmosphere in which we are living. It is by no means dull — a mixture of the age of the Maccabees, a dash of quatre-vingt-treize, and a little Agatha Christie to enliven the whole. We ourselves, however, are quite well and comfortable, as far as one can be with so much unhappiness around one. S. goes on painting his lovely little birds and flowers. Poor J. has most of her time taken up with cooking and housekeeping, but occasionally finds a moment for brushes and canvas. As for me, I have plunged into a work which is probably absurd, but serves to distract me and often leads my thoughts to you. I am trying to cast an infinitely small ray of light on a minute portion of the English language for the benefit of French students.[8] When the time comes it will want a little of your sympathy and even collaboration.

And you? I hope and expect that you have been able to work a little

5 Nadine Vogel.
6 The American friend of Gide and the Bussys, Keeler Faus.
7 Yvonne Davet was at a workers' camp in Jena.
8 This would be *Fifty Nursery Rhymes*, which she considered a more important work than *Olivia*. It was published by Gallimard (N.R.F.) in 1951.

in spite of events. Rumour says you are going on with your Journal. May this be true! I am still awaiting the last pages of *Hamlet* which I hope are properly finished. Do try, somehow or other to write us a real letter. Roger firmly believes that you are still with the H.'s[9] and that you have no intention of leaving them in spite of what you wrote in your Red X message. If that is so give them our love. But I like to think you have carried out your intention and are in the neighbourhood of 'Simon's belle-famille'.

Love from us all three
I am (do you recognize me?)

Yours as ever
D.B.

198. André Gide to Dorothy Bussy

220 rue Michelet
Algiers

10 October 44

Dear dear dear friend,

An occasion presents itself . . . I am given to hope that this letter will reach you soon;[1] but Nice these days seems further away from Algiers than does Paris – from which place, at last, I was able to have some news. Who led me to believe that the three of you had returned to London? . . . When shall I stop trembling for your safety? The skies over London were still very uncertain. And in Nice I picture you emaciated to the nth degree. I won't attempt to make you understand how dearly I want to see you – oh, not for a passing visit, but to live a long time with you. I wait for that as for the reward of too long an anticipation; I think of it constantly.

I dread finding in Paris (which in any case I can't return to without an *ordre d'appel* that I hope will arrive any day) nothing but troubles, problems, fatigue, and cause for sadness; I shouldn't like to stop there for more than a short time. I also dread the cold, which I have become ridiculously sensitive to, and am done in by the first gust of

[9] Jacques Heurgon and his wife Anne Desjardins lived in Algiers.

[1] There are no letters from either correspondent between 21 September 1943 and 8 October 1944.

north wind ... And toward what southern place could I escape? Even Nice, without heating, frightens me. Will the hotels have re-opened? First I must know whether it is true that you are still there ... Roger spoke of returning to Nice (letter from Figeac). I live in a state of the greatest uncertainty, and when I quit Algiers shall leave all my belongings here, should I have to return.

What news of your sisters –? with whom I expect you've been able to correspond. A thousand affectionate wishes to Simon and Janie. A fond and tender hug from

your
André Gide

199. André Gide to Dorothy Bussy

220 rue Michelet
Algiers

22 October 44

Dear friend,

You most likely (at least I hope so) received my letter at the same time I received your postcard. So long as the postal service is not entirely restored, it will be easier for me than it is for you to take advantage of certain people returning to France.

With beating heart, I read, reread, savoured, your blessed cartolina. I had been without news of you, and frightfully worried – as I was for those in Villars de Lans who were said to be in serious danger and threatened with 'reprisals'. They should be back in Paris by now. Pierre Herbart was able I think to drive Mme Théo and Andrée Vienot[1] there, also her mother and the two adopted children. We also feared for Mme Desjardins whom we had no news of. Finally, the day before yesterday, a letter from her. She had remained in Cérisi, which was occupied by the Germans, and just escaped the American bombardment that completely annihilated the little village, but spared the château which was liberated soon afterwards. No new cause for mourning among our friends.

Everything I hear about Paris dissuades me from returning right now. I'll try, instead, to bring the petite dame here; she endures the

---

[1] The daughter of Mme Mayrisch and widow of Pierre Viénot who had recently died in England while serving with de Gaulle.

cold almost as little as I. I therefore declined the offer of returning by plane which was made me – a bit late thanks to a certain malevolence at this end. I feel I have neither the heart nor strength to face the difficulties, worries, sadness that await me in Paris. I also believe that here I am of some comfort and support to Anne (Jacques is busy in Rome, at the Farnese Palace)[2] – at least, her kindness would persuade me that it is so, and persuades me to overlook the malevolence and caddishness of her two terrible elder children. Very trying! – Otherwise, I am well. My letter told you, I think, that I even worked, and wrote, last May–June, in a state of indescribable joy which I had believed I would never again experience, a *Thésée* I'd had my heart set on for a long time and which I almost despaired of ever carrying through. Since then, nothing more than a few very untimely pages of *Journal*, and, to fill the emptiness of my days, I have set myself to reading Latin again, with tremendous zeal.

Have I told you that the charming Raymond Mortimer has sent me from London, Hogg's *Memoirs of a Justified Sinner* (1824), certainly one of the most extraordinary books *I ever read*[3] – which you are probably familiar with. But how is it that this masterpiece is not more generally known?

I hope you will now be able to correspond with London. May you receive only good news from those dear to you!

The war is not yet over; we must tell ourselves that repeatedly. The initial exaltation of deliverance is followed by a distressing malaise, and . . . but what good talking about it? '*Happiness . . . not unmixed*', you say. I am nevertheless hopeful; but we shall still have a very severe period to endure.

Give Louis Gautier-Vignal my very fond wishes. As for Simon and Janie, embrace them both for me. Oh how sweet it would be to see you! to spend a good long time with you! When will it be possible? *Utinam . . .*[4]

With you, with all my heart. – Indefectibly yours,

André Gide

---

[2] The French embassy.
[3] Gide's preface (translated by D.B.) was published by The Gresset Press in England in 1947 with a new edition of the book before appearing in France with Dominique Aury's translation of Hogg's memoirs, *Confession d'un pécheur justifié* (Charlot, 1949).
[4] 'If only . . .'

200. Dorothy Bussy to André Gide

30 Oct. '44

Dear Gide,

At last a letter from you – the one in answer to my post card – one you wrote before that has not yet turned up but I expect it will. I am glad you are not thinking of going back to Paris just yet. It doesn't sound at all pleasant there. The excitements, the transports have died down and the inevitable reactions have set in. – and there is no coal, no gas, no wood. Mme Théo will be wise to join you – if she can. Here too things are not pleasant. People are starving and quarrelling and saying in a whisper, how much they prefer the English to the Americans, but that is only because the English are not here and the Americans are.

I have just had my first letter from England for more than a year and it brought me melancholy news, though long expected. My beloved eldest sister Elinor Rendel died last July. It is a very great loss to all of us and when we were in England her home was very much the centre of our lives. It made me feel for a time that if I never see England again I shall not miss much personal joy. But I don't think she herself had anything more to expect from life. As for me I have recovered from my dejection and still dream of going home. There have been no further losses among my family and friends. And even 51 Gordon Square is still intact and the warmth of maternal affection will still inhabit it.

Dear Gide. It is no use telling you that I am growing very old, that my hair and teeth are falling out, my eyes, my ears, my memory failing, that I hardly dare walk without a stick, that perhaps you wouldn't recognize me.[1] *But*! I prefer to think of you and your 'joie indicible'. As far as my experience goes, there can only be two causes of such a state – human love or Divine Grace. In your case I make my choice without much hesitation. Allez! Je ne vous en veux pas! But I admit I am more *sincerely* rejoiced that you should have written your *Thésée*. One of the moments at which you seemed to one at your most brilliant – and, for other reasons at your most lovable, was one afternoon in October 1938 (Munich) when I was resting in your 'chambre d'ami' Rue Vaneau, and you talked to me about *Thésée*.

---

[1] D.B. was then seventy-nine.

And I remember as we were going up in the lift together, for you had invited me to stay with you, you said 'Now I shall have you to myself!' What an illusion! For no sooner in at the door than I was pounced upon by Mme. Théo and carried off to be made comfortable in *her* 'chambre d'ami' and the only moment we had together was that afternoon when you talked about *Thésée* and I admired and liked you. There's a pinch of ash saved (for me) from the embers of the past.

Well I have had no 'joie indicible' to help me through these last two atrocious years . . . But I *have* had a help, in the shape of what has become for me a very serious and passionately interesting piece of work, and I think too it may possibly interest you. It is about the English language and English usage and is intended to help French students of English such as you were 30 years ago – who are cultivated and want to understand or appreciate *literary* English – so, you see, my public won't be very large. As a matter of fact though and without false modesty and I hope without undue vanity I think my book, which is in an unusual form, may be of interest to a good many people and even to English people themselves. However, this may all be self-deception. If however you show the smallest sign of interest in it, I shall soon send you my Introduction and Table of Contents, and whether you are interested or not, I shall eventually very earnestly ask for your help in revising and criticizing it – as a reward for *Hamlet*! By the way a few pages of *Hamlet* are still due. What are you doing about it?

I am longing to hear what Latin you have been reading – Poetry I expect, but that is too difficult for me, but I too have been reading it diligently and made one of the most pleasurable discoveries of my life – namely Cicero's letters to Atticus. Thrilling from every point of view, drama, *psychology*, modernity etc. etc. How wrong of all those highbrows at Pontigny to despise Cicero. I was deceived by them for a long time.

Dear Gide. I could go on talking to you for ever. You seem to me sometimes the only person I *can* talk to about *everything*.

Very friendly messages to Anne. I am very glad to have news of Jacques and Mme. Desjardins.

But what about those children? My blood runs cold!! J. and S. send you their fondest love.

Yours as usual

D.

201. Dorothy Bussy to André Gide

40 Rue Verdi

19 Nov. [1944]

Dearest Gide,

Your letter was very sweet to me. And what more is there for me to expect or desire, from you at any rate? Even the 'revoir' would add little and if it should never take place, I think I should depart satisfied. And there is one thing I desire more than that 'revoir' and that is to see Janie rescued from this God-forsaken town, where there is less and less I can do to help her, where there is no companionship, no possibility, no time for intellectual interest. I don't mind. I really don't for the present – mind getting old myself, but I hate to see her getting old. I long for her to have a rest from all her harrassing cares, to be comfortable, to be warm, to be able to paint and to read, to have companions and friends once more. To leave these dreary streets where we and she especially, have suffered, where we feel now in a desert island, impossible to move in any direction, where even letters, even now hardly ever reach us. And as a matter of fact, I see, no, I see only the dimmest and most distant prospect of escape or rescue. There are to my mind insurmountable difficulties between us and England. The promised land. Roger seems rather hesitating on the verge of coming back here rather than going to the Tertre, greatly damaged. It would mean an immense difference to us but I daren't urge it, hardly dare hope it, the food situation is so bad.

There! I ought not to sadden you with our woes, but I told you I should write you everything. And I know that almost everyone in the wide world is a great deal more miserable than we are. You too perhaps my dear? I have been anxious too about Catherine for some time past, not because of what people say about her, but because of what they don't say. The petite Dame's and Beth's letters to me seemed strangely to avoid mentioning her. What can she be up to? However, if the petite Dame and the Herbarts manage to get to Algiers, I shall be jealous, but still very glad that they should join you. You will all be happier.

Now to return to Latin literature! What a relief! But first you advise me to get Hogg's book from a bookseller or library. But one of the Gestapo's charming little acts before leaving the town was to go into every bookseller's shop and forcibly cart away all English books. Our Anglo-American lending library which I once showed you and which was really a very decent library of good English books old and modern, history, letters, fiction, works of reference (very good) was completely stripped, its shelves left empty, *seven thousand* volumes removed. Some people say all these books were burned. This is not certain but very likely. I had a long talk with Mr. Denny, the American librarian, whose work this library was and who devoted himself to it as a labour of love for the last 20 years or so. The library itself was founded in 1865. Altogether the book situation in Nice is very serious . . . a famine there too. Nothing new arrives, not that I want to read anything new, except *Thésée*. When? And everything old has gone. However, this summer I managed to get a school edition of Sallust and was reading it perhaps at the same time as you and with great enjoyment. But you had the advantage reading it 'sur place'. And no doubt you have all possible helps to a serious study at Algiers. I've nothing here. How I should like to have you as a schoolmaster for the *Eneid*. I know it very ill. Horace much better. I think we approach Cicero's letters from a different point of view. What I enjoyed in them, and intensely, was not the amusement of one or two letters here and there, 'recompensantes', but the characters, the psychology of Cicero, the whole dramatic and tragic situation. Cicero, torn between Pompey whom he loved and despised and Caesar whom he feared and admired, Cicero's weakness and mingled cowardice and courage, his love of life, his passion for letters, his passion for the Urbs, his affection for his ungrateful son and worse nephew and heartless brother, all the tangled web of his private and political life and over it all the impending doom of Caesar's assassination. What could be more thrilling than Cicero's describing the dinner he offered Caesar about three months before the final act – a good dinner, says he for it had to be of my best. And then we see the two great – each equally great in his own way – talking brilliantly, discussing letters and grammar, 'but nothing serious,' and each knowing what was in the other's heart. And then after the event that extraordinary scene at Brutus' house with his wife and mother and Cassius . . . and Cicero's bitter discovery that the tyrant had been killed but not tyranny. Oh! I must stop this tirade. But wind up with a quotation from a poem about Virgil. Do you know it? If not, I will send you some more of it for I think it is a good poem.

'All the charm of the Muses
Often flowering in a lonely word.'[1]

Forgive this almost unreadable scrawl.

Simon seems very well working as usual all the hours of daylight.
A telegram yesterday from London to say they are all well.

Farewell. Au revoir, my beloved.

Your,
D.

202. André Gide to Dorothy Bussy

Algiers

27 January 45

Very dear friend,

I languish in expectation of a letter from you and doubt whether
you've been receiving mine. Nothing from Roger either, since a brief
note announcing his arrival in Nice, with a promising 'letter follows'.
Sometimes the mail strays, is sometimes lost; certain letters arrive
after considerable delay. Such silences are less easily borne since the
postal service has supposedly been resumed.

I have given up waiting for Pierre Herbart. His departure has
encountered such obstacles! and travel has become so difficult that I
have come to the point of advising the petite dame against attempting
to join me here. Instead, I shall hasten my return to France, with,
perhaps, a stop over in Nice before going on to Paris. I have even
proposed to the petite dame a stay at the Adriatic, if the management
can provide two comfortable rooms with the possibility of heat, and
if the journey were not too exhausting. (I am well, but have no
resistance and tire very quickly.) You and Roger might look into the
first item (the Adriatic).

I had the joy of finding *Persuasion* at the English library; delved
into it immediately, but will only speak to you of it when I've
finished.

Received yesterday a telegram from Madame Brasillach: 'Beg you
to intervene in favor of clemency for my son Robert sentenced to
death.' The poor woman had undoubtedly learned of my efficacious

---

[1] From Tennyson's 'To Virgil'.

intervention in the case of Lucien Combelle who had long been my secretary. We held no opinion in common, but I esteemed him highly despite all our differences. I knew him to be incapable of a base or even simply 'interested' action. Which is what I explained as best I could in a letter to his lawyer, which he was able to read in the course of the trial, and which, he told me afterwards, saved the life of that poor boy who had been led astray by *Action Française*. For Brasillach I feel no compunction to do anything and shall leave his mother's petition unanswered.[1] I only know Brasillach from his articles, which in the past moved me to indignation. To pardon such poisoners is to harbour a public danger and set the stage for other Salengros.[2] I cannot approve Mauriac for having interceded in favour of the hateful Béraud. In three years' time we shall see him reappear, with sharper teeth and more malice in his heart. I hope at least that judicious laws affecting the press will manage to curb calumny (in the manner of judicious England).

Has Roger settled down to work again? Did he receive my letter welcoming him back to Nice (and containing a copy of my article on Benda?) If you knew how I hungered for the slightest word from you, you would not let me fast this way. Wholeheartedly with you. A thousand fondnesses for Simon and Janie.

André Gide

203. Dorothy Bussy to André Gide

Feb. 6th 45

Dearest Gide,

Your complaining(!) letter of Jan 27th reached me yesterday – in bed with a bad cold and temperature. Better today, but still in bed, so excuse handwriting, style, contents, etc. It is true that one's letters no matter where from often take an unaccountably long time to reach one. I have an idea though that all yours have come through to me. As for me I posted you a letter on Jan. 12th. (Had you not got that before you wrote on the 27th?) You wrote me one on the same day

[1] The petition, which was presented to General de Gaulle, was signed by sixty-one writers and artists including Valéry, Mauriac, Claudel, Camus, Colette, and Gabriel Marcel. Pardon was denied and Brasillach was executed on 6 February 1945 for collaborating with the enemy.

[2] Roger Salengro was Minister of the Interior in the government of the Front Populaire. A series of defamatory articles led to his suicide in 1936.

... the 12th which I got on the 20th and answered on the 23rd. I always think of you, you know, as being submerged with letters, so that I sometimes feel it's a positive charity not to write to you – especially as there's nothing cheerful to say, is there? Life here seems to get more difficult, more laborious, more Kafka-like every minute. Every single action is an exhausting struggle and in nine cases out of ten fails in its object.

Well, Janie went off to the Adriatic to ask about rooms for you. They were extremely polite and regretful but said it was absolutely impossible – three days ago the whole hotel had been rigorously requisitioned by the American army which apparently is going to descend upon us again to the tune of 15 divisions – but this is rumour – and what to do. God knows. At any rate when asked if he could recommend any other hotel the manager said he believed every decent hotel in Nice was in the same case as his. The military have also lately evolved another pleasant little regulation calculated to facilitate and enliven the existence of the Niçois. Nobody is allowed to quit or enter the department without a 'sauf-conduit' which takes on an average 9 or 10 days to get. Janie consulted Roger on the telephone as to your idea of coming *here* with the 'petite dame'. He considers it perfect madness. The difficulties of travel are practically insufferable, the difficulties of feeding oneself more and more crushing. Our ravitaillement is worse and worse managed than before. But perhaps this is a *slight* exaggeration. The only thing that can be said in favour of Nice is that the sun shines magnificently nearly all day and every day. But they take advantage of this to reduce our gas pressure so low that it is practically impossible to cook anything at all and to cut our electricity ruthlessly. We are only just saved from extinction by our Mirus.

Well, in spite of all this or because of all this we are embarked on a frenzied struggle to get to London. The devoted Vincent is evidently making desperate efforts on his side, helped by the no less devoted François.[1] We have received magnificent letters from various ministries saying that they desire our presence in London, and armed with them we all three spend hours wrestling with officials at the Préfecture, the Commissariat de Police, the British Consulate (oh Kafka!) who in their turn spend hours in writing 9 copies each of innumerable formulas (with 8 photographs attached) all this as the preliminaries for getting the necessary *ordres de mission* and *visas*

[1] François Walter was in London, working with the Comité de Libération.

de sortie et d'entrée. These *preliminaries* have, we are told, been accomplished and we may hope for a favourable answer, the French officials say, 'in two or three months', the English, 'in three to four'. That was last week. So you may judge! As a matter of fact however, it will do us no harm to postpone this alarming journey until weather conditions are more favourable. If however, we do manage to get off in a month or so, if this ferocious winter abates its furies, if you are still inclined to make a stopping place of Nice on the way to Paris, remember that when we have left Rue Verdi, it is entirely at your disposal! Two bed rooms, mine and Janie's for you and Mme. Théo. at your choice (Simon – jealous of I don't know what always locks his up when he goes away); a sufficient quantity of linen (poor stuff, mais que voulez-vous?), vaisselle, couverts, and more precious than anything very likely, the services of our priceless Rina. Our little sitting room which you know well, all too well, is singularly un-attractive, but the Mirus warms it and thanks to superhuman efforts by Simon, doesn't smoke. There are also two or three small electric heaters and a réchaud for boiling water. Our big drawing room's chiefly used now as a repository for potatoes and wood, but I fear not much of these articles will be left.

We have no intention whatever of letting the apartment so no hesitation on that ground is necessary. All our letters, M.S.S. auto-graphs, books, etc. will be left open to inspection or purloinment and we would lend it only to persons of umblemished virtue. We think you and the 'petite dame' may just come up to standard, but Roger doubts it! However we are willing to risk that much!

Dear Gide, it would be almost as harrowing to have you here without us, as for us to be at Rue Vaneau without you. Still con-venience mustn't be sacrificed to sentiment, and in any case, if it suited your convenience, it would be very soothing at the same time to our sentiments. As for getting *ordres de mission* that would pierce the Nice 'barrages' I don't doubt that you have enough 'influence', the two of you, to achieve that. Remember that Gaston Berger is 'Directeur régional de l'Information à Marseille', a powerful and important situation, and that he is much attached to us all. But you no doubt have all the powerful friends you want as far as that goes. Remember that March and April too may be very pleasant here and still highly unpleasant in Paris, and that you would certainly be doing a very good turn to Roger, who will soon be finding Nice as appalling a place as Figeac. . .

We had a very pleasant visit the other day from a young English officer called *Vernon*[2] who said he had much enjoyed meeting you in Tunis and that he had seen a good deal of Jacques Heurgon at Rome, to his great pleasure. He knew a great many of our personal friends in London, and we had a friendly talk about old times in Bloomsbury – quite refreshing!

It must be very agonizing to act as a Court of Appeal in the case of men condemned to death. But there is a great deal to be said it seems to me about all these condemned, not only on the condemnations themselves, but on the manner in which the trials are conducted. No publicity is given to them, no reports. What the accusations are and what the defense, it is hard to tell. There never seems to be a pretense of justice. Just a mere haphazard falling of vengeance. Sometimes, I doubt not, but who can tell? Public opinion, conducted by a decent press which should be our safeguard has been ruled out of courts. There isn't paper enough to give us an impartial account of any trial. A stroke of luck saves M. Combell and another M. Béraud.

None of this turns upon *facts* but on personal appreciation, highly dangerous, we have been taught to believe, in a court of law.

The Nice press is infamous, and it is practically all we see, occasionally le *Monde* which seems free enough in its criticism of high quarters.

Au revoir, dearest, your loving,

D.B.

204. Dorothy Bussy to André Gide

13 March '45

Dearest Gide,

It seems to me ages since I last wrote to you. Not that I don't think of you. The weather must be fine in Algiers now, so perhaps your cold is better. Here the weather is spring like. Flowers blooming everywhere. But the 'ravitaillement' is still very bad and the authorities say cheerfully that it is going to get worse.

Oh dear Gide, I don't feel a bit inclined to write to you tonight. Nothing is in my mind and heart but lamentations. It isn't only

[2] John Vernon (who was made a captain in 1944) visited the Bussy family frequently during 1944–5 when he was stationed in Nice. He had met Gide in North Africa through the Heurgons.

'ravitaillement' that is getting worse, but *everything*. Even what they call 'Victory' is horrible. One is filled with a kind of deadly nausea. The only thing to do is to try not to think. But when I write to you I seem obliged to think a little and I feel it very difficult – in fact impossible to write the contrary of what is in *my* mind and heart to *you* so it's best for the present not to write at all – better to wait till I am out of the Slough of Despond, which perhaps I may be one of these days. . .

A very kind affectionate letter from the Petite Dame this morning (March 17th) but I can't say it has helped me out of the Slough – rather on the contrary. But I won't tell her that. And it is only to you that I feel the need of being strictly truthful.

Your,
D.B.

205. André Gide to Dorothy Bussy

Algiers

25 April 45

Dear friend,

The weather is so lovely, the air so mild this morning that I join you again; besides, the letter I wrote yesterday could satisfy neither of us, since it spoke only of arrangements for your passing through Paris, and was intended to give you immediate reassurance. I was taken up by my correspondence and could give you no more than a few moments. But after answering six urgent letters, my mind is a little clearer. I even managed to enjoy a bit of Cicero.

But my dear friend, it's horribly difficult! . . . I think you must be much better up in Latin than I am. I should be incapable of understanding anything (in the letters to Atticus) without a facing translation to which I have continually to refer. I recognize that the very tone of the letters is moving, quite different from that taken by Cicero in *De Senectute* or in the orations. And then I feel that you're reading them (these letters) with me. I intend to read them all.

Had I really nothing to tell you of our trip? The only real joy I felt was through the petite dame,[1] for whom it was all new. For myself personally, it held no surprises. And not the smallest adventure! My best moments were spent in the company of Virgil.

[1] Gide had arranged to have Mme Théo 'abducted' and flown to Algiers.

Great disappointment at Biskra, where dates abound, at not being able to make the smallest shipment. Authorized for military personnel alone. My regret became keener still when I learned that Janie had such great need of agreeable nourishment, yet was so deprived of it. I hope she is now, nevertheless, completely recovered.

No, as I have already told you, the recent glorious events bring no more joy to me than they do to you. Dresden, Nuremberg, Cologne, in ruins! All that too was ours . . . And constantly I think of Berlin, of that surrounded population, with unbearable anguish. I keep telling myself: it was necessary; it is necessary. But it doesn't calm me. It's atrocious, quite simply . . . and deserved (which is hardly consoling!)

Have you read Mauriac's *Trois grands hommes devant Dieu* (Molière, Rousseau, Flaubert), 1930? Until yesterday I was un-familiar with the book. One of the most interesting, most meaningful, best written, and most exasperating by our friend (four of whose novels – which I can't manage to like – I have just read, one after another).

The opening of *Antoine et Cléopâtre* has been postponed for a few days, so I have no news of it yet.

Au revoir. Soon, I think. Affectionately,

André Gide

206. André Gide to Dorothy Bussy

Algiers

28 April 45

Dearest friend,

Our letters chase after one another; it's infuriating. Not one responds to the last written, but always to the preceding – which another soon comes to rectify. This morning I get one dated the 23rd, that renders quite useless what I wrote you the day before yesterday concerning lodging in Paris. With or without help from Stoisy or Simon's sister, don't be worried. And I shall try to precipitate our own return, since it happens that your trip is to be hastened. It would be nonsense to miss you. . .

Together with your letter, I received an exquisite one (oh, yours was exquisite, too!) from Roger, who speaks of you in the tenderest manner: 'I am deeply fond of her, and always increasingly so: she is a friend,' (the underlining is his) and it moves me a great deal to hear him say that. But he describes the three of you as being at the end of your resistance and 'skeletal'. I hope he is exaggerating and that I find a bit of flesh to hug. May you successfully endure the long, tiring trip which Roger worries about for you, as do I. May you also receive Miss Pell's package in time! No, I have received no letter from her.

I'm very worried about poor little Davet; fear that she has been placed in a very bad, and false, situation, and I tremble when I read in the papers that the Germans have set fire to I forget which 'workers' camp. Shall we ever see her again? Her distress, doubtless, is terrible; and she must think herself forgotten . . . What a nightmare!

I'm delighted by what you say about Virgil. I go on reading him with ever increasing satisfaction. But now I have dropped Book IV (which is where I am – my fourth reading) to take up again with you, this very morning, the Laocoön episode. Despite all my efforts, I'm having trouble taking a fancy to Cicero. Pleased you found the *Aeneid* '*much easier and more amusing than expected*'. His management of the story I find to be of the most accomplished artistry . . . the suspension of interest, the intervention of the gods, the proportion of all the elements, the involvement of the landscapes – I read it all like an adventure novel, and know none that is more beautiful. And what verse! (Oh do learn to scan it!) Beside that, Ovid, whom I am also reading, strikes me as a deflated '*couille molle*' (Sorry!)

The petite dame sends her best wishes, and I embrace you fondly.

Yours,
André Gide

Your telegram has just arrived. Your letter, mailed the same day, preceded it!

207. Dorothy Bussy to André Gide

Address still
51 Gordon Square

July 16th [1945]

Dearest

I find the greatest difficulty in writing to you. I haven't any idea why.

Nothing to say? There is heaps to say, of course, as usual. I think in reality I am still emotionally tired and writing to you – even on the

driest subject seems always to come perilously near making a call –
even a distant call – on the emotions – (I don't mean yours but mine.)

Where are you? Simon told me you had been at Cuverville.[1] There
you are! How think of that without emotion? What are you doing?
Are you able to work yet? Are you free yet from your crowds of
friends – and victims, I called them in my last letter? But of course it is
you who are the victim. Dear Gide, you see how I am trying to avoid
anything real. Reality exhausts me.

England, from which I have been absent so long, interests me
profoundly. I try to realise what it has gone through, in what way it
has changed. Perhaps only a temporary change. Perhaps it is only
because I am old or French & am supposed to have suffered starvation, that everyone is extraordinarily kind and attentive and unselfish
– Bus conductors, the travellers in buses and trains and tubes,
policemen of course, but food officials too and the ladies in this kind
of pension where I am staying (generally – formerly – so unbearable),
my sisters of course, my young nephews & nieces, my acquaintances,
the people one knocks up against in the street. But no, this is not an
illusion, it is the very spirit of fraternity, born of that terrible time of
blitz & 'doodlebags' to which people will hardly allude except with a
smile, of that time too of a nation's, of a people's *unity*. I hadn't
realised it. It's really terrific power. But then only the deadliest
danger and agony can evoke it. London's ruins which are now a
garden of grass and wild flowers, green & pink and yellow, springing
of their own accord in the wastes.

In spite of food and friendship Janie and I are getting depressed at
the difficulty of getting Simon over. He himself talks always of your
& the petite dame's kindness but . . . you can finish the sentence
yourself. And we are still hopeful all the same that we shall eventually
succeed. Then we ourselves are in considerable difficulties about
lodging ourselves. It is almost impossible to get service in London or
to get rooms.

More people want to lodge in 51 Gordon Square than there is
accommodation available for them. So I have gone away to stay in a
kind of boarding house in the country, but I hope it won't be for long,
though I have time here to return to the *Aeneid*.

I saw our English publisher[2] the other day who wants to bring out,

---

[1] Due to difficulty in obtaining a visa, Simon remained behind at rue Vaneau with
Gide and the petite dame.
[2] Secker & Warburg.

I gather, a re-edition of the English translations of your works. I said decidedly I would not undertake the *Journal*, but asked him to let me know any other developments. He said he had seen 'Blanche' Knopf a day or two before who had recently seen you in Paris. So we are again in her clutches! A mistake, I think, of Schiffrin's.[3] *Then* would have been the time to break with her.

It is most frightfully difficult to keep in touch with France here. No French papers that are not a week old. All English papers seem carefully to conceal everything we want to know. In private conversation, great sympathy & affection is expressed for everything French – with one exception. The General has bitterly and irretrievably alienated from himself English public and private feeling. This seems to be a matter more of *manners* than of anything more serious. A very great pity. And it dates from the first days. I was quite unaware of it.

Two more letters from Davet. The first letter I wrote her was very severe. But she has taken my severity in good part & admits it was deserved.

I had wondered whether it would be a good thing to publish her letters from Iena. (*I* should have expurgated them!) But she tells me that she is following your advice & has begun an account of her experiences.[4] Much better.

Have you said good-bye to Valéry?[5] Alas! But to have known him a little and, for a week, almost intimately, is one of the million things I owe to you. I saw him for the first time at Mme. Lucien Muhlfeld's when you took me once to tea.

After all, it is not so difficult to write to you as I have been fearing.

Your ever devoted
D.B.

208. André Gide to Dorothy Bussy

Mont Dore

16 August 45

Dear dear friend,

Your good letter at once alarms and reassures me . . . somewhat. You are paying today the accumulated interest on the fatigue and

---

[3] Jacques Schiffrin had been living in New York since the beginning of the war. He was the publisher of Gide's *Hamlet* (Jacques Schiffrin-Pantheon Books, 1944).

[4] These were never published.

[5] Paul Valéry had died on 20 July.

privation you suffered in Nice. The interest? I should say (with a dreadful pun) the *'usure'*.[1] I wish at least that you would feel my thoughts were constantly with you; there is nothing here to divert them from you. Pleasant as our last talks were, there were still many things I wanted to say, this in particular: that I have not been a single day without a certain brief note from you, carried in my wallet like a talisman and which I no longer needed to read because I knew it 'by heart' – and which you have perhaps forgotten. It is dated simple *'Wednesday evening'* before my departure for Tunisia. *'Tear this into a thousand pieces and drop them in the sea'* you said in the last line. You won't resent me for not having had the heart, will you.

Quickly, in order not to miss the next post, I embrace you

Very tenderly,
André Gide

209. André Gide to Dorothy Bussy

Permanent address:
c/o Légation française,
Cairo

Cataract Hotel, Assouan

22 January 46

Dear friend,

Your letter (of 6 December) is the only one which Mme Théo., recognizing your handwriting (and with a perfect sense of priorities), has forwarded to me; the only one, among the others which, she tells me, by regular mail should reach me I don't know when. In the meantime, you have received, I hope, an insignificant note from me, postmarked Luxor (and giving you the Chevriers' cordial remembrances). Age, accumulated fatigue, the climate, everything here reduces me to <u>insignificance</u>. I rummage about in my brain without discovering anything *'worth mentioning'*. This lecture which I shall be asked to give in Cairo terrifies me. I have requested that it be postponed until February, the end of February. They're expecting it; they've announced it . . . and nothing is written. I have told myself that I shall speak extempore – yet I fear drawing a blank, finding nothing to say. Don't know how I'll be able to manage it . . . Meanwhile, I think about it as little as possible. To tell the truth, I don't think about anything. The days go by, ineffably empty – spent

---

[1] *Usure* means both 'wear' and 'usury'.

I don't know how – in growing old, in waiting for the return of clement weather, of the seasonal return of life ... Your letter is exquisite ... and absurd. My life is only near you, with you – and all your amiable pessimism doesn't prevent you from knowing it.

I embrace you tenderly,
André Gide

210. Dorothy Bussy to André Gide

51 Gordon Square W.C.1

10th Feb. 1946

Dearest Gide,

Your letter from Assouan (Jan. 26th) reached me on Feb. 3rd (I think). I was in the middle of influenza. We have all had it with the rest of London. Not badly but very unpleasant, especially when your 'help' is one of the victims too and one has to take it in turns to do the housework, the shopping, the cooking and the nursery. Fortunately we were only in bed one at a time. However, if I go on complaining there would be nothing else in my letter – only it wouldn't be about food, over which the English are making the most ridiculous and ungrateful fuss.

Well, Gallimard's contract[1] has at last arrived – thanks, no doubt, to the efforts of a great many friends, chiefly yours. And whatever my sins I don't think ingratitude is one of them. So for your introduction to your cousin Edouard I send my best thanks. Indeed I haven't at all rejected any proposal that may eventually come from him, answered him very politely and given him all the information I could about the English translation and rights. And my morals don't go so far as refusing a profitable job even if it involves countenancing the impiety of not allowing Gertrude to be blind. After all that's your look out. But I'm very glad that Beth exaggerated the story.[2]

Now, dear Gide, do tell me the *truth* about *Thésée*. What is there in it so different from the style of all your other books that makes it not my 'affaire'? You may, not unnaturally perhaps, want a change in the style of your translator. You may perhaps think that, considering my age and years of wear and tear, my capacity has in all

[1] For *Fifty Nursery Rhymes*, which was not published until 1951.
[2] Concerning the film version of *La Symphonie pastorale*, produced by the Société Gibé, of which Edouard Gide was a director.

probability diminished. You may perhaps have had complaints of
my past work. All those things I could understand, but I can't
understand that *Thésée* is not my affair. Never mind. I'll accept that.
What I find it hard to accept is that you should give it to another
translator without consulting me. I am willing to be modest about
my talents as a translator, or perhaps I should say my talents as a
writer. But I do not believe that a more talented writer would
necessarily be a better translator. I do believe, however, that if you
might possibly find a better translator than me, you will not find a
better judge of translation than me. Especially translation from the
French which I think I know better than most English people, and
from you, whose works I have such a long experience of. The fact is,
as perhaps you are guessing, I have an uneasy suspicion that you have
once again fallen into the toils of Mrs. Knopf. . . that Mrs Bradley[3] is
enraged that I never answered her kind letter offering to act as an
agent for me on procuring the rights of translating your works,
introducing and recommending me to you. You know that I have the
greatest mistrust of Mrs. K. from every point of view. I may be too
severe in some of my harsher opinions of her but I am certainly not
wrong in thinking that I am a better judge of English prose than she
is. Let me know whom you have chosen as translator of *Thésée* and
upon what grounds. If you ask me I will do my very best to get you a
good one or to give you a sincere and impartial opinion of anything
you may show me.

Morgan Forster is in the very centre, the heart's core of Bloomsbury. The intimate friend of many of my intimate friends, though I
barely know him personally. The *Voyage to India* [*sic*] has been on
my shelves for about 20 years. He never struck me, or I think anyone
else, as being a writer of difficult English. I wonder what you mean.
But he is certainly a novelist of mark.

After these months of finding my way about post-war literary
England, I have come to the conclusion that perhaps the most shining
light that has emerged is Cyril Connolly. Do you know him? He is a
brilliant writer and a very pleasing critic and as cultured as it's
possible to be. Hasn't written much so far.
The Unquiet Grave by Palinurus, (he knows Virgil).
The Condemned Playground, (a book of Essays which I enjoyed
greatly.)

[3] Jenny Bradley, the wife of literary agent William Aspenwall Bradley, who
assumed direction of the agency after her husband's death.

The day I got your letter I happened to be reading in it an Essay on *Les Faux Monnayeurs* (not very good) but I was pleased that he recommended it to English readers and said, 'It is very well translated.'

Dear Gide, I am sorry you are passing through a Slough of Despond. I have had a few months of it too, but am determined not to leave my bones in it. Better indifference than despondency. And now I am looking forward to a good deal of work in polishing *Nursery Rhymes*. I am truly delighted that they are to come out under the dear letters N.R.F. though extremely astonished.

Dear Gide. Do you really hope we shall meet again? Really meet again? You must get out of your Slough of Despond then and I will make another scramble up and away from the shores of Indifference.

Yr. loving
D.B.

211. Dorothy Bussy to André Gide

11th May '46

Beloved Gide,

Your last letter reached me five minutes after I had posted my last to you. I am very much grieved you have caught one of your horrid colds again and hope to goodness it is better by now.

And then Roger Senhouse – your – or rather Mrs. Knopf's English co-editor of your books – rang me up yesterday and said 'Miss Enid McLeod[1] has just told me that Gide is coming to London to give a lecture at the French Institute. Is it true?' (I don't know why I am supposed to know.) I answered that I didn't know but I should be rather surprised if it were. I suppose it means that the British Council, of which Miss McLeod is an influential member, has invited you. I really believe you would tell me if you had accepted!

Thank you for your Aragon cutting.[2] But I can't think what you are complaining of! M. Lalou has after all succeeded in publishing his Anthology. If you succeeded in preventing M. Aragon from

---

[1] The friend of 'Whity' and Elisabeth, Enid McLeod was director of the British Council and attachée at the British embassy in Paris. She is the translator of Colette and Supervielle, and the biographer of Héloïse, Charles d'Orléans, and Christine de Pisan.

[2] Of a review of René Lalou's anthology *Les Plus beaux poèmes français* (in *Lettres Françaises*, 3 April 1946, p. 5) in which Louis Aragon objects to inclusion in the collection of three poems by Charles Maurras, who had received a life sentence for collaborating with the enemy.

publishing his foolish article, *that* would be a case of interference in the liberty of the press. *My* idea of the liberty of the press is that *both* M. Aragon and M. Lalou should be allowed to publish their opinions. If *either* of them (or even you) accuse each other of criminal acts punishable by law let them then, and their publisher, be punished and fined after a fair trial.

If Aragon really asked for your head, bring an action against him!! As a matter of fact do you really think that Aragon's idiotic attack will do anybody any harm except Aragon himself? And has not just this excessive violence actually been the reason of the Communist set back which is obvious in the vote on the referendum? (And isn't it true that Maurras' poem which A. gets so excited about is really very like some of his own late and charming verses?) No, my dear. I really don't think there is the smallest chance of your ending your days in Ste. Pelagia.[3] You are after all, even by your own showing, a more popular author than Monsieur if not Mme. Aragon.[4]

There is here a 'crise de traducteurs' – Janie and I are perpetually being asked to translate French books and we steadily refuse. We think it is high time to strike, like everybody else, for better pay. Hermine Priestman – Auguste Bréal's daughter is one of the chief personages in the French section of the B.B.C. She is bilingual and very clever. They submit all the translations of French texts to her and she says that the average is deplorably poor. People are not paid enough to spend the necessary time on this very expert work. I will not translate your *Thésée* but this is not my reason. I confess I should have liked to. I should have been proud to. But now I know your reason – I believe you – I can't.[5] And now I am going to say something very serious. I realise at last that I have been one of the greatest disappointments of your life. You would have liked (for sentimental not rational reasons) to be translated into English by a young man – especially *les Nourritures*, especially *Si le Grain ne Meurt*, especially *Thésée*.

This is what you really mean in your subconscious at any rate, by your 'voix grave'. How can you, who pride yourself particularly in

[3] A Paris prison that had been demolished in 1899.
[4] The novelist Elsa Triolet.
[5] On 1 May Gide had written: 'Dear friend, you are Absurd and Ridiculous when you speak of the aforementioned *Thésée*. I have entrusted the translation of that masterpiece to no one, and your amiable jealousy is totally wasted. It simply seemed to me that a woman's vocal chords were inappropriate for so deep a voice. But be assured there is still time to prove me wrong.' (*Theseus*, translated by John Russell, was first published in 1948 by Horizon.)

imitating a woman's, a young girl's voice, think that the opposite impersonation, especially in a translator who has nothing to invent, is impossible. Tell me that a woman is incapable of translating a good book, that there are [*sic*] a much greater choice of good men writers than women and therefore a greater choice of good translators and I will admit and in the latter case agree with you. On the other hand I will tell you that the infinite patience and conscientiousness and fidelity that is necessary in a translator is more often found among women. And moreover a man who is more gifted than a woman is less likely to devote himself to the subordinate task of translating. He wants as a rule to work for *himself*.

But I don't suppose you want a particularly bass voice for Descartes[6] (is a philosopher necessary?) and I will undertake him with pleasure. And at any rate I hope you'll send me the Beyrouth lecture.

It is nearly 1 a.m. and I must go to bed. I don't think you need take my jealousy of your secretary seriously enough to let it interfere with your pleasure in writing to me – as you threaten in your last letter.

Will you tell Gallimard that the foreign correspondents of the B.B.C. send on an average 100 letters a month imploring them to recommend an English grammar, and they have promised to recommend mine and give readings from it. But he'd better look out or they'll be bringing out one of their own – and that would be a great pity.

Oh! You'll never get through all this! My best love to the Petite Dame. A year ago we were staying with her – and you.

Your
D.

212. André Gide to Dorothy Bussy

22 June 46

Dear friend,

Someone informed me yesterday, in an off-hand manner, of something very disconcerting, which I refused to believe but which he assures me is indisputable: the days are beginning to grow shorter. It seems there is nothing to be done about it. Opposition would be

---

[6] Gide had asked D.B. to translate a short piece on Descartes for one of the English journals.

futile. We shall have had no spring. It rains everywhere without stopping, I think in London as much and as hard as in Paris. Nevertheless, tomorrow morning I take the train to Brussels where on Monday I am to address the young barristers' association, or, more exactly, read my Beyrouth lecture. I shall be back on Wednesday, n'sh'Allah! Between now and then I shall have no time to write to you, which is why I am replying quickly to your excellent letter of 17th June. No, I'm hardly in the mood, nor have I strength enough, to reply to entreaties from London; I cannot, could not, decline them totally and categorically, as I do those from Brussels . . . Furthermore, since it would necessitate leaving from Paris (plane or train), there would still be time to change my mind when I return from Belgium. But I have . . .

– no possibility of going on – Continuous interruption . . .

Soon.

Tenderly yours,
André Gide

213. Dorothy Bussy to André Gide

29th June '46

Dearest Gide,

Your funny letter about your 'consternant' meteorological discoveries amused us very much. The weather is atrocious here too and doesn't seem much better in the Midi. I had a nice letter from Beth a few days ago telling me about Catherine. I am glad to feel that this turn of events has made her so happy – and you too, she says. Beth says too they are going to ask Simon to be 'témoin' at the marriage.[1] This will flatter and please him very much, as long as this post doesn't entail any religious performances. You told me the young man's family was Catholic and I believe Catherine herself was rather inclined that way herself once upon a time.

Nothing sensational has happened lately to me personally – except receiving from Zézette Charlie's book on Benjamin Constant.[2] You can hardly call this sensational, but I am reading it with extreme interest and have temporarily abandoned poor Dido. It seems to be her fate!

[1] Catherine Gide and Jean Lambert were married in August 1946.
[2] *Grandeur et misère de Benjamin Constant* (Paris, Corrêa, 1946).

I really think Charlie is sometimes very good. He has got of course a subject admirably suited to him, and it seems to me he treats it admirably. There is a great deal in it that is new to me, and he very rarely irritates me. But the subject, perhaps, interests you less than it does Charlie and me? I wonder. Dear Gide forgive this very dull letter. I console myself by saying that if I had been as brilliant as Mme de Staël you would have probably liked me less. . . ?

Yours ever
D.B.

Good news from Simon. Will you be going to Cabris for C.'s wedding?

214. Dorothy Bussy to André Gide

[July 1946]

Dear Gide, your last letter was exquisitely flattering and made me smile as all flattery should. Particularly pleasant too because you incited the beloved Roger to take part in it. But as you rightly guess I highly disapprove of both your attitudes towards my misjudged sex of which I am not at all an exceptional member.

Joking apart, almost my deepest impression in this return after six years absence to my native land is the magnificent development which the improvement of their position has brought to English women. Seriously I don't think this is an illusion. Responsibility has been given them and a very near approach to equality. My admiration for the way in which they have borne the frightful test of these last terrible years is unbounded and the virtues they have displayed are those which men used to claim as exclusively their own. You and Roger belong to the generation who believed that women were constitutionally unfitted to drive motor cars. You, who believe in progress should open your eyes and see what changes may be worked in the constitutions of slave populations by opportunity and education – just beginning to be allowed to women. But in reality I think that Englishwomen, though no more capable of development than their continental sisters, have had one great advantage. For about the last 80 years or so they have learnt that there are two million more women than men in their country. That two million women, especially of the upper bourgeoisie, must not look forward to marriage. They need no longer wait upon the tastes of men to secure a livelihood. They must look elsewhere for a livelihood. They need no longer think it a virtue to stifle their own personalities and inclinations. They need no longer assume qualities and charms they don't possess to please their masters. And strange to say and very surprising, they have discovered that very often their masters prefer it too. There! You have brought upon yourself this feminist elucu-bration. Tant pis!

I believe Mr. Shawe-Taylor is going to send you proofs of the Poussin translation.[1] I don't think you need bother about them. Again tant pis. But ask Davet to send them back as soon as possible.

What a thought to go to sleep with (for I, I am ashamed to say, sleep very well as a rule) that you too think of me often 'with the natural inclination of heart and mind'. With that thought I almost grudge going to sleep.

P.S. Enid's flourish was, as I suspected, a mere flourish. She has admitted it.

Your,
D.B.

215. André Gide to Dorothy Bussy

22 July 46

Very dear friend,

The news from London is hardly reassuring and I worry a good deal for you. I picture you feeding yourself even less well than you managed to do in Nice in war time, and with even greater difficulty. May John Strachey's ingenuity lead England rapidly toward some measure of ease![1] and may you endure this period of terrible scarcity without suffering too much. I am beginning to think that Simon at the rue Verdi is better off than you – and I myself am almost embarrassed to be in want of so few things here . . . I mean material things, for as to the rest, this solitude is quite hard for me to bear, especially since Roger left Paris. But I am too busy, too harassed by numerous trifling little tasks to find the time to be sad; besides which, you know that melancholy is not my forte. Nevertheless I think of

[1] The editor, Desmond Shawe-Taylor. The proofs are of D.B.'s translation of the preface which Gide had written for *Poussin* (Paris, au Divan, 1945).

LETTER 215

[1] John Strachey had recently been named Minister of Food.

you very often and of the time we shall be together . . . and find
nothing to say to each other! . . .

23 July

Interrupted yesterday. Endless solicitations, enough to drive one
mad. This morning I am to *luncher* at the Heurgons with Jean
Schlum. and A. Maurois, back from America. A few months ago he
would have got himself torn to pieces; but it seems that resentment is
calming down. Aragon's hateful wrath makes him odious to nearly
everyone, even to those of his own party (which has grown more and
more weak and discredited). People are beginning to realize
. . . I lack the time to develop my thought. Just enough to embrace
you fondly.

André Gide

216. Dorothy Bussy to André Gide

51 Gordon Square W.C.1

26th July '46

Beloved Gide,

Two letters of yours to answer and the text of the preface to
Hogg's book to acknowledge. I will give Shawe-Taylor the message
that you would like me to do the translation, and there's no need for
you to write. He suggests I should send you the proofs of the Poussin
but I don't think I will, I don't suppose you could do much about it
even if you wanted to. To be really improved, it would want an hour
or two's collaboration such as we used to have sometimes in the old
days – but there's obviously no chance of that.

Janie and I laughed at your concern for our food. We have *masses*
to eat! The English who complain don't know what it is to be really
short. We – everybody – have at least ½ a litre of milk every day,
bacon, a good allowance of butter and fat, plenty of sugar, meat 3 or
4 times a week, unlimited heaps of fish, plenty of jam, chocolate, very
good tea, not bad coffee, biscuits, potatoes, etc. etc. etc. It is the
anti-labour newspapers who have got up this scandalous racket
about starving England. We are not very good cooks here and 'ces
Messieurs' after a tour abroad where they have fed in first class Paris
restaurants on black market produce, come back and compare it
with the meals provided by their unfortunate wives who are harassed
to death with housework. All this because bread is rationed! A good

job too. If you had seen the 'ordures' – the pails put in the streets to be filled for pigs and choked with untouched loaves. A frightful sight!

The rationing is no doubt not yet very well organized by Cousin John and the bakers are furious at having to cut off 'coupons' and weigh bread which all of *us* had to do for four or five long years. No. The fact is everyone is cross and tired, sick to death of intolerable bureaucracy, and a real scarcity of everything *except* food.

Janie has had to spend hours in queues lately – not for food, but for passports, visas, permits, tickets, etc. and comes home exhausted by struggling with innumerable officials who are still far too few and are ignorant of their jobs, which appear totally useless. Enough! (But even [with] these I feel we have nothing to complain of, compared with France and the continent. We have good comfortable punctual trains. Amusements easy to get to. Good omnibus and taxi service. The English have no right to complain and I think most of them realise it.)

I enjoyed my week's stay with the Mirrlees. I shall not enjoy my three weeks in the country with the Dick Rendels so much – though they are all very nice and kind and Dick excellent company, but I'm afraid he won't be there.

I like to think you will be seeing Simon. Janie too, I hope. I am very glad too he is going to be Catherine's 'témoin'. I hope we shall get to know the young couple.

You will be a fine 'family reunion'. (T. S. Eliot wrote a play with this title.) I hope to hear all about it – though not from you I fear. Simon is not an extra good reporter but if Janie is allowed in, she would be.

My love and blessing to Catherine. Love too to the Petite Dame and to Beth and amitiés to Pierre. What to you? You may choose.

Yr.

D.

217. Dorothy Bussy to André Gide

Owley
Wittersham
Kent

22d Aug. 1946

Dearest Gide – Mon vieil ami

I haven't yet thanked you for your *Thésée* which I got many days –

if not weeks – ago, just before Janie left for Nice and I moved down here.

I read it once very hastily, as usual, and, after a first reading – and very often after many more than that, didn't understand it in the least. I understood however why you didn't want to offer it to me to translate. You were quite right. It isn't the tone of voice (I think) nor the language that is too masculine for me to find words for – it is the spirit that I don't like or, more probably, don't understand.

I don't like your *Thésée*. I don't want the coming generations to learn and follow his lesson. So, Hitler might have advised and written, if Hitler had known how to write, which, fortunately, he didn't.

By some curious chance, I have lately found myself in circumstances where there was nothing whatever for me to do but to re-read *L'Immoraliste*. I was obliged to. How strange! I had forgotten it, forgotten how extraordinarily beautiful it is, how every sentence is a kind of divine music, something the kind of pleasure, I imagine, that you have in listening to Mozart. Teaching? What care I for teaching? It is '*délectation*' I want. At the same time in soberer moments a part of us still wants to understand. And there your preface to a later edition gave me some help. 'Nul ne me sut gré de l'indignation qu'il ressentait contre mon héros; cette indignation, il semblait qu'on la ressentît malgré moi; de Michel elle débordait sur moi-même; pour un peu l'on voulait me confondre avec lui.'[1]

So, I need not confound you with Thésée – or think that you entirely approve his lesson. In fact, is not that shown by the dreadful punishment he suffers, in the destruction (due to himself alone) of Hippolytus, the younger generation for whom he had toiled and fought and laboured? To whom does he leave his teaching and his example? To a youth whom that very teaching has destroyed.

But Thésée's misogyny (and you pretend that he is *not* a misogynist!) I find very hard to forgive and almost impossible not to impute to you. Only two women in his world – one, an intolerable bore because she likes poetry and of course deserves to be abandoned, the other, with the only attraction of swinging indecently, has no qualities but the inherited lusts of a particularly lustful family. One might have thought that Oedipus might have given you, if not Thésée

[1] 'No one was grateful to me for the indignation which he felt against my hero; it was as though one felt that indignation in spite of me; from Michel it overflowed on to myself; one nearly came to confusing me with him.'

himself, an opportunity for mentioning an exception to this general view of the female race. But no! The fruit of his incest has been merely two infamous sons. He forgets that he ever had a daughter!

Dear Gide. It won't do. You will never build up a new world by simply scratching out the greater part of mankind. Try at any rate to make use of it.

But perhaps, after all, these are the very lessons you wish to convey to the succeeding generations and it is only my perversity which misinterprets you. (I have not seen a single review of *Thésée*. I should like to. Nor spoken to a single person who has read it – not even Janie. My remarks are uninfluenced by anyone.

Unadulterated
D.B.

P.S. Another letter soon. I must get this off my chest.

218. Dorothy Bussy to André Gide

40 Rue Verdi

Oct. 29th, 1946

Dearest Gide,

Just a line to tell you that I have come out of my state of '*euphorie*' as senselessly, I expect, as I got into it. The atmosphere of Nice, in spite of sun, is too overpowering. I am back again in those frightful war years; every step, every glance, every object reminds me of that hideous time – Solitude, fear, horror. You, my best friend, absent, or if not absent, worse – alienated. I know you are unconscious of this and would – which, of course, made it worse – deny it. But there it was, as plain as daylight for everyone to see – too much occupied with your private hopes and disappointments to be aware of ordinary friends. It was better when you were away in Tunis. But then came the nightmare of the occupation, growing fear, growing starvation, growing despair. And we were the people, no doubt, least to be pitied in the whole affair. But I can't forget it, as I did more or less in England. I miss my brothers and sisters very much, and my friends, and intelligent conversation, and life, all the same, in the streets, and respectable activity about one. There is nothing of all that here. Nice is a horrible town. And the worst of it is that I know Janie is feeling the same. Her youth – hardly any left – and talents completely wasted.

Simon, to be sure, is, I think, more or less happy, painting away as ardently as ever, with no one to look at his work or take the smallest interest in it – nor any hope that any one ever will.

Well, the only thing for me to do is to give English lessons to three nice little girls who are quite incapable of understanding a single thing that I might teach them. Waste again!

This letter is called a 'grouse' in English slang.

Will you please give my best souvenirs to Mme. Davet and tell her the cake and the sweets were delicious, and thank her again from me and Janie.

No dear Gide, I don't feel a bit alienated from you now and you must take this grousing letter as a proof that I feel we are real friends now and forever.

Your
D. B.

219. André Gide to Dorothy Bussy

1st November 46

Very dear friend,

I don't know what oasis of friendship awaits us on the other side, but the winter months are going to be hard to endure. Your good but sad letter yesterday was sufficient, alas, to convince me of it. And I was foolish enough to be overjoyed by your return to Nice! I hope at least that friend Roger will join you soon; you can console each other ... Here occupations and preoccupations of all sorts dispel the tedium. The faithful Marguerite last week left the petite dame (not definitively I hope), and I sense that she has suddenly grown older, shrunken. She says she is too tired to take her meals in a restaurant and finds the means to feed herself with I'm not sure what – very inadequately I'm afraid. Every morning I light her fire beside which she huddles all day long. I'm planning to take her to Brussels for a week; we leave together on the 4th or 5th. I shall take some work (?) so as not to die of boredom at the hotel, then return to tend, with Barrault, to the staging of the *Procès*.[1]

---

[1] Gide and Barrault had collaborated on the dramatic adaptation of Kafka's novel, *The Trial*.

No sooner had you left than I wanted to write and tell you again what I'd managed to express so poorly in our last conversation: I think you do not fully realize, modest as you are and as I like you, what you have been for me – always, and more and more. Hang on, despite troubles, tedium, disgust, and sadness – for the love of your faithful friend

André Gide

220. André Gide to Dorothy Bussy

Brussels

9 Nov. 46

Very dear friend,

Here we encounter cold, fog, lugubrious weather, and I continue to be haunted by the plaintiveness of your last letter. Yes, these winter months are going to be painful, hard to get through . . . and as I was about to leave Paris the day before yesterday, bad news of you from Roger . . .[1] We set about immediately to find that remedy you require and which cannot be found in Nice. You must have received it twice, from Jean Schlumberger and from Yvonne de Lestrange, who both had been alerted. Is it in fact <u>that</u> you wanted? May those mysterious candy drops have a salutory – and immediate – effect.

As soon as I am away from Paris and its constant (and exhausting) excitation, I feel a frightful weight of accumulated fatigue crash down upon me. I had planned to discharge a good deal of back work here, but drag about in a state of torpor, without curiosity for anything, nearly incapable of effort. I tell myself that some little virtue might yet be made of our coupled deficiencies – and am grieved to think you are so far away . . . Rarely have I felt so deprived by your absence. If only you could draw a little comfort from that avowal! and from sensing that I am more deeply than ever your friend

André Gide

Mme Théo, in Brussels, feels like a fish in water; all young again – it's marvellous.

We return to the Vaneau on the 14th.

[1] D.B. was suffering from vertigo.

221. André Gide to Dorothy Bussy

25 Jan. 47

Dear friend,

The day after my arrival in Geneva, a telegram from Elisabeth informed me of Mme Mayrisch's death[1] and of her (Elisabeth's) departure for Cabris. Was she able to stop and see you on her way? . . .

How many useless torments are brought to an end by that lamentable death! How much terrible anguish! You may have glimpsed some of it, may even have suffered as a result of it. I remember two conversations with that poor, proud, possessed woman where really I drew back terrified by the discovery of such an inner hell. Everything in her grated, was discordant. She could only find rest and calm in death . . .

I hope Elisabeth will not remain too long in the south, for Mme Théo must feel very much alone . . .

Geneva is lugubrious. An icy wind blows through it. The food is very poor. But I am learning to sleep again, which for me is enormous, and will soon permit me to return to work.

Nothing else to tell you today, '*absolutely nothing*' as Lytton used to say – but I embrace you fondly.

A.G.

222. Dorothy Bussy to André Gide

40 Rue Verdi

28th Jan. '47

Dear Gide,

I was glad to get your letter from Geneva. Your funeral oration for poor Mme. M. was pretty terrible. I myself only knew her superficially and superficially thought her very charming, elegant, graceful, and . . . harmonious! She came to see us once or twice in London. Perhaps she was one of those people – there are many of them – who are better when they are away from their own belongings. Elisabeth telephoned to us from the Messuguière but we didn't see her. She told

---

[1] She died at Cabris on 19 January.

us of their plans, the ceremony at Colpach and that she was going to pick up the petite dame in Paris and do the journey with her. Since when this awful weather has come on and I have been feeling very anxious about them. How have they fared travelling across ice-bound, snow-bound Europe on such a doleful mission? The weather here is hellish too and there is nothing to eat. Janie has just come in from her marketing and says it is as bad as during the worst days of the war. Shouting, fighting queues, hours of standing and coming home with nothing – not even potatoes, which have been destroyed by frost!

Our only other news is that we have let the Souco to Mr. West, Segonzac's[1] brother-in-law, for three years, quite advantageously.

Nothing, absolutely nothing else to say except that I am

As ever
Your affect
D.B.

223. Dorothy Bussy to André Gide

40 Rue Verdi, Nice

3rd April, '47

Dear Gide,

I do hope your change of air and surroundings is doing you good, and that you have been having better weather on your Swiss-Italian lake shores than we here – though at last it has changed and we have had two days real spring.[. . .]

We have had somewhat of a blow lately – in fact a considerable one. Simon was invited by his London picture dealer, probably the best there is, to have an exhibition there this spring – in June. He has spent the winter preparing, varnishing, stretching, *framing* (difficult and very expensive) all his work, oil pictures, for the last ten years. There are about 150 of them. At the last moment we realised that it was impossible to get these works into England without a very solemn undertaking not to sell a single one of them in England, in fact, to return every one of them to France.

Only painters so famous as to despise sales will be able henceforth to exhibit to the British public. Other artists may sell their books,

---

[1] The painter André Dunoyer de Segonzac was a friend of Simon Bussy's.

their films, may perform their music, others again may send their boxers and their racehorses to extract its precious gold from the English public – only painters and sculptors are discriminated against. And this is the doing of a government who spends large sums of money and prides itself on '*encouraging and disseminating Culture*'!

I hope Simon will succeed in having an Ex. in Paris. I believe that his work deserves and might very well have a great success. It is not in the fashion obviously. It is not on a gigantic and monstrous scale. But have the French lost their taste (so well defended by you) for *perfection*? The last ten years he has spent in perfecting his art, materially and spiritually. It has amused me lately to compare him in my mind to La Fontaine. His contemporaries were on the gigantic scale, but it didn't prevent the beauty, the finish, the elegance, the wit etc. etc. of his tiny pieces from being recognised. About animals too! Birds and flowers and fishes! Absurd no doubt.

It was pleasant to get the *Figaro Littéraire* again once more. (Oh! these strikes of democratic Culture).

I have always seen it spelt 'Oyez', at any rate never 'Oyess'. In case you reprint the article, remember that the name of the place you mention is 'Elephant *and* Castle' which alas is nearer to its transformed guise. Do you know the other celebrated public-house sign: '*The Goat and Compasses*', said to have been derived from '*God Encompasses Us*'?

We are leaving here towards the end of the month and shall be in London at the beginning of next. I shall go and see Gallimard in Paris and try and make him note my change of address, in case by any strange event he may be sending me proofs.

> Love from all
> Yr.
> D.B.

224. Dorothy Bussy to André Gide

51 Gordon Square, W.C.1

11th May 1947

Dear Gide,

I wrote to Miss Starkie two or three days ago and got her answer last night. We are somewhat disillusioned and I don't quite know what to advise. I had imagined that Miss Starkie occupied the chair for French Literature at Oxford University. My sister Pernal who is, as you know, in the know about University matters tells me very decidedly that this is not so. She is no doubt a Dr. and a Professor of French but only at Somerville College which is one of the two *women's* colleges of the University. From her letter it is clear that you would be the guest of *Somerville*, and feminist as I am, I don't think this is grand enough for the first reception of a person like you at the University of Oxford. If you are offered the Honorary Degree (L.L.D.) of the University it would be a very different matter, but this appears to be still uncertain, though Miss Starkie still has some hopes of it. The worst of it is that Mauriac has already been offered this distinction and is coming over in person this summer to receive it. I am not alone in thinking (and Miss Starkie herself thinks) that it would be infuriating if not discreditable to English letters, if dear Mauriac were so pointedly preferred to you. We must remember too that there still reigns at Oxford the Roman Catholic tradition and strong R.C. influence. We don't know what cooking is going on in the background.

The Bryce lecture was offered to and accepted by M. Herriot[1] who recently cancelled his acceptance on account of the 'political situation'. It is very honourable, but purely a Somerville affair.

What to say to Miss Starkie? After reflexion I think I shall tell her straight out, that I consider that it would be unworthy of the University of Oxford to allow a man who is universally considered the greatest French writer now living to visit Oxford more or less professionally as the guest of any College whatever and not of the *University* itself. I shall say I have advised you to accept the very kind invitation to Somerville and the delivery of the Bryce lecture, *if it is accompanied* by the bestowal of the *Oxford Degree, otherwise not*, and this for the sake of *Oxford* and not of *you*, M. Gide, who can afford to overlook such trivialities.

Poor Miss Starkie! Her letter to me, which was very long, was not very sensible, confused and unaware, I thought, of proper proportions, though *fundamentally* all right. But I don't think I *can* advise you to go to Somerville and expect you to enjoy being entertained at dinner by an Italian professor – even though at Magdalen College.

As a matter of fact I only asked Miss Starkie to tell me the exact date that was proposed for your lecture and to give me details of

[1] Edouard Herriot (1872–1957) was elected president of the Assemblée nationale that year.

trains so that I could help at this end of your journey. She did neither in her answer. For I think the date of June 2nd which she mentioned did not refer to the '*Bryce*' lecture, which was left vague.

I need hardly say that my advice here is highly disinterested as I am afraid we shall loose, if you take it, the chance of seeing you for a brief moment in London.

Dear Gide, I will write you a better letter soon.

Your

D.B.

225. Dorothy Bussy to André Gide

51 Gordon Square, W.C.1

12th May, 1947

Beloved Gide,

I am afraid the letter I wrote you yesterday about coming to Oxford was very discouraging. Before you make any decision you must wait for another letter from Miss Starkie. She may have heard that the University have decided to offer you a degree in which case all would be well.

We are terribly distressed to think that this may prevent us from seeing you in London and hope and pray that you may consider us and London as well worth a visit as Starkie and Somerville. We can put you up in our house – and feed you – so Janie, the housekeeper, says. And we can invite anybody you like to come and see you – or no one. Would you care, for instance to see Morgan Forster, the author of a *Voyage to India* [*sic*], who has recently paid another visit to that country – or a ravishingly beautiful youth lately picked up by Duncan Grant and preparing to be a monk, or perhaps Saint Denis and Laurence Olivier and have a talk with them about *Saül* and the English stage?[1] Of course the world is all before you where to choose and at any rate you might have a rest from Davet and writing letters.

We have only just really settled in and seen no one so far but the family. But at last our telephone is in working order and we are beginning today with Raymond [Mortimer] – who is the general gossip.

---

[1] There is no evidence of *Saül* having been performed on the London stage. In any case, the translation which was eventually published (in *My Theater*, Knopf, 1951) was by Jackson Mathews.

Dear Gide, I think of you a great deal with all the usual longings and regrets. I don't think I was at all 'nice' last time in Paris. I am afraid I said a great many things I wish I hadn't, and failed to say others I wish I had. But it is ever so. Of you I remember, and always shall, one strange word. It was 'unique'.

Your affectionate
D.B.

226. Dorothy Bussy to André Gide

51 Gordon Square, W.C.1

13th May '47

Dear Gide,

My last two letters must be counted 'nulles and non avenues' (except for one or two trifles). Poor Miss Starkie has been working very hard to get your University degree voted in time for a visit in the near future. She seems to have achieved it. And evidently your prestige must be very high – even in Oxford! – to get through all the formalities in so short a time.

Miss Starkie was very much upset, I fear, at my suggesting that a college lecture was not as grand as a University degree and to give the former to you and the latter to Mauriac was not to be borne! The authorities themselves have now realised this and I am very glad of it. A University degree is a very pleasant distinction and I hope with all my heart you will accept it and not let *anything* stand in your way. If you have to pay for it by giving a lecture, no matter. Something in the style and even on the same subject as your Beyrouth one would be very suitable, wouldn't it?,[1] and, I am sure, greatly appreciated, and perhaps not very difficult for you to compose in so short a time. And your reception at Oxford will take on a very different colour and be far more amusing, as the recipient of a degree rather than a Bryce lecture, though that too, as Miss Starkie assures me, is highly distinguished.

I have been invited too to assist at your Honours and rather feel inclined to. A bribe from Miss Starkie to use my persuasion in her favour! *I do.*

Your,
D.B.

[1] Gide was dissatisfied with the Oxford lecture and refused to have it published.

227. André Gide to Dorothy Bussy

Echarcon[1]

16 May 47

Dear friend,

Your last letter (of the 12th) has succeeded in reassuring me. I am therefore changing nothing in my plans. Although the date of the lecture (a very pretentious word for the brief allocution I expect to give) has been postponed one day, I shall nevertheless arrive in London on June 1st, together with Elisabeth who has been invited by the other Enid.[2] Can you arrange to let me know where I am to stay – and all the better if it can be at 51 Gordon Square! Conelly, whom I saw yesterday before he returned to London, assured me he would contact you immediately and arrange everything with you. For heaven's sake don't have me meet too many new faces: Forster however, very gladly. And among the already known, yes, I'll be happy to see Saint-Denis, Laurence Olivier, and Raymond Mortimer. Conelly had proposed to invite Lehmann to lunch with me, and who else? . . . and to contrive to let me have a nap after the meal. I told him again how quickly I tired – and not to overtax my energy. But in a week there is, all the same, time to do and see a great deal.

May I not show myself to be too far beneath what is expected and wished from me – considering all those honours and apparent warm feelings! . . . Your friendship will support me; I am already taking great comfort from it –

Soon. I embrace the three of you.

André Gide.

One thing more: I had given over to Conelly (I'm afraid I misspell his name) the text of *L'Art bitraire*, with a view to its publication in *Horizon*. When I reconsider, it seems to me that its publication would be <u>most ill-advised</u> – and to be avoided. I should like to let him know as soon as possible, before he takes the trouble to translate it – but don't know his address. May I rely on your kindness to inform him of my decision NOT to submit the text – to *Horizon* or elsewhere.

---

[1] Gide is visiting Mme de Lestrange.
[2] McLeod.

228. André Gide to Dorothy Bussy

22 May 47

Dear friend,

Enclosed is a copy of the telegram I have just sent to Miss Starkie.[1] My regrets stem only from missing an occasion to see you; as for Oxford's welcome and the honour to be conferred on me, I believe, I feel, that my situation, so soon after Mauriac's triumph, could only be very awkward. Add to that the fact that I am again very tired and fear I might cut quite a sorry figure in Oxford. And then the text I had drafted strikes me as mediocre – and I lack the time and energy required to remedy its inadequacy – or to begin again with a new idea. It would be courting disaster. Overwhelmed as I am with work (if this constant harassment can be called work), I can't explain further today. Will write you better in a few days – but please go ahead and express my keen regrets to those I looked forward to seeing – and keep the keenest for yourself.

Yours,
André Gide

229. André Gide to Dorothy Bussy

26 May 47

Dear friend,

Yesterday I sent a cable to Miss E.S., reassuring her; she has perhaps informed you of it. Her fine argument, although it doesn't overcome my fatigue, at least convinces me to disregard it. As for my lecture, it will be what it can. Roger M. du G. to whom I had read it, declared it to be very mediocre, unworthy of Oxford and me. It was in good part his judgement, coupled with my fatigue, that had discouraged me. But when I take it up again, the text no longer seems to me as bad as a smoky, rather doleful reading had led us to believe . . . A few sleepless nights had sapped my energy; I felt 'outdated' and wanted only to withdraw from the game. For the past two or three

---

[1] 'Enid Starkie 41 Saint-Giles, Oxford: LEARN FROM *FIGARO* FRIEND MAURIAC TO BE ENTHRONED AT OXFORD THIRD JUNE STOP FEAR AWKWARDLY IRONIC APPEARANCE OTHER SIMILAR CEREMONY SO SOON AFTERWARDS AND CONSIDER PREFERABLE POSTPONE NEXT YEAR STOP PLEASE RELAY DECISION AND BEST WISHES ANDRÉ GIDE.'

days I have felt better and am regaining confidence; shall go ahead with the original plan and arrive in London, with Elisabeth, on the evening of June 1st. Let us keep, then, the appointments made (R. Mortimer and Connelly). As to Lord Berner's amiable invitation, I leave you to judge of it, but I'm afraid the *country house* might take too much time from such a brief stay . . . (N.B.: I have no dinner-jacket.) Please convey my warm thanks – and accept or refuse *as you like*. A visit (and probably a rest) at the French Embassy would seem indispensable, inevitable – to be included in my schedule. Joy to say: soon.

André Gide

And please excuse, and have the others excuse, the momentary confusion that caused my wavering; it is true that I felt at the end of my tether.

230. André Gide to Dorothy Bussy

12 June 47

Dear friend,

You probably heard that our Golden Arrow only left at 11 o'clock, and, as we were at the station at 8:30 . . . Over two hours to regret for not having spent them with you.

Trip without difficulties, in an empty train. The crossing as beautiful as it was going over. And, thanks to the British Council and its auto, we were delivered home by about 7 o'clock (French time).

Here, nothing *worth mentioning*. Everything well. Everything poorly. Everthing continues . . .

To kill the two-hour wait, in London, I set off to Piccadilly in search of a 'Biro'. Enormous shop. 'We fill and take orders here; we don't sell.' So that what I'm writing to you with is the kind Raymond M.'s implement. This you may tell him, but it's in secret that I tell you my first (and so far only) errand in Paris has been to see to his red ribbon.[1] Massigli and the English authorities were notified at once (since it seems their consent is required.) I expect it will go off 'without a hitch', and, I hope, quickly, for there has been unanimous approval. It takes about two months I've been told. I have never 'taken steps' with greater pleasure.

[1] Of the Légion d'Honneur.

Nothing more to tell you today that you do not already know: that is, the fine memory I have of this 'English week' – and my deep gratitude.

I'd like to believe that your brother didn't allow himself to be beaten at chess out of kindness!

Don't yet know, given the strikes, whether it will be possible to join Roger at Bagnols – but I shall not forget the messages I am to give him – and not leave Paris without clearing up the matter of Simon's exhibition at the Charpentier gallery. – I wish I had talked more with Janie . . .

I embrace the three of you, together and individually –

Toujours yours,
A.G.

231. Dorothy Bussy to André Gide

Private and Confidential   17th–20th June, 1947

My very dear. I have been reading your agonizing little book[1] since you left—more agonizing, I think, for me than for any other of your 18 recipients. Did not the fringe of your tragedy touch the heart of mine? But can I call mine a tragedy? I suppose not. It brought me, I suppose, more riches than pain – a 'love begotten by despair upon impossibility'.[2] But it was the impossibility that saved it from being a tragedy for me. Twice in the course of our 'friendship' you gave me permission to imagine myself in Madeleine's place. I should have made a worse, a more lamentable failure of it than she did. There are certain things I could not have reconciled myself to as she eventually did. No, I don't think I could. Our – your and my – two conceptions of 'love' are too different and I should have had no religion to help me bear it. And it's a mistake, I think, to say that it was piety and education that caused her misunderstanding, it was something even more innate than that – something which I suppose *your* innate nature prevents you too from understanding, something which is innate in me too. 'Feminine' you will say, but a femininity (if it is that) which a good many men share too. Once when I was young, I enjoyed for about ten years an equal love with a man. I know what it

[1] *Et nunc manet in te*, the story of Gide's marriage to Madeleine Rondeau. It had been published that spring.
[2] From Marvell's 'Definition of Love'.

is. Consummation of desire was not necessary to my happiness (for I was happy) but an equal desire, an equal understanding were. That would always have been impossible with you and I could not have borne it.

Dear, I think of all people now alive, it is I who have known you best. For the boys you loved were too young, too ignorant to understand what it was you gave them. But I was neither too young nor too ignorant to know what it was you gave and what you withheld. I have known for a few brief moments which I daresay you have forgotten, your tenderness, the part of you that is divine, the part of you that makes me believe in the supreme beauty of the human soul – in certain human souls.

Oh Gide it's no use going on. Farewell. In spite of everything, in spite of the past and the present – our friendship, our 'love' has been something unique for *me*, something *you* would have been poorer not to have known. Am I 'too bold'?

Yr.

D.

232. André Gide to Dorothy Bussy

15 Evole
Neuchâtel

19 Nov. 47

Very dear friend,

In the avalanche of letters – friendly and official congratulations[1] – this one in particular moves me; would you please pass it along to Janie. I answered Bernd Schmeier[2] at once and said I would tell you of his joy.

Elisabeth, Catherine, and Isabelle have left Neuchâtel for Ascona, where Jean Lambert, arriving from Paris, and then Nicolas[3] and his nurse, will quickly join them. Everything goes well – in that domain at least.

For myself, the prospect of a trip to Sweden (although Roger is doing his best to persuade me that it is indispensable) is terrifying. I

---

[1] Gide had been awarded the Nobel Prize.
[2] Unidentified.
[3] Nicolas Lambert, born 16 October of that year.

have no strength for it – all the less since my heart has been giving out lately. Besides, what good are those honours to me? They only mean inconvenience, and I had rather spend working or meditating the little time left me! . . . Impossible to judge the quality of what I write these days, but rarely have I felt better disposed. So I go straight on and don't allow myself to reread anything . . . We shall see later what it's worth and whether it is more appropriately polished or torn up.

I embrace you fondly with all my faithful heart,

André Gide

233. Dorothy Bussy to André Gide

40 Rue Verdi

20 Nov 47

Dearest Gide

This isn't going to be a letter of congratulations – rather of condolences. I imagine you swamped, engulfed in the former and with no secretary to help you – or have you sent for her? – and cursing the day that has inflicted on you world-wide celebrity. How much pleasanter from every point of view is obscurity! Why couldn't they have waited just a little longer – for you to be safely and comfortably in your grave? Such, I imagine are your reflections. For us, your friends, it is different. We have the pleasure, the satisfaction, the reflected glory, without any bother – practically no letters to answer, no thanks to bestow, no charities to distribute etc.

The Swedish academy's little accompanying note to explain and justify their choice was, I thought, very well expressed. The English radio gave it, the French omitted it from their announcement – an omission which made me furious.

We are settling down here quite comfortably. After our first week the weather turned beautiful and still remains so. We have got a bonne, who promises well and cooks our lunch quite satisfactorily. She is a great help to Janie, who has had time to dust and re-arrange the books. There is hardly anybody we know in Nice and we have seen no-one but the Père Valensin.[1] We talk about Milton, he is under the impression that the English people are quite unaware that

[1] Auguste Valensin, whom Gide had known since about 1941 and whose *L'Art et la pensée de Platon* serves as point of departure for a passage in Gide's *Journal* (11 June 1948).

M. is a great poet. I alone have discovered this fact and convinced him of it. But then *I* am a phenomenon!

another subject.

No, my dear. I have never followed, nor thought it right to follow, worldly, pedantic, silly old Polonius' advice – or was it Laertes? (He was his true son) and keep 'within the rear of my affection', or been afraid of tumbling over the edge – I have always been regardless of the danger of breaking my neck or my heart, or my vanity, or – more important still, the esteem of others – or of *one*.

When I was still a child it was the fashion to make calendars with a Scripture text for each day which one used to consult superstitiously. My mother amused herself by making a choice of Lay Texts, (a pretty little volume) and took special trouble in her selection for her children's birthdays. I will copy you out mine which I re-read only the other day. What do you think of it? Is it good advice or not? Have I followed it or not? Wisely or not? 'Persons lightly dipt, not grained in generous honesty, are but pale in goodness, and faintkneed in sincerity. But be thou what thou virtuously art and let not the ocean wash away thy tincture.'

Sir Thomas Browne

This reminds me of *your* birthday. How are you spending it? Are you with the Lamberts yet at Ascona? What news of Paris & the petite Dame? Everything sounds alarming. But more forebodingly than actually.

Your loving
D.B.

P.S. I reopen this to tell you that Simon was very much grieved to hear a few days ago of the death of his first & oldest friend Eugène Martel the painter. He died suddenly & unexpectedly of a heart attack.

234. André Gide to Dorothy Bussy

15 Evole
Neuchâtel

22 Nov. 47

Dear Friend,

Your letter this morning quickens this flagging heart that keeps me here incapable of effort. Still totally taken up with correspondence, excuses and regrets addressed to the Swedish Academy, seconded by a medical authority who declares me (after extensive examination) clearly incapable of making the trip and who condemns me to a period of complete quiet. Excellent for work.

I know how old and faithful the friendship was that bound Simon to Eugène Martel. Tell him how well I can understand his sorrow.

Happy to know a 'bonne' has finally come to Janie's assistance! What a sigh you must have breathed!

Tell the Père Valensin that I have read *Paradise Lost* from beginning to end and am having today the great pleasure of rereading it, only to admire it all the more. Does he know *Samson Agonistes*?

I leave you. Just enough strength to embrace you fondly,

André Gide

235. André Gide to Dorothy Bussy

15 Evole
Neuchâtel

10 December 47

Very dear friend,

Received your telegram last night; answered this morning. Is it those 'notices' in the papers that worried you? or Davet who panics and alarms you? No need. The lengthy examination by an eminent local cardiologist, the results of which he communicated to Stockholm, showed very clearly that I was in no condition to risk a voyage. My heart required a prolonged rest; thanks to which I have felt better the past two days. Tomorrow another visit from the doctor. In any case, all moving about has been put off until I don't know when. No question, for the moment at least, of returning to Paris or of travelling to Nice or Ascona where the Lamberts settled two weeks ago. But this enforced rest allows me happily to work, and I wish (for the moment) nothing more. My hosts[1] surround me with tender cares and kindness and, <u>provided I attempt not the slightest effort,</u> I don't feel at all poorly.

I hope you, in Nice, didn't suffer much from the strikes, etc. Considerable delay in mail delivery. Enough for today.

I embrace you very fondly

André Gide

What pleasure a letter from you would give me!!

[1] Gide is at the home of his friend, the Swiss publisher Richard Heyd.

236. Dorothy Bussy to André Gide

40 Rue Verdi

29 Dec 1947

Dearest Gide

Just a line to send you all my best wishes for to-day, tomorrow and all the other days that are to come and may they be many.

It seems to be ages since I have had any news of you or from you and I don't know how you are, where you are or what you are doing – Still, *I* imagine, at the Heyds at Neuchatel, but Roger whom we saw yesterday (yes, thank goodness, they have come at last) seemed to think you couldn't still be there. Yes, I imagine you still in your spare moments, to rest you from 'work', answering congratulations about the Nobel Prize – Even *I* suffer from this & some of your devotees think that *I* ought to be congratulated as well as you! For instance, Miss Pell who irritates me madly, though she is kindness itself and smothers us with presents of all sorts.

Roger brought me the last packet of my proofs[1] from Festy. They added a considerable weight to his already considerable luggage. But when I have finished with them & done the indexing there will be nothing left to do but the binding. This it seems will no longer be Festy's business but Allard's and will take a very long time – still according to Roger.

The weather here – since we are reduced to talking about weather – has been fine lately. We have an excellent gas stove in our drawing room and not at all bad central heating. The hotels here are empty for lack of English visitors and bitterly complaining. The prices of food and everything else are getting more & more catastrophic every minute but still things seem to go on much as usual. News from family & friends too much as usual. John Lehmann writes to me about Mascolo[2] and his fashion of conducting the business of rights for translations of Valéry.[3] Roger Senhouse does *not* write to me about the publishing of the translation of *Les Nourritures*,[4] which he

[1] Of *Fifty Nursery Rhymes*.

[2] Dyonis Mascolo, who was in charge of translation rights at Gallimard.

[3] *Dance and the Soul*, D.B.'s translation of Valéry's *L'ame et la danse*, was published by J. Lehmann in 1951.

[4] The translation of *Les Nourritures terrestres* and *Les Nouvelles nourritures* (*The Fruits of the Earth*) was published in 1949 by Secker & Warburg, and by Knopf in the States.

has been talking about for more than two years. He is one of those who talk more than they write.

I have still got a lot to say to you which I think can only be said & not written.

I am doing a translation of a chapter of a book by Malraux on Lawrence or *Le Démon de l'Absolu*.[5] It is extremely interesting but oh, dear, I am accustomed to people who bestow more care on the construction of their sentences. Translation is a severe test & one doesn't know which is the more difficult, to deal with good writers or bad. At any rate I think Malraux might profit by Flaubert's example and take a little more trouble over his '*qui's*' and '*que's*.' It is sometimes quite confusing.

Prof. O'Brien's *Journal* is I think having a success.[6] I send you a note I got from him this morning. Yes I did make a few criticisms (very mild) about his vernacular, the tone of which, rather than the language, does not seem to me quite in tune. But it is a prodigious work all the same, & there is every reason to be grateful to him.

But some day I shall write a criticism, not of the translation of the *Journal*, but of the *Journal* itself, & the critics, & perhaps the author, will be perhaps surprised.[7]

All well here. The painters painting. How I should like to hear that your heart has ceased to trouble you.

Yours ever
D.B.

A kind sister has sent me a copy of Baron Corvo, author of *Hadrian VII* which I talked to you about in Paris. I would pass it on to you if I thought you would read it. But it is too precious to be lost. (A tattered, dirty, shilling Penguin.)

237. André Gide to Dorothy Bussy

2 February 48

Dear friend,

If Nice were not so far, if I felt surer of my strength, I would be there with you. I wish it constantly, being aware of how quickly the

[5] D.B.'s translation, 'Was that all, then?', was published in *Transition: Forty-eight* (no. 2, pp. 44–59).
[6] Volume I of Justin O'Brien's translation of Gide's *Journal* had been published in September of that year by Knopf.
[7] Never published; most likely never written.

days pass, of how little time is left us – and that I could put to better use . . . And here I have now let myself be persuaded to accept – almost – an extraordinary invitation from the U.S.A. for the beginning of next spring. A matter of a lecture in Baltimore,[1] then of a rest in Florida in some villa which has been placed at my disposal for two months. Pierre Herbart would accompany me (for I fear travelling alone). The invitation was conveyed by the kind Keeler Faus, then by Alexis Léger (St.-John Perse)[2] in so pressing a manner that . . . all of it without commitment, subject to a state of health that is still far from satisfactory. I am better however, and can once more tie my own shoes. Even watched over by Pierre H., even with the assurance that I would be spared any kind of 'reception' . . . this sudden lurch into the New World terrifies me.

The post has just come, bringing its daily Tablatura: Anne Marsan, the editor of the book on Poussin informs me that *Town and Country* is publishing my text, embellished by all the reproductions. Question: it is your translation they're printing? I shall write to Schiffrin at once and ask him to find out.

And India! And the Gandhi drama![3]

I think of you constantly. Yours,

A.G.

238. Dorothy Bussy to André Gide

Feb. 23rd 48

40 Rue Verdi

Dearest Gide

Thank you for Henriot's article on Carcopino's book[1] – I was very much interested by it, but there's a great deal might be answered – at any rate to M. Henriot.

Cicero, I should have thought, has already been 'debunked' for at any rate a period of one, if not two generations. We are no longer in

---

[1] An international congress on criticism was to be held on 13–15 April at the Johns Hopkins University. Among others invited were Benedetto Croce, Sir Herbert Read, Allen Tate, John Crowe Ransom, and R. P. Blackmur. Gide did not attend, but sent his paper to be read.

[2] The French diplomat and poet, and Nobel laureate for 1960, was then living in Washington.

[3] Gandhi had been assassinated on 30 January.

LETTER 238

[1] *Les Secrets de la correspondance de Ciceron*, 1947.

need of being told that he is a 'rhéteur sententieux, verbeux et creux'.[2] Everybody had discovered that – common talk at Pontigny 20 years ago – when M. Henriot was in his cradle! What is wanted is not to attack Cicero's morals, but to explain his extreme interest not as a writer – though I can't help thinking he has some good points even there – but as an illustrious case of neurotic psychology which has become of interest, of growing interest, since Freud's great discoveries. Les Messieurs seem not to have heard of Freud or they wouldn't be so surprised or so terribly shocked by his 'secrets' – taking up the same attitude to him as the virtuous did for so long to Rousseau. 'Dans la fortune montante de César il a opté pour le vaniteux et inefficace Pompée.'[3] This of course is Cicero's great drama. He was perfectly aware of Caesar's superiority & Pompey's hopelessness, and yet this (according to Carcopino & Henriot) barely self-interested & ambitious man deliberately chose the losing side. Why? All the letters in which he struggles over the great decision he had to make are deeply interesting psychologically and very far from entirely base. Even his attitude to Caesar's murderers is not to my mind base. Even his luxury and love of art and books and pictures and statues and brilliant conversation does not seem to me wholly despicable! I am surprised they don't accuse him of committing incest with his daughter as some of his enemies do. He didn't love his wife! Dear! dear! But they can't deny he was capable of deep affection. He had 27 slaves! But how did he treat them! With what generosity & care & friendliness. How amusing, how unaffected, how human his relationship with the two boys – son & nephew.

Oh! I must stop this. But I will try and read Carcopino.

In the mean time I must confess to you a little adventure of my own. I think it must be 15 years ago that I showed you a M.S. of a short story.[4] Oh how could I be so idiotic? 'Ariane, ma soeur'[5] I didn't know or realise then that that was enough to make the hero and founder of cities 'débarque' (We don't want women who write in our cities!) you on the island of Naxos. Anyway, I had a copy, re-read it & didn't think it so bad and last year I took it with me to London.

[2] 'Hollow, verbose, sententious rhetorician'.
[3] 'As Caesar's star rose, he chose the vain and ineffectual Pompey.'
[4] *Olivia.*
[5]   Ariane, ma soeur, de quel amour blessée
             Vous mourûtes aux bords ou vous fûtes laissée?
                                    (Racine, *Phèdre*, I. iii).
D.B. identifies with the blue-stocking Ariadne, abandoned by Theseus.

I showed it to three people – all women – one was Rosamund Lehmann. They astonished me by the – almost – violence of their approval, especially Rosamund and in writing, in letters too, not personally. 'It is a work of literature' she said, 'far too good to lose. It *must* be published' and she inveighed me into showing it to her brother John. He too professed admiration. He would like to publish it but small books are very difficult now-a-days etc. and he offered me a place in a great magazine he is editing[6] with works by all [the] swells in it. Sitwells, Bowen, etc. But that was not my idea at all and I sent it to Leonard Woolf who has merged the Hogarth Press into the big publishers Chatto & Windus. A man, I thought, he won't like it & I shall be saved any more trouble. But he too surprised me, for he was more enthusiastic than anybody else – 'amusing, terribly moving, characters done *superbly*'. And he is not at all gushing as a rule. *But* he must show it to his three partners. He writes now to say that they all agree with him, they are 'enthusiastic' and all want very much to publish it; enclosed is an agreement with what seems to me a very good offer and hopes of bringing it out this autumn. So now, dear friend, perhaps you will have the glory of having rejected two best sellers – Proust[7] & yours truly! But you won't write me such a nice letter as you wrote him. P.S. my book is to be anonymous and *please don't mention it to any one* – though I have told Roger.

I hear you are going to be driven to Paris – when it is warmer, I hope. (How I wish it could be via Nice) And there you will settle about America. A very nice letter from the Petite Dame and from Beth too with news of you. I hope M. Heyd is getting on well. No need to answer this. If there is any news, no doubt I shall hear it.

Your
D.B.

239. Dorothy Bussy to André Gide

début Mars 1948[1]

Dearest Gide

It was nice (O shade of Henry Tilney!)[2] getting a real letter from you after this long abstinence. But you know I would rather have no

---

[6] *New Writing.*

[7] The N.R.F., of which Gide was a founder and editor, had rejected Proust's *Du Côté de chez Swann (Swann's Way).*

LETTER 239

[1] Written by Gide.

[2] The unsentimental hero of *Northanger Abbey.*

letter than feel you had been overtired by writing one.

The poor Heyds.[3] What a wretched time for you all. Terrible for them and not very restful for you.

You say something about an Exhibition for Simon. He wrote to Charpentier some time ago, asking if he could now suggest a date, but so far there has been no answer. Have you heard anything of it? So Amrouche[4] is going to convoy you back to Paris. And then we shall hear your decision about America. You know what my feelings are about that. But I shan't tell you for fear you should be encouraged to do the contrary! 'Ariane, ma soeur.' How appropriate for me to say that! Why did Theseus dislike and disembark her? Simply because she was fond of poetry and tried to write herself. I have been slightly, though certainly not *very* injudicious in that respect myself.

The little work you have so completely refoulé,[5] when you come to re-read it, as I hope some day you will, will make only too clear a) the reason you disliked it and b) the reason why I wish it to be anonymous.

It is a very serious effort – not like the play which was just for fun. You might as well suggest publishing *Le Treizième Arbre*[6] in the same volume as *La Porte Etroite*.

I began this story with a very lofty and unattainable ambition before me. Like people who gaze at the Himalayas and long to climb them. Impossible – never mind. Let us try. My dream was to add another to those few volumes which are so special and so peculiar: *La Princesse de Clèves*, *Adolphe*, *Dominique*, *Werther*, *Volupté* and *La Porte Etroite*. A personal experience – almost nothing but a personal experience, transfigured, transformed by memory, by later knowledge of life, by piety, by an aching love of art. It was to be simple, direct and unaffected almost to bareness, to have only one centre to which every word should converge, to have no characters that were not essential, to develop to a climax which should be *tragic*, and fade and dwindle, like life itself, into a melancholy peace. Such was my wild desire – a failure of course, and when, foolish Ariane, I showed it to you, your only comment was three crushing words, 'Pas très entrainant'. All the same, from the reactions of the three or four persons I have since shown it to, I think it cannot have

---

[3] Three weeks earlier, Richard Heyd had undergone an operation for a liver ailment.

[4] Jean Amrouche was one of the founders of the review *L'Arche* and a member of Gide's entourage.

[5] *Olivia*.

[6] Gide's little-known play.

been *wholly* a failure. *Some* of what I wanted has got across. And at any rate they one and all said that having begun it they couldn't put it down. But, though every one who knows me will at once recognize me as the writer, it is too intimate for me to want to put my name to it. And please believe that attaching as I do very great importance to your opinion, I greatly prefer that you should have totally forgotten it than that you should dimly remember it as uninteresting, and moreover I am very glad, that I waited so long before wanting to – do I really want to? – publish it. Grateful to you for that as for everything.

I shall go on reading Book X with greater pleasure if I feel that you are actually accompanying me – not only preceding me. You must know that I am at present without any '*crib*' & have to hammer it out by myself without any help but the notes in the little book you gave me, which like all notes, constantly infuriate me by explaining things which are crystal clear and making long technical grammatical remarks when what one wants is the *sense*. However I have been able to appreciate at times, dimly, I admit, the (what Charlie called) 'tempo' of the battle.

I am very glad you don't defend Henriot on Cicero & I feel sure you are wrong in thinking the latter more difficult than Virgil. You got stuck up in the first letters about money matters to his banker – like modern stock exchange talk, incomprehensible to the laity, and didn't get on to the really interesting ones. But no doubt, though more interesting to the psychiatrist, he is less so to the poet than Virgil.

I didn't know about Mme Michaux, nor herself personally. It sounds horrible.[7] And I'm very sorry Marc should be unhappy.

Our weather here is marvellously beautiful and we are all well.

Ever your

D.

240. André Gide to Dorothy Bussy

8 March 48

Very dear friend,

Your long exquisite letter came forwarded this morning from Neuchâtel. As you did not date it yourself, I have written at the top:

[7] The wife of the poet Henri Michaux had died of accidental burning.

beginning of March – and save it, even more preciously than many of the others (but I keep them all, in any case, locked in a special box).

Madame Théo wrote yesterday to Roger giving him (and you) news of me, and excuses for not writing myself. (Nearly completely incapable of the least effort. – No pain, but I only feel well lying down and thinking of nothing. Any book I attempt to read (with the single exception of Virgil) falls from my hands after five minutes – the letters dance on the page; I no longer understand any of it. – I don't despair of feeling better in a few days – but in the meantime I can only embrace you fondly and tenderly.

A.G.

And how much there is to say to you! . . .

Di Jovis in tectis iram miserantur inanem
Amburum, *et tantos mortalibus esse labures*![1]
[Aeneid] X, 758

241. André Gide to Dorothy Bussy

9 April 48

Dear friend,

The idea of seeing you in Paris makes my heart beat faster. As regards the question of a hotel, I shall consult with Mme Théo; I don't know what she will say, but I do know that for myself it would be a great disappointment not to have you right here – all the more so since I move with increasing difficulty and walking very quickly puts me out of breath. Add to that an incapacity for work which means that all my time is free.

Despite my near unavailability, I have concerned myself a good deal with Simon's exhibition since I returned, and if I have not written sooner it is because I wanted to have something definite to relate. I have the 'almost assurance' that Charpentier (his representative) will himself write to Simon. It appears that very truly he is not free to offer his additional rooms just now; but, somewhat embarrassed to disappoint us, he is all the more intent on committing himself definitely for the 1st exhibition following the vacation. As to

[1] 'The gods in the palace of Jove took pity on the vain wrath/of both, which it is so much the lot of mortals to endure.'

terms, there would be nothing to pay; he would simply deduct a percentage from the sales. They would like very much to present, in one showing, a <u>double</u> exhibition (in a manner of speaking); that is to say: to present to the public, besides the canvases that Simon planned to send, others (pastels or studies) from very different periods, which would be likely to enlighten the public and interest it by not showing it only a single aspect or facet of the work of an artist whom it cannot fully <u>discover</u> at a single glance. By the time you receive this letter, Simon will perhaps have already received one from Nacenta Charpentier. Curious to know what he (N.C.) proposes and whether it conforms to received assurances. I should like so much for it to turn out well! Also, he says he would take advantage (Charpentier or his representative) of Simon's stop-over in Paris at the beginning of May, to decide everything with him and to begin assembling the works. It would be important to show a few works of which one might already say 'from the collection of . . . Vic. de Lestrage – or A.G. or X or Y. . .' so as to stimulate public interest. I think this would be excellent tactics. Shouldn't he also show a few portraits? (I am thinking particularly of the extraordinary Lady Ottoline, so . . . *exciting* – or Lytton, or myself.) This as an appendage or supplement to the body of the exhibition as he had originally conceived it.

Don't tell Simon that, also, I promised to write a few pages of presentation for the catalogue,[1] for I shouldn't want him to have cause to think my intervention had in any way assured the victory.

What else can I tell you today? Am I feeling a little better? Maybe . . . Certain nights of quite painful nervous and cardiac anguish. Yesterday I ventured a little outing on foot, which nearly had bad results; but what I especially suffer from is an increasing imbecility. I had committed myself to send a contribution to the Johns Hopkins University . . . which I am incapable of finishing. – Nominated none the less Doctor Honoris Causa at Columbia U. All this comes when it no longer gives me any pleasure. But I think Claudel is getting soft-headed even faster than I.

This article on your friend Cicero may interest you.

Au revoir. I would have so much more to tell you, but Amrouche is waiting to throw this letter into the postbox.

A thousand fond remembrances to Raymond Mortimer. I com-

---

[1] This text was also published in *Le Figaro* of 23–4 October, five days before the opening at the Galerie Charpentier.

pletely lost my temper and made a scene over his red ribbon, but your letter leads me to believe that it is now a closed matter, and I applaud

your
A.G.

Delighted with the Poussin cheque!

242. Dorothy Bussy to André Gide

31st May 1948

Dear Gide

This morning I posted you a copy of my *Olivia*. I feel very remorseful about it & beg you not to think yourself obliged to waste any time reading it & still less writing about it. But one of these days get Davet to make a parcel of it and send it back to me.

Justin O'Brien has sent me Vol. II of the Journal. I think it is better than Vol I & in fact quite good. The Index, though much trouble has been taken over it, still occasionally makes me shudder.

Ever your
D.B.

243. André Gide to Dorothy Bussy

OVERSEAS TELEGRAM
[4 June 1948]

Dorothy Bussy 51 Gordon Square
London

As repentant and embarrassed as with Proust   Gide

244. André Gide to Dorothy Bussy

5 June 48

Very dear friend,

I was so tired yesterday after I finished reading the book – and so overwhelmed by it – that I put off writing until today and contented myself with a provisional telegram. I read, I devoured the whole thing in two long sittings of several hours, 'all business ceasing', hungrily, delightedly, with anguish, intoxication . . . At the same time I recognized it all and discovered it all; for it all came to life anew, from inanimate letter it became palpitating life, suffering flesh, poetry and reality at once. Freud alone could say and perhaps explain what scales covered my eyes the first time I read it. For it's not at all comparable to my earlier mistake concerning Proust (despite what my telegram says). I had done no more than 'scan' – and with a hostile eye – a few pages of the *Temps perdu*. Here, I have no other excuse than the excuse of friendship, yes, of friendship's prepossession . . . but it's useless to dwell on it. Only this matters: your *Olivia* seems to me an extraordinary tale, as accomplished and perfect as possible in its feeling, its decorum and tact, its secret lyricism, its restraint in indiscretion, its wisdom acquired through reflection, in the moderation of its ardour (without the ardour being in any way diminished), in its eloquent reserve, in its quality at the same time of modesty and candour . . .

Let me however venture one petty criticism: this sentence, these few words in the last chapter I object to: '*She had been disgusted.*' You may have been sincere in thinking it true then; you are doubtless no longer so in writing it. You know very well that what causes her to draw back is not disgust, but fear – fear of herself and of the allurement she glimpses. And you seem to me much more in the line of truth when you ask: in the name of what does she resist? In another sentence you express it almost cynically, excellently. And it would have been awkward to stress it. I admired the art of the entire story.

I embrace you very fondly and tenderly

André Gide

You mustn't hide this little masterpiece under a bushel.

245. Dorothy Bussy to André Gide

9th June 1948

Dearest Gide

Thank you for your letter. I am glad that Olivia after so many years of patience, has at last succeeded in touching you, as she would have wished.

Do you yet recognize, I wonder, that it is your presence in my life, your teaching, your example which brought her to life?

Now we will rest from thinking of Olivia.

Your
D.

246. Dorothy Bussy to André Gide

June 9th
10th 1948

Dearest Gide

Your telegram which I got this morning cheered me up a great deal & made me laugh heartily. Thus I shall go down to posterity bracketed in one of your immortal sentences with Proust! But, but, but . . . Can you guess what 'but' is? I hope not.

Janie is away for a weekend. Simon working, even on a Sunday morning, at the Zoo. So that I am left dawdling at home with nothing to do but to send you my love.

Yr.
D.B.

247. André Gide to Dorothy Bussy

Torri del Benaco
Lago di Garda

22 August 48

Dear friend,

I have only strength enough for a few lines (being yet only poorly recovered from otitis – with a bursting of the eardrum – and from the worrisome fatigue of the heart that followed) to reply to yours, an excellent one, of 16th August, received this moment. So I select the most important, or rather, the most urgent: Delighted with your proposal to translate my *Feuillets d'automne* for *Transition*.

Roger has no right to mutilate the beginning of *Olivia*.[1]

[1] In translating *Olivia*, Roger Martin du Gard worked from a French version hastily drafted by D.B. herself. He complained of her awkward style in French and lamented that his lack of English did not allow him to appreciate the qualities of the original. Despite a difficult start, the project was carried through to a successful conclusion. *Olivia*, translated 'by Roger Martin du Gard and the author' was as well received in France as it was in England.

Cyril Connolly's . . . what about my Beyrouth lecture??[2] *. . .* With all my very tired heart, *I love you,*

André Gide

Simon should shake up Charpentier through Lassaigne[3] . . .

I don't know at all whether I shall be in a condition to leave here . . . for a long time. I never leave my room, in which – nearly total rest.

248. Dorothy Bussy to André Gide

51 Gordon Square W.C.1

28th August 48

Dearest

I got your letter this morning with bad news of your heart. It gave me an ache in mine which I wish could relieve yours. But things aren't arranged so in this world. I hope and suppose Pierre Herbart is still with you.

Thank you for your permission to translate your *Feuillets d'Automne* & give it to *Transition*.

Roger has written me a very sweet letter. (One of the advantages of growing old (for a woman) is that your gentleman friends are no longer so terribly afraid of being affectionate!) What *I* call '*férocité*' he calls '*franchise*'. But I have tried to appease him without giving in on what seem to me vital points. Did I tell you that Duncan Grant has been commissioned to design the loose cover which will certainly be a good advertisement. Are you allowed to read during your enforced rest? London is talking about two books. One is the report (verbatim) of Oscar Wilde's trials.[1] The other is by the most famous novelist who has emerged since the war – Graham Greene. He is a Catholic convert & his latest book *The Heart of the Matter* is said to have caused a schism in the Church. It is reported that Jesuits, Dominicans & Carthusians support his thesis which is that a man who has

[2] It was to have been published in *Horizon*, which Connolly edited.

[3] Jacques Lassaigne, who, with Jean Amrouche, edited the review *L'Arche*, wrote the 'Chronique Artistique' of *La Revue Hebdomadaire*.

LETTER 248

[1] *The Trials of Oscar Wilde*, etc., edited, with an introduction by H. Montgomery Hyde (London, W. Hodge, 1948).

committed all the crimes & sins possible may still be a saint and discover Heaven & perhaps will get it without absolution. What does the Holy Father say? And what about the Supreme Judge? Query! We are all discussing it!

I believe I said that Cyril Connolly had played us a 'dirty trick'. (Probably libellous). After having first ordered & then accepted my translation he has never published it. Well and good, but he then excused himself by saying he was prevented because another translation of the same lecture had already appeared in another magazine. This was false, the truth being that a short quotation in the original French had been quoted in a review.

I hope all this stuff won't bore and tire you. Dear Gide, at any rate it won't make your heart beat as one sentence in your letter made mine beat this morning. But then I say to myself, 'He doesn't know English well enough to quite realise what he was saying!'

Oh dear! What nonsense from your friend aged 83 last birthday 24th July. Born on my father's birthday and hence called by my mother Dorothy 'the gift of God.'

D.B.

P.S. One word more – a postscript – the postscript to my life. I do believe those three English words in your letter. I believe, I know, you understand, you mean them.

D.B.

249. Dorothy Bussy to André Gide

40 Rue Verdi

25 Feb. [49]

Dear Gide

As you may have guessed, I had made a vow not to write to you again unless you signified you wanted me to.

But who am I that I should pride myself on keeping a vow? And why should I care what you want or not?

So here I am again, as ever,

Your wishing, hoping, loving

D.

P.S. All well here and no news at all. In fact nothing whatever to say.

Rumours, brought yesterday by Roger, to the effect that you had not been well but were now better which accounts for this effusion.

Roger and I have been very busy over his translation of *Olivia* which is now finished.[1] We quarrelled a great deal. He calling my style (which I am rather proud of!) a 'galimatia poétique' and accusing me of using 'mixed metaphors' and in fact trying to eliminate any approach on my part to a metaphor of any kind, which indeed I consider I use very sparingly. I have had a kind of promise from the Hogarth Press that it – *Olivia* – will appear in the middle of March. And I shall make bold to send you a copy.

As for Roger, in spite of his violence against my style, he filled me with admiration – so scrupulous, so conscientious, so hard-working, so determined to do justice to every syllable and every fleeting expression! And on the whole I think the result is very satisfactory.

I sometimes spend a waking hour in the night (in thinking of you, you will expect!) No, that is not what I was going to say but . . . in writing an imaginary letter to M. Gallimard.[2] Don't be alarmed. I shan't send it. But it relieves my mind even to imagine telling him what I think of him, without any regard to politeness.

Dear Gide. enough of this nonsense. I don't even ask you to imagine or remember what is behind it.

Yr.
D.B.

250. André Gide to Dorothy Bussy

5 March 49

Very dear friend,

If I found a little energy it would be to write to you –. They tell me I'm better. It's possible. But I am emerging from my little crisis completely imbecilified. I'm afraid I don't know English anymore! and just enough French to hesitate at the smallest phrase. The days are spent in useless attempts at working. I am constantly tired as you would not believe. I fantasize myself, wish myself, in Nice, near you;

---

[1] The French translation of *Olivia* by 'Olivia' was published by Stock in the spring of 1949, shortly after the book's publication in England and America.

[2] D.B. was angered by the delay in publishing *Fifty Nursery Rhymes*; Gallimard was disappointed that the more profitable *Olivia* had been given to Stock.

and it would be to say nothing. But let this disappointing note at least tell you I think of you tenderly (very inadequate word).

Your
André Gide

251. André Gide to Dorothy Bussy

10 April 49

Very dear friend,

I am beginning to think (I should say: to hope) that our next meeting, which I think of incessantly, will take place not in Paris but in Nice itself, where I am doing everything possible to arrive between the 20th and 30th of this month. Worn out, exhausted, insomniac, my heart beating only with one wing, I'm floundering about in the daily mesh but have the firm hope of getting free of it before the end of next week – before being kaput!

Too tired to write to Roger. Please inform him of my plan – without elaborating . . .

I have only enough strength left to embrace you.

Your,
André Gide

252. André Gide to Dorothy Bussy

23 June 49

Dear friend,

Yesterday a letter of 'advice' concerning the film to be made of *Olivia*,[1] but let it not be said that I only write to you on business matters! Nucki's[2] return to the Semiramis served as a lucky pretext for going to your hospitable apartment. With trembling emotion I entered your room. I came out with the first volume of Tacitus' *History* under my arm. Without the facing translation I would understand almost none of it. (How easy Virgil's language seems

---

[1] The film *Olivia*, with Edwige Feuillière in the role of Mlle Julie, was released in 1950.

[2] 'Stoisy' Sternheim's eldest daughter, who had been in the concentration camp at Ravensbruck towards the end of the war.

next to Tacitus'!) The numerous indications jotted by you spur me on. I feel I am reading <u>with</u> you; your thought hardly leaves me. It's also with you that I am reading and rereading your translation of the *Nourritures* (the *Nouvelles nourritures* especially), endlessly astonished by your poetic ingenuity – and I feel I have not told you enough how grateful I am to you for having so well triumphed over the traps and pitfalls of that very difficult task.

I am better (another blood test on Sunday will tell whether I may consider myself 'cured') and feel, and should like you to feel, that I am deeply,

your
André Gide

I'm having my *Anthologie*[3] sent to you.

253. Dorothy Bussy to André Gide

c/o Colonel Rendel
Owley
Wittersham
Kent

Aug. 9th, 1949

Dearest Gide

How nice to get a letter from you – I am staying in the country – not with Vincent, but his elder brother, plunged in farm life and rural administration! Very instructive!

Roger & perhaps you, are, I think, unnecessarily concerned about the effect newspaper reviews may have on me. They don't touch me much either one way or the other, though I think they are sometimes more likely to make *you* detest *me* than the other way round. That you & Roger should be accused of being the authors of *Olivia* is so silly, however, that I can't even take it as a compliment though you might more justifiably take it as an insult to you! But though almost all the articles have been complimentary, I think it is only one or two private letters which have really pleased me. One or two unknown correspondents who have not pierced my anonymity. I may say too that the English papers have been very much more respectful of my

---

[3] The *Anthologie de la poésie française*, which Gide had begun in 1937, had just been published (see Letter 156).

desire for anonymity than the French who have constantly shown the utmost indiscretion in every respect.[1]

I don't know what more we can do to protect ourselves from the machinations of the films. So far I have done nothing but sign a three months option. I suppose all the precautions will have to be taken when the final agreement comes to be signed. I don't think I shall have any opposition from the clergy (how monstrous about the *Caves!*)[2] but some say I shall from the English censor.

I like to think of your having a villa to yourself at Juan les Pins, to which you can invite your own friends. We are going to try now and recuperate the Souco, if only we can succeed in turning out our present tenant.

But the law is so peculiar now-a-days that who knows whether we shall succeed. Both Simon & Janie would like it and so should I very much. S. & J. have gone to Edinburgh for a change while I am in the country. They hoped to do some painting but of course the weather changed and became impossible. I expect we shall all be back again in London on August the 15th.

I am glad Dr. Angier is satisfied with your health. If your spirits too were as good as Matisse's all would be well.

I see now my fate is to be jealous of a dog![3] But as I always say in these circumstances, 'If it makes you happy, I am content.'

But I don't like dogs!

Farewell, dear Gide. Forgive my nonsense.

Your devoted
D.B.

254. Dorothy Bussy to André Gide

40 Rue Verdi

30 Nov. 1949

Dearest Gide

I was very glad to get your letter about [J. W.] Mackail's *Latin Literature* & delighted that you like it. I had barely finished reading

[1] *Olivia* received a very favourable press. What annoyed D.B. was that the French reviewers either assumed that the book had been written by Gide and Martin du Gard, or revealed her identity while stressing Gide's influence on the 'vieille octogénaire' who was his close friend, the wife of an English (as one critic supposed) painter, the sister of a famous biographer, etc. The book had considerable success; within two years of its publication, it had been translated into seven languages.

[2] Opposition had forced the abandonment of a plan to film *Les Caves du Vatican*.

[3] Gide had acquired a poodle named Xénie.

it when Roger rang up with his shocking news. It really was a shock for he had seemed greatly reassured about poor Hélène a day or two before. We have not seen him yet but Christiane has arrived and says he seems better than she could have hoped. Will this event bring them together? What a good think that would be, but I fear Christiane is too much of a goose to improve much. The funeral is tomorrow. Simon & Janie will go to it but I think I shall stay away – as Roger & Christiane beg me to.

What will become of Roger now? I wonder all the time. He said once that if he were alone he would go away and live by himself in the West Indies. But what a grief that would be for us! I think that he really likes you and the Petite Dame better than anyone in the world. Will he leave Nice? Will he stay in Paris? Too early to think of such things now, but still I do.

What a mystery it is that he who is so outstandingly good should have so small a circle of intimates! I know it is his own doing and probably the result of his own virtue.

Dear Gide. I can write of nothing else. And I have left unanswered a very sweet and affectionate little 'message' you sent me a few days ago.

And I don't know your country address and you don't put it on your writing-paper!

Yours ever
D.B.

255. André Gide to Dorothy Bussy

Wednesday [7 December 1949]

Dear friend,

I am meddling as little as possible in this inextricable imbroglio poor ex-Miss Pell seems to have been caught in by Mr. Runes.[1] It's very unpleasant, very painful for me to have to grieve such a sweet creature, of such evident good will . . . but I don't see how to get out of this fix. The Mercure assures me they went about it in such a manner as to reserve all [translation] rights for you. But Y. Davet has just informed me that you are unacquainted with the volume (a copy

---

[1] Editor of Philosophical Library which published Elsie Pell's translation, *Autumn Leaves*, in 1950. Unaware that translation rights were included in the agreement with the New York publisher, Gide had expected that D.B. would translate *Feuillets d'automne* (Paris, Mercure de France, 1949).

of which I am sending you at once). I think it's very un-nice of you not to have received a copy of the special printing before general distribution.

A sad and very beautiful letter from Roger, with this sentence: 'Christiane stayed with me until Saturday. She was <u>perfect</u> (the underlining is his) and it grieved me to see her go . . .' Happy about this, for him and for the other one.

Very tired lately, to the point of wondering in the morning whether I shall have enough fuel to reach evening.

I embrace the three of you, and linger a bit with you, my friend.

André Gide

256. André Gide to Dorothy Bussy

9 March 1950

Dear friend,

My life has slowed, has diminished, to such a point . . . I hardly notice that the days go by and I haven't seen you. At 9 in the morning, with great difficulty, I rub the sleep from my eyes; at about 10:30 I go back up and sleep until about half past noon; then again from 2 until 5. Jean Lambert, fortunately, has been helping me a great deal with a correspondence I could not face without him. This state of constant torpor must be abnormal; I shall look into it. Add to that a sort of sciatica that immobilizes me –. And the fine optician in Nice gave me a new pair of glasses thanks to which I can no longer see much of anything. What is most astonishing is that despite all the above, I am rather pleased with my work. Yes, every night I get up at 2 (a practice I can't now do without) and for about two hours I set myself to *Arden*[1] (it's almost finished) or to the *Caves*[2] which I have been reworking miraculously.

If you see Roger, excuse me to him; I feel incapable of the least letter, and what's more, I can see only very imperfectly the marks I make on the paper. But I embrace you all the harder.

André Gide

[1] Nearly twenty years earlier, at Antonin Artaud's request, Gide had translated a fragment of *The Tragedy of Mr. Arden of Feversham* which was later published in the issue on the Elizabethan theatre of the *Cahiers du Sud* (June–July 1933). Gide had again taken up his translation, this time for Barrault, but never completed it.
[2] See Letter 260.

257. Dorothy Bussy to André Gide

Tuesday [April 1950]

Dearest Gide

Please forgive this further outcry about *King Lear*.[1] I do want your judgment. I would like you – oh! so much! to reconsider it in writing. I am afraid that with your immense authority you may lead astray whole generations of young Frenchmen into misjudging a work which really deserves a little more respect than you give it. Etc.

What are you doing? How are you? You are quite capable of going off to Taormina without a word of farewell to us, without giving us your address, without attempting to come & see us again.[2]

You will get this to-morrow morning (Wednesday). Why not get one of your satellites to ring us up and fix on a day for coming to lunch, with Amrouche, whom we should like to see very much.

If not – good-bye. We are going to London on May 10th & shall not break the journey in Paris, as this is much more fatiguing than going straight through.

Your still passionate (though passion now-a-days is kept for such subjects as King Lear)

D.B.

I want to add a few words to the talk we had the other day about King Lear.

Do you remember the epitaph engraved on Swift's tombstone? It is in Latin, of which I only remember one or two words. 'He is at rest now where *saeva indignatio* will no longer *lacerate his heart*.'

I remember reading a discussion once about the proper translation of the word 'saeva.' There are two English words which might do: 'ferocious', an objective, or 'fierce', a subjective passion. Swift's heart was lacerated by *'fierce indignation'*. Shakespeare's too, I believe. With Swift was it the cause or the effect of madness? Shakespeare in King Lear seems to me to be hovering on that same brink. In the fierceness of his rage, he was in no state of mind to care about classical composition or to try and avoid imitating Victor Hugo.

Of course Lear is 'sénile, gâteux, fat, sot.' That is where the whole

---

[1] D.B. was annoyed by Gide's comments on *Lear* in his *Journal* for 1 and 2 December 1946.

[2] Gide was planning to spend May and June in Taormina.

point of the work lies. He impersonates the luxury, folly, indifference and selfishness of the wealthy and powerful, who have never come into contact with reality and who are suddenly forced to experience all its horrors. His sufferings are caused partly by his own folly and intemperance, partly by the crimes of others and partly by the ferocity of the Gods in Heaven and by the senseless, overpowering forces of Nature. Shakespeare is not trying to be human here; he doesn't want (unless incidentally) to move us to pity or to wring our 'tripes'. His subject is more than that. 'Enormous', you say with scorn. 'Factice and faux'! What work of art is not? Must men then never be ambitious? Must they never even attempt greatness? At one stroke you would abolish *The Book of Job*, *Prometheus Bound*, *Paradise Lost*, and Dostoievski's novels. (The 'époustouflant' temple of Abu Simbel too.)

That such works can never have the quality of perfection is more than likely. I do not claim it for Shakespeare – neither here nor anywhere else – and it is perhaps a pity that his only available tool was the drama, which, I expect, requires *perfection* more than any other form of art, and which enabled you to compare him (last insult) with Victor Hugo!

You complain too that all the characters, good and bad alike, are confounded at the end in an indifferent hecatomb. What other end was possible to such a subject? Would you, like the 18th cen. have preferred Edgar and Cordelia to make a happy marriage and live happily every after? Shakespeare, at any rate sometimes, was able to resist the snare of a happy ending.

There are other things too which one might have thought would appeal to you. That kind of prefiguring and redoubling of incidents, which you admire in Hamlet and, I believe, in other cases too, here you brush away contemptuously. In spite of your friends Tiresias and Oedipus, you see nothing suggestive in the fact that it is only when Gloucester's eyes are put out that he sees the truth. The questions of bastardy, of adultery, of men and women's sensual behaviour, which Lear harps upon have apparently no interest for you, though they seem to be treated with some originality. All the horrors of the play 'faux and factice'! Is it for us who have lived through the last ten years, is it for us to say so?

Shakespeare, no doubt, almost recovered from his nervous *break-down*. In his last three plays (*The Winter's Tale*, *Cymbeline* and *The Tempest*) he has more or less climbed out of his pit. Not altogether, though. For there too we find the wicked violences of Leontes, the imprecations of Pauline, the monstrosities of Cloten and Caliban. But he has consented in these, as he did not for Cordelia, to bestow a final and lovely happiness on Perdita, Imogen, and Ariel. And you must be hard-hearted indeed, if you do not find in Cordelia's first meeting with Lear after the break, and her death in his arms, the most exquisite, the purest, the divinest poetry.

258. André Gide to Dorothy Bussy

Easter Monday [10 April] 50

Juan-les-Pins

Dear friend,
Dear friends,

Gilbert[1] has now gone, taking Catherine first to Switzerland where she is to pick up Nurse and children, then back to the Mivoie.[2] Without news of any of them, I am in a state of expectant anxiety, waiting for Pierre Herbart, immobilized on this terrace (which is very pleasant actually, but which I don't dare go down from since there is no lift to bring me back up) – and of uncertainty concerning even the nearest future. As always, our last conversation continues to reverberate inside me. Oh, you must be right about *King Lear*; you are certainly right. If I had to suppress from my *Journal* all errors of judgement on works, events, and persons, it would often be found simplified to the point of insignificance. Ah, how young I felt you to be the other day, in your passionate protest – and how much younger than I! who am too tired to hazard more than a near immediate acquiescence . . .

Completely forgot to tell you of my very long conversation with Claude Gallimard, the day before I left Paris, on the subject of your *Nursery Rhymes*. I parted from him only after receiving near assurance that we shall very soon see the volume come out; and all the same very concerned, for if nothing is done to promote the sale of the book, what good is it to know that it's '*out or sorti*'? It was also on this point (advertise and 'push') that my efforts were especially spent. Hence, a discussion extending to nearly an hour . . . which I

---

[1] Gide's valet and chauffeur.
[2] The house in the Vallée de Chevreuse where the Lamberts lived.

cannot summarize in a few lines. – This waiting, held here on my terrace, is trying in the extreme; there are hours when I feel I can't bear it any longer . . .

How good we thought Janie's luncheon the other day. The Lamberts, daughter and son-in-law, particularly asked me to tell you again.

I think it's this morning that L. Gautier-Vignal is expected. He will give me superficial news of you.

A fond embrace,

André Gide

259. André Gide to Dorothy Bussy

The garage of the 'Provençal'[1]

12 April 50

Dear friend,

Your good letter breaks my heart – and all the more as, if I could . . . but you don't seem to have understood that without a car, reduced to myself, I can't do anything, am no more than an invalid. Since I left the 'Oiseau Bleu' I have been captive on this terrace that is as lovely as one could wish, but that I don't dare leave to take myself down to the real world because I'm not sure I should have the strength to come back up these two flights that isolate me. By what means am I to come to you? How many days has this purgatory gone on, I don't count them any more; but I don't remember having lived through a time that was harder to bear stoically. And I don't at all know, not at all, what awaits me afterwards. What is most annoying is that I have rarely felt better disposed for work. I can't speak to you of what it is that holds me back, that prevents me from working; but I have never understood better, and approved more, the unsociable withdrawal of our friend Roger. Alas, the state of my health and 'relations' no longer allow me to be independent.

All the same, I embrace you fondly,

André Gide

[1] A property belonging to the American, Florence Gould.

260. André Gide to Dorothy Bussy

Albergo Grande Italia
Rapallo

5 July 50

Dear Dorothy,

I think discretion keeps you from writing to me. It doesn't keep my thoughts from flying to you – often. But my imagination wearies not knowing where you are or what sort of life you are leading. Gordon Square must be very hot, very trying. I'd like to think you were in some tranquil Haslemere, with a few young friends.

I have been feeling better lately, but went through a period of painful fatigue which was also the cause of my silence. I learned a new word: anorexia, which means: absence of appetite. Yes, I was suffering from a quasi total anorexia, moral as well as physical, and dragged from day to day with no more curiosity than desire. However, the Comédie Française's plan of putting on the theatrical adaptation of my *Caves du Vatican* has somewhat dispelled my torpor. I had put it together, hastily (28 or 30 years ago), to be performed by the students of Lausanne. One of the theatre's board members learned of that text, assembled the committee directly, held an enthusiastic reading. It was unanimously accepted. The manager and the principal director came and hunted me down at Juan-les-Pins and told me of their intentions: to stage the play as soon as possible, after various changes which claimed my immediate attention and which I was able to impart to the director[1] (who is to play the role of Protos) when he came to spend three days with me in Taormina. Perfect agreement. Rehearsals, which will require my presence in Paris, are scheduled to begin in September. Following Claudel, it's expected to create a lovely scandal![2]

Give Simon and Janie my affection, and to your sisters who are there, my best wishes.

This is the longest letter I have written in weeks or months. And in fact I have come to the end of my strength. I have just enough left to embrace you.

Your
André Gide

[1] Jean Meyer.
[2] Gide's play opened on 13 December, shortly after the closing of Claudel's *Soulier de satin*.

Yes, this project has somewhat restored a taste for life which I had lost. The actors appear to be extraordinarily excited; no more so than I. Claudel believes a *coup* has been set up against him; yet I did no more than assent to an initiative which others (the Comédie Française) had taken. If the success matches their expectation we shall have a good laugh. Oh if only the opening could coincide with your stop over in Paris!!

Thinking of your reading Ariosto, I plunged into Tasso (without however abandoning Virgil), but I would need a *teacher*; by myself I slosh about and guess at a good deal more than I really understand.

Yesterday at Portofino, the author of *I, Claudio* [*sic*][3] was presented to me. Lives on a boat, athletic, half naked, very nice. I told him that you'd had me read his book. He spoke very amicably of Lytton. Read nothing *worth mentioning* in a long time.

I write to no one, not even to myself; which is to say that I no longer keep my *Journal*.[4] Pierre Herbart was here with me – whom 'business' recalled to Paris; so that I am now alone, with the faithful chauffeur Gilbert, sadly insufficient company. But for some time now I have stopped thinking I would depart this life before the end of the day.

261. André Gide to Dorothy Bussy

Grasse

9 Sept. 1950

Very dear friend,

If I still wrote letters, it would be to you. Am I growing hard hearted? I don't believe so; but my hands shake and I have trouble forming my letters – above all, I can find nothing much to tell you. I belong to the past; and even when I think of you (which I often do), it is very very far back that my recollection begins, and I take pleasure in hearing again numerous of your sayings that remain for me as actual as they were in those first days. Back in Paris before the end of the week, I shall be taken up by a number of tasks (certain of which will be most interesting: rehearsals of *Les Caves*) and left no time to breathe. So I'm writing to you quickly, before plunging back into the tumult.

[3] Robert Graves.
[4] Gide's last Journal entry is dated 10 June 1949.

Have I ever before seen so long a string of such lovely days? Pity that so many abominations spoil the time we are spending here. In Nice I was able to see no one but the very nice Nouki, who expresses much gratitude for your renewal of hospitality. She talked to us (to Mme Théo and me) for more than an hour about Berlin, and related so many nearly incredible things: Stalin's portrait banned throughout the entire Russian zone, replaced by Lenin's. Explainable by who knows what secret motives. Unimaginable misery and moral collapse . . .

I read little (Jane Austin [*sic*] and Renan); try a little to write, but without much knowing what the result is worth . . . Have you taken steps for your play?[1] With all my heart I wish you would. Under the auspices of *Olivia*, its reception would be enthusiastic it seems to me. I put your letter away so well I can no longer lay my hands on it. It contained however two points I promised myself I would respond to . . . In any case, this: I don't believe a single of your letters was ever lost pursuing me through Sicily or Italy. Didn't you speak of an exhibition of Janie's work?

I embrace you very fondly, very tenderly.

André Gide

262. André Gide to Dorothy Bussy

5 December 50

Dear friend,

Three days off (which is to say that rehearsals at the Comédie Française will, for three days, do without my presence.) I take immediate advantage by running to rue Verdi. I was so tired I began to be afraid I wouldn't last until the thirteenth, the date of the 'opening'. To give out at the last minute would have a disastrous effect and risk being understood by the 'press', very unfortunately, as a disavowal. 'Gide withdraws because too displeased with his interpreters,' someone would surely say. To be avoided.[1]

Beyond that ordeal, I see nothing. I shall be in great need of rest, but where? Problem (complicated by the question of secretary and

[1] *Miss Stock.*

LETTER 262
[1] Gide did manage to attend the opening of his play.

chauffeur). 'Visibility zero' as the weather bulletins say for aviation. We'll discuss it later.

The Herbarts return tonight; they will help me 'get my bearings'. Circumstances being favourable, I should be very well disposed for work . . . oh yes! naturally I'm thinking of Nice, but (there are a heap of 'buts') . . .

And after all, despite the assurances (and the self-assurance) of the actors, I consider it perfectly possible that *Les Caves* may flop.

In the meantime I embrace you very fondly, but without daring to say: soon.

Steadfastly yours,
André Gide

263. Dorothy Bussy to André Gide

40 Rue Verdi
11th Dec. 1950

Dearest Gide

Perhaps this will reach you in time to bring you our wishes and congratulations for *Les Caves*. But – but . . . I have every confidence in *Les Caves* – but a good deal less in *you*! Success at the Français is not worth making yourself ill over. You have had quite enough success in your life and really what does the success of the *Caves* as a play matter? This will certainly make you very cross. Please forgive & realise that it is much more important for me at any rate – without counting the rest of the world – that you should keep in good form some time longer.

And, perhaps, come to Nice for the winter. It is all quite comfortable now. You would have friends here – but not too many – and very discreet!

There! That's all I can say to entice you!

Roger seems greatly delighted at his work with Pierre over the *Thibault* film.[1] It is indeed an excellent idea.

Farewell, my very dear, and let us say 'Au Revoir' all the same.

Yr.
D.B.

[1] Martin du Gard was working on a scenario of his novel, in collaboration with Pierre Herbart.

264. André Gide to Dorothy Bussy

28 December 50

Dear friend,

I need to write to you, without however having anything to say. If I were at rue Verdi, I would sit with you and say nothing; it would be enough to feel you there. Myself, I seem to be very little 'there' any more. I feel as if I were going off, slipping away; I am diminishing. My mind is holding fast – and what is customarily called the 'intellectual faculties'. But when it comes to moving, I am a pitiful sight . . . no pain or distress, but a respiratory discomfort so great I cannot take a step.

Elisabeth H. thinks she can convince me that this won't prevent our going to Morocco by car. I'm waiting for the medical examination to tell me whether it isn't madness. Add to that, a total lack of curiosity for anything a new country might offer.

The Gallimards had indeed promised me your book[1] would 'come out' before the end of the year, even before December. I don't think too much about it for fear of becoming enraged. (And I know the book is <u>ready</u>.)

I am past the age where the success of *Les Caves* at the Comédie Française could – could have, delighted me.

I think of you and embrace you fondly.

Your
André Gide

265. André Gide to Dorothy Bussy

8 (?) Jan. 51

Dear friend,

I have been feeling a bit better since I decided I was too poorly to go away. (And surely you wrote me the winningest letter!)[1] I have too much to say to you and should like to speak only of your book –

[1] *Fifty Nursery Rhymes.*
LETTER 265
[1] The letter has been lost.

which I've been living with for the past two days. But first, let's clear away old business:

1. Yes, I agree to all Secker & Warburg's wishes (which seem very reasonable to me *'provided that the omissions are notified in the book'*. How marvellously produced the *'limited edition'* is!)

2. Pleased that Beatrix Beck[2] wrote to you concerning *Olivia*. – As for the *Nursery Rhymes* ... dismayed by the purchase price: enough to discourage the very students most likely to be enthralled by the book. Obviously of very comely appearance, but not at all what I expected (shall talk to Gallimard about it); hadn't we agreed that it was to be hardbound, like a schoolbook? Your introduction is perfect; but despite what you say, it is unclear for whom the book is intended.

If only some scholarly critic would take the trouble (let's hope it happens), what an interesting study could be made, showing that your book only very rarely (may as well say never) duplicates the dictionary, even the monumental Harrap's. What particularly amazes me is the great choice you give, whereas the dictionary claims to be exhaustive. But what I enjoy the most are the little comments (where I am pleased to recognize your voice), and the less 'little' they are (id est: the more expanded they are), the more I like them. And it's they, obviously, that constitute the book's value. It's they that fasten the reader's attention.

Concerning 'publicity' (complimentary copies). I have already spoken about it to the nice Justin O'Brien, on his way through Paris, and especially to Dominique Drouin who is very devoted to you (relations with colleagues of his father's) – Want to discuss it with Jean Schlum. and, naturally, with the Gallimards themselves. And first of all to find out how many copies they are granting you. – Then with Enid [McLeod] and Whity. I propose offering it (I shall) to Keeler Faus, rediscovered. (He is presently in charge, officially, of production of books for the blind.) Today I feel well and take great pleasure in writing to you; but these past days, I felt non-existent. All the same, very much

your
André Gide

Completely reworked the last dialogued scene (Lafcadio and Geneviève) of *Les Caves*.

[2] Gide's secretary since October of the previous year.

266. André Gide to Dorothy Bussy

9 Jan. 51

My dear friend,

I need very much to write to you; the letter I sent yesterday satisfies me so little. Since then I have barely left you. The few reservations I put forward vanish one by one, first of all the duplication of the dictionary. Inevitably there are some 'overlappings', but much less important than it seemed to me before a closer examination; and in fact, they give value to your book. It's when the dictionary is silent that your voice (and only then) can rise. And what pleasure I take in listening to you; I am there with you (*utinam*!) Then the amusement of saying to oneself; Ah! I already knew that! On the whole I already knew, thanks to you, many things. Then there are others that I sense so well!

This morning I'm feeling better, and now at last am once more 'outward bound'. But where. . . ? Completely reworked the last scene of *Les Caves*.

Fond embraces.

[No signature]

267. Dorothy Bussy to André Gide

40 Rue Verdi
Nice

28th Jan. 1951

Dearest Gide

Just a line to tell you a little piece of personal news.

We have won our lawsuit with our tenant of La Souco and been given the right to return to our own house. He has been told to quit and the lawyers say that with luck we may get him out by the middle of April. It now depends on the Préfet. Claude Bourdet gave us a letter to a M. Hugues saying I was the author of *Olivia* and a friend of yours. We saw him yesterday when he declared he was much impressed by these two items and promised to do his best for us. People seem to think now we have a good chance.

And where are you? I imagine you on the way to Morocco & that you don't dare to tell me so. I expect when we are safely out of Nice you will come back to it – according to custom. Will you ever come to La Souco again?

I had a helpful letter from M. Hirsch about the Service de Presse of *Nursery Rhymes*. And I daresay that between us all we shall sell a few copies.

And after all if you go to Morocco I shall take it as a sign that you are feeling better and try to forgive you as usual.

Your
D.B.

[Gide was too ill to answer this letter. He died at his home in rue Vaneau on 19 February.]

EPILOGUE

[Among the papers found by Roger Martin du Gard's literary executors was an envelope marked 'Notes de Madame Simon Bussy'. It contained more of those pages on her meetings and relationship with Gide, which Gide referred to as her 'black notebook'. According to a note written on the envelope by Martin du Gard, Dorothy Bussy had given him the papers on 11 May 1949, before leaving for London. She asked that he show them to Gide (then in a clinic in Nice) and that he take them back and preserve them among his own papers. To the envelope, Martin du Gard added the following page of his own:]

Nice, 25 May 1949

Gide's condition is noticeably improved. The day before yesterday I gave him Dorothy's envelope. When he returned it to me, he said: 'This love of Dorothy's has been a pathetic thing. There are some overwhelming passages in these notes, overwhelming to me, and for any reader, dear . . . And by depositing these papers in your archives, Dorothy certainly hopes that they will one day be exhumed . . . There is an astonishing page where she tells herself that she has been, in my life, the only woman who might have been the cause of my 'infidelity' – of my infidelity *vis-à-vis* my wife, and that that is why she frightened me, why I protected myself against her love; and that this unique place which she held in my life has been a curse to her; that if she had mattered less, she would have obtained more . . .' I interrupt: 'Fortunate illusion . . . in which she likely found her one consolation!' He makes a gesture of vague hesitation, as though he were not aware that Dorothy deluded herself, quite willing, perhaps, to accept, retrospectively, this psychological subtlety, precisely because of its subtlety . . . But I who have heard his confidences concerning Dorothy since 1920 and in the following years, I remember with no possible error that he never felt for her more than a compassionate and deeply tender *friendship*, that he was always incapable of returning any of that frenetic passion she felt for him, that he avoided her, fled from her, so as not to have to repulse her and cause her too much pain, and that it was from natural incapacity and not at all from conjugal fidelity that he brushed aside her too ardent love. He says: 'You cannot imagine, dear, what attraction I feel for her face, and always more so, truly, with the years . . . Yes. I find the expression of that face exquisite . . . I look at her now, with more emotion than ever.' He adds: 'She gave me, some time ago, a whole packet of notes, notes concerning me . . . If ever my health permits me to return to Paris, I shall send them to you, so that you can join them to this envelope, dear. It will form an ensemble, which will have some interest perhaps, later on.'

R.M.G.

INDEX